Your Toddler

Head to Toe

Also by Cara Familian Natterson, MD

Your Newborn: Head to Toe

Your Toddler

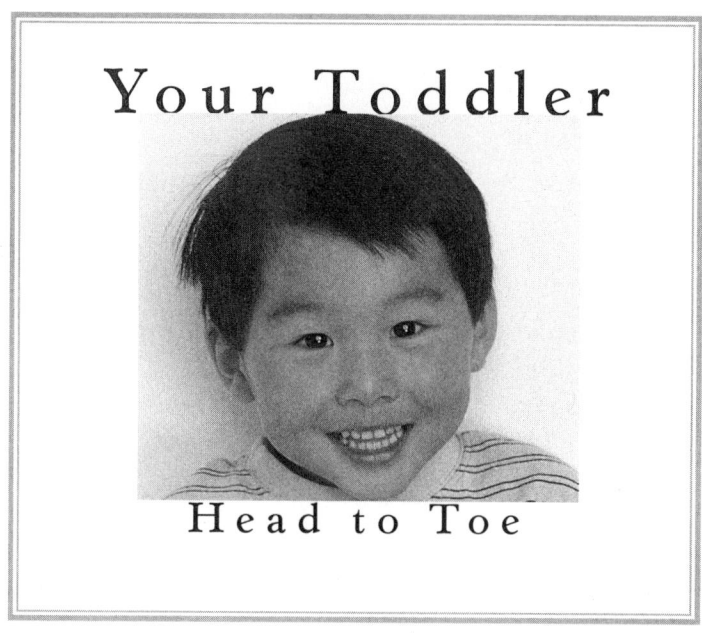

Head to Toe

Answers to the Questions
You Meant to Ask Your Doctor

Everything You Want to Know About Your Child's Health Through the Toddler Years

CARA FAMILIAN NATTERSON, MD

LITTLE, BROWN AND COMPANY

New York   Boston

Little, Brown and Company
Hachette Book Group USA
1271 Avenue of the Americas, New York, NY 10020
Visit our Web site at www.HachetteBookGroupUSA.com

First Edition: June 2006

The information in this book is not intended to replace the services of trained health professionals. You are advised to consult with your child's health care professional regarding your child's health on a regular basis, and in particular with regard to matters that may require diagnosis, a specialist referral, or medical attention. Anytime there is a particular concern about a medical problem, you should call your doctor, or, if it is an emergency, call 911. The medications and medical advice described in this book are generally in accordance with the standards of care set forth by the American Academy of Pediatrics.

Library of Congress Cataloging-in-Publication Data

Natterson, Cara Familian.
    Your toddler : head to toe : everything you want to know about your child's health through the toddler years / Cara Familian Natterson.
        p. cm. — (Answers to the questions you meant to ask your doctor)
    Includes bibliographical references and index.
    ISBN-10: 0-316-01014-6 (pbk)
    ISBN-13: 978-0-316-01014-6 (pbk)
    1. Toddlers — Health and hygiene. 2. Toddlers — Development. 3. Toddlers — Care. I. Title. II. Series.

RJ61.N343 2006
618.92 — dc22   2006001170

10   9   8   7   6   5   4   3   2   1

Q-FF

Printed in the United States of America

For Paul, Tali, and Ry

Contents

Acknowledgments

I am grateful to all the physicians who reviewed my materials to make sure my advice was accurate and salient. You continue to teach me how to be a better doctor. Thank you, Moise Danielpour, Andy Fine, Heather Fullerton, Robert Kleinman, David Krasne, Deborah Lehman, Ira Skolnik, Lisa Stern, Shannon Thyne, and Ken Wright. For curbside advice anytime of the day or night, Ron Bahar, Andrew Freedman, Catherine Fuller, William Hohl, Harley Kornblum, Dan Levi, and Joanne Low.

For their daily support, good cheer, and unbelievable smarts, my partners at Tenth Street Pediatrics.

Finally, to my family and close friends, who put up with me while I wrote another book, had another baby, and continued full-time practice. Especially to my husband, Paul, who has the most awe-inspiring mind I know and at the same time has the ability to handle two kids effortlessly while sending me off to write. I married well.

Introduction

I wrote this book for the same reason that I wrote its predecessor, *Your Newborn: Head to Toe*. It seems obvious to me that you, as parents, want — and need — a resource to go to when your child is sick or hurt. You want something on your shelf that you can pull down at 2:00 in the morning before calling your doctor. You want a resource that you can go back to after you have seen the doctor, because you have already forgotten half of what was said or you have ten new questions. You need a hands-on medical book written explicitly for you.

You will likely approach your child's toddler years with more comfort than you had in the first year of life. Caretaking is easier because you know your child. You have fallen into the groove of parenting. Yet the need for clear, concise advice does not end with your child's first birthday.

Just when a rhythm establishes itself, it is time for socialization. Toddler groups and then preschool experiences are critically important for your child's cognitive and social development, but with these comes a series of new medical challenges — constant colds, skin infestations, lice. This is why I call this my "gross book." One of my goals is to cover all those illnesses and ailments that you need to know about but are sometimes too squeamish to ask about. While there is a lot in this book that is not at all disgusting, there is an equal amount that, well, is. . . . When I was writing this book, I would have two screens open on my computer at any given time. I would flip between Microsoft

Word, with its black-and-white text, and my staple Internet reference sites. People would glance over my shoulder as they often do in coffeehouses packed with writers on computers. I knew they were looking at my screen from the gasps I would hear as I clicked on to a giant picture of a hair louse or as I looked up yet another scaly, pustulating rash on Dermatlas.

The format follows that of *Your Newborn*. Each chapter focuses on a part of the body. Within each chapter are sections about the most common ailments affecting toddlers. These are broken into distinct parts: What is happening inside my child's body? What can I do? When does my doctor need to be involved? What tests need to be done, and what do the results mean? What are the treatments? What are the possible complications? This framework provides enough information to understand the nature of your child's problem and the solutions that may be suggested. Unique to *Your Toddler,* however, is the detailed illustration at the start of each chapter depicting the featured body part. The illustration can be used as a point of reference as you read through sections in the chapter.

Throughout the text are medical terms written in bold italics. These are meant to help you identify those catchphrases you may hear in the hospital or doctor's office.

At the back of the book, there are chapters dedicated to lab tests, vaccines, and developmental milestones. These subjects generate a significant amount of debate among parents. The primers included here are meant to provide background information so that you may ask your pediatrician about these topics in an informed way.

Perhaps the most important part of each section is the list of Web sites at the end of the text. The Internet has fundamentally changed the way medicine is practiced. Parents use it in an effort to collect information and help their child. But researching your own child's particular ailment online is simply ludicrous. There is no way to tell what information is valid and what is preposterous. Some of the prettiest Web sites have some of the most misleading information. This is why every section of the book has Web-site addresses listed at the end. If you need more information, you can go to these sites rather than to a general search engine. I have chosen them because they contain more detailed information or pictures, presented in a way that a nonmedical person can understand. Most important, the information is accurate.

The topics in this book were chosen by sheer volume: these are the issues that I see in my office every day. There are many topics not included in this book, namely uncommon illnesses and complex subspecialty issues. Hopefully, the Web sites referenced in each chapter will help direct you if your child has a problem that is not discussed explicitly.

While the book technically covers the toddler years — approximately ages one to four — many of the topics discussed occur in younger or older children. I hope you find *Your Toddler: Head to Toe* a helpful springboard of information.

Part One

Head to Toe

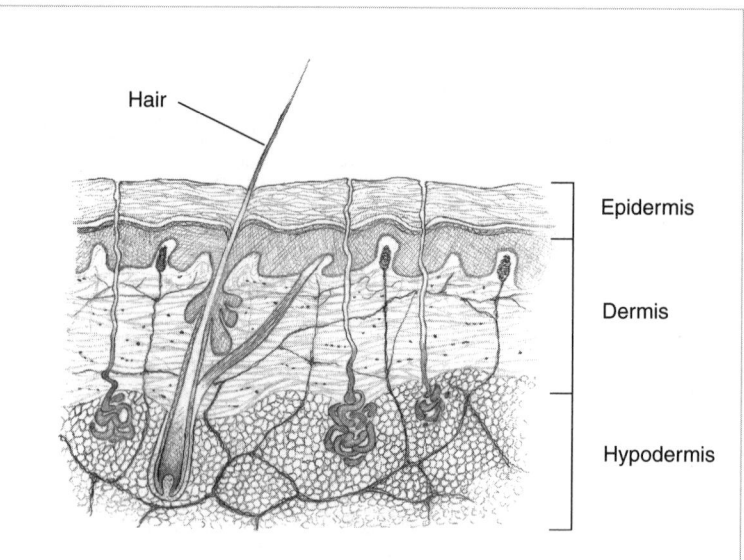

The skin has a thin upper layer (epidermis) and two thick
lower layers (dermis and hypodermis). Any of these
can be involved in rash formation.

1

Skin and Rashes

CHICKEN POX

What is happening inside my child's body?
Getting chicken pox is almost inevitable during childhood — or at least it used to be. Chicken pox, also called ***varicella,*** is a viral infection that causes fever and a rash that evolves from red spots to blisters to scabs over 48 to 72 hours. The hallmark of this illness is that spots of all ages are clearly visible, from young and pink to old and crusted. The spots are small, ranging from 1 to 5 millimeters.

Because the rash tends to be extremely itchy, children will often scratch and unroof the blisters. When this happens, the open sores can become infected with bacteria. Infected pox are more likely to scar. The open skin also provides an entry point for bacteria into the body, creating the potential for more serious complications.

Chicken pox is very contagious. If your child has skin-to-skin (or face-to-face) contact with a child who is infected with chicken pox, the virus can be transmitted easily. For this reason, a child with chicken pox is considered contagious until every last pock has scabbed over. But the contagious period begins before the first pock even appears. In the earliest part of the illness, before the rash emerges, the virus is shed through **respiratory droplets.** A respiratory droplet is a tiny particle of moisture that comes out of the mouth with a cough. The older the child with chicken pox, the more vigorously she can cough, and the farther a respiratory droplet can fly. With the combination of coughing and rubbing a runny nose with bare hands, the virus lands on doorknobs, toys, and just about anywhere else you can imagine.

The incubation period for chicken pox is 10 to 21 days. This means that if your child is going to get chicken pox, she will develop the rash and fever 1 to 3 weeks after exposure.

In years past, parents often had "chicken pox parties." These gatherings were an effort to expose children who had never had chicken pox to a child who had a new case in hopes that the uninfected children might pick up the infection. Now that the chicken pox vaccine is available and the potential seriousness of the illness is appreciated, chicken pox parties are a rare occurrence.

The chicken pox vaccine, called **Varivax,** has recently become part of the standard childhood vaccine schedule. It is strongly recommended (and in most states required) prior to entry into kindergarten or day care. This vaccine has been in used for decades in Japan. It has become increasingly popular in the United States in the past 10 years. About 10 percent of the children who get the vaccine may still get chicken pox, but they will get a significantly milder case with a much lower risk of a secondary infection or other complications. The vaccine is discussed in detail in chapter 20.

Shingles is a reactivation of chicken pox. Once a person has had chicken pox, the virus remains dormant in the body, housed in compartments called **ganglia** located along specific nerves. When the body is under significant stress — for instance, when it is fighting an infection or when the immune system is suppressed — the virus located in the ganglion nerve roots can reactivate, traveling along the nerves to the skin. The rash that appears looks very similar to the original chicken pox rash, starting as small red spots and then becoming blisters and eventually scabs. However, unlike chicken pox, the shingles rash appears only in the specific segment of skin served by that one nerve root. Therefore, the rash is isolated. Also, with shingles, the activated nerve tingles or burns as the virus is moving along it. This is why shingles tend to hurt as well as itch.

What can I do?

If your toddler has been exposed to chicken pox and has never received the chicken pox vaccine, she should get a dose of Varivax as soon as possible. Studies show that if Varivax is administered within 72 hours of exposure, the severity and duration of the illness are significantly reduced.

However, many times parents do not know that a child has been exposed. Exposures can happen just about anywhere — the park, the shoe store, school, camp — and the illness is contagious just before the infected child breaks out with the rash. Although most parents with an infected child will try to notify contacts, they cannot warn families if they do not realize that their own child has the illness.

Varivax cannot be given to children younger than one year. The only thing to do when you know that your infant of 12 months or younger has been exposed is to watch and wait. Maternal antibodies can remain in a baby's body for up to one year, though, so the baby of a mom who has had chicken pox may very well be protected by lingering antibodies that were passed through the placenta during fetal development.

The scenario is similar for children who have already received the vaccine: watching and waiting is all you can do. These children are as protected as they can be. About 1 in 10 vaccinated children will break out with a mild chicken pox rash within a couple of weeks.

If your child gets chicken pox, use a fever reducer when necessary. It is critically important, though, not to give your child aspirin. In the presence of varicella, aspirin can lead to a form of liver injury and ultimately brain injury known as **Reye's syndrome.** Acetaminophen (Tylenol) is the safest alternative.

Pain management is important for a child with a significant case of chicken pox. You can bathe your child in an oatmeal bath made with lukewarm water. Use store-bought oatmeal or pre-packaged oatmeal bath solutions available at most supermarkets and drugstores. When you take your child out of the tub, do not wipe off the skin completely. Instead, try to pat the skin dry so that the starchy film coating the body remains. It is this film that provides anti-itch relief. Other medical treatments directed at itching are discussed in the treatments section.

Perhaps the best thing you can do to minimize the complications associated with chicken pox is to trim your child's fingernails, because if she does scratch, she is less likely to break the skin. This sounds simple, but its importance cannot be overstated. Scratching the pox and breaking the skin leads to the most common complication of chicken pox: secondary skin infection.

Some cases of chicken pox are extremely mild — so mild, in fact, that not even a single pock may be visible. This is why an adult who thinks she has never had chicken pox has a 95 percent chance of having immunity to the virus: she likely had a case so mild that she never knew she was infected.

When does my doctor need to be involved?

Complicated chicken pox needs to be evaluated by your doctor. This means that if your child has a high fever that does not respond to fever reducers or if any of the pox look infected (red, pus filled, more tender or painful than the others), your doctor should be involved. Likewise, if your child is refusing to eat or drink because of mouth or throat pain, see your doctor.

Call your doctor if your child's fever returns once it has already broken. This can be a sign of a secondary infection.

In very rare cases, the chicken pox virus moves into the body, affecting the liver, lungs, or brain. If your child has a significant cough or difficulty breathing, ask your doctor to check your child. If she becomes increasingly aggressive or sleepy or she cannot keep her balance while walking, you should speak with your doctor right away.

What tests need to be done, and what do the results mean?

Chicken pox is a clinical diagnosis. That means that if you know what the pox look like, you can make the diagnosis. Most doctors can diagnose chicken pox within seconds of beginning a physical exam.

The only time a lab test is necessary is when there is a complication. If your doctor suspects that the chicken pox has spread to an internal organ, he will order blood tests.

What are the treatments?
The most effective first-line treatments for chicken pox are the remedies listed previously. However, serious or complicated chicken pox may warrant medical intervention.

If your child's case of chicken pox is severe, an antiviral medicine called acyclovir (Zovirax) can help shorten the course of the disease. The medication is generally used only when there are hundreds or even thousands of pox or when the virus gets into the bloodstream, lungs, brain, and so on. Acyclovir can also be used in cases of shingles.

An antibiotic may be necessary when there is a secondary infection. The antibiotic will not affect the course of the chicken pox itself because a virus causes chicken pox and antibiotics treat only bacteria. However, bacterial infection of the skin — usually due to scratching — has its own set of potential complications, so antibiotics may be very important for children with secondary infections.

If your child's itching cannot be controlled with oatmeal baths, you may want to try an antihistamine. Antihistamines are available over the counter as diphenhydramine (Benadryl) or loratadine (Claritin), or by prescription as hydroxyzine (Atarax) or cetirizine (Zyrtec). Some of these anti-itch medications, especially diphenhydramine, alter the level of alertness. Most of the time, this means that the medicines will make your child sleepy. But there is also a chance that they will do just the opposite and make your child hyperactive. About 75 percent of children become sleepy with diphenhydramine, and about 25 percent are revved up.

What are the possible complications?
If the pox spread down the throat, swallowing can become unbearably painful. This can lead to **dehydration.** To prevent significant dehydration, a strong pain medication (such as codeine) can be prescribed. Your child will be more likely to drink if her pain is well managed, helping to prevent dehydration. If she does become dehydrated, she may need IV fluids.

In rare cases, the virus can travel through the bloodstream to various organs, such as the liver (causing *hepatitis*), lungs (causing *pneumonia*), or brain (causing *meningitis* or *encephalitis*).

Equally unusual is a complication involving clotting of the blood. If the bloodstream becomes overwhelmed with the virus, there can be blood vessel spasm or clotting along the blood vessels, with subsequent formation of blood clots (*thrombi*) or infected clots (*septic emboli*). When these clots travel throughout the body, they do their own damage. Examples of complications from blood clots include breathing problems from a clot in the lungs (called a *pulmonary embolus*) and significant problems in the brain (such as *stroke*).

Additional Resources:

http://www.cdc.gov/nip/diseases/varicella/

http://www.mckinley.uiuc.edu/ (Go to "search" in lower left-hand corner and type in "chicken pox.")

http://dermatlas.med.jhmi.edu/derm/ (Go to "search" and type in "chicken pox.")

http://www.who.int/immunization/en/ (Go to "search" in upper right-hand corner and type in "varicella.")

◆   ◆   ◆

COXSACKIE VIRUS (HAND-FOOT-MOUTH DISEASE)

What is happening inside my child's body?

This infection is appropriately named because it causes a rash on the hands and feet and in the mouth. The rash consists of small blisters (1 to 2 millimeters) on a red base. The blisters do not itch, but they can be tender.

Coxsackie is the virus largely responsible for the dreaded hand-foot-mouth disease. Coxsackie is a member of a group of viruses known as the *enteroviruses.* Even though Coxsackie is by far the most common culprit here, other viruses in the same family have been known to cause a similar rash.

The blisters are especially tender in the mouth. As your child's throat becomes increasingly sore, first eating solids and then drinking liquids can become extremely painful. Some children cannot even swallow their saliva because it hurts too much. When a child is so uncomfortable that he can neither eat nor drink, he can become dehydrated.

Hand-foot-mouth is associated with fever, adding to the discomfort. The fever can run as high as 104°F.

The rash of hand-foot-mouth varies. In young children, it can spread up the legs to the thighs and diaper area. In these places, the rash is not made up of blisters, but rather of small, flat, red spots. Although the rash almost never itches, when it is in the diaper area, it can cause discomfort.

It is important to know that despite its name, hand-foot-mouth does not always cause a rash in all three places. In fact, in mild cases, there may be only a blister or two in one of the three areas and nothing else.

Coxsackie is extremely contagious. It is passed through saliva and can live on toys, doorknobs, and other surfaces for up to two weeks. For this reason, school outbreaks are not uncommon. The incubation period is 3 to 7 days. This means that if your child is going to get Coxsackie virus, you will begin to notice symptoms within a week of exposure. The rash itself usually lasts 7 to 10 days.

Although Coxsackie can appear anytime during the year, it is most common in the summer and fall.

Theoretically, once a child has had hand-foot-mouth, he shouldn't get it again. However, because the disease can be caused by more than one type of enterovirus, it is possible to pick up different enteroviruses and to get hand-foot-mouth more than once.

What can I do?

If your child has hand-foot-mouth, you want to make him as comfortable as possible. Keep his fever down with fever reducers when needed.

The rash on the body does not need any creams or lotions, because it typically does not cause discomfort. However, if your child has blisters in his mouth, he is likely to have pain there. If he doesn't want to eat solid foods, stick with liquids to help keep him hydrated. Cool liquids will soothe the throat, whereas warm liquids may burn. Popsicles, smoothies, shakes, and the like are usually the best options.

Sometimes the pain at the back of the throat is so severe that even cool liquids hurt. The easiest over-the-counter remedy is a concoction called "magic mouthwash." This mixture of Maalox and Children's Benadryl Allergy Liquid helps coat the throat while reducing inflammation.

When does my doctor need to be involved?

If you are sure that your child has hand-foot-mouth disease, you don't need your doctor to confirm it. But you do need to call if you think your child is at risk of becoming dehydrated. Also call if your child's pain is so severe that the home remedies do not offer any relief.

What tests need to be done, and what do the results mean?

Generally speaking, infection with Coxsackie virus does not require any tests. However, if the rash becomes secondarily infected, or if your child gets dehydrated, blood tests may be necessary. These tests include a complete blood count, blood culture, and electrolyte panel. Each of these tests is reviewed in chapter 19.

What are the treatments?

Because Coxsackie is a virus, there is no medicine that can shorten the course of the illness or help get rid of the infection sooner. Therefore, the medical treatments for hand-foot-mouth are aimed at pain relief.

When pain limits the intake of fluids and magic mouthwash is not enough, prescription pain relievers may help. Codeine is effective, but it can cause side effects such as drowsiness, upset stomach, and constipation. It is uncommon that a child with Coxsackie is in so much pain that he requires codeine.

If the skin becomes secondarily infected, an antibiotic will be necessary. However, since the rash of Coxsackie does not itch, children rarely scratch, and secondary infection is unusual.

For extreme cases of hand-foot-mouth that lead to dehydration, IV fluids may be necessary. This often requires a visit to the emergency room or an overnight stay in the hospital.

RECIPE FOR MAGIC MOUTHWASH

There are many versions of "magic mouthwash" suggested by health care providers and Internet health sites. All of these recipes contain one ingredient to coat the mouth and throat and another to reduce inflammation. Together, these ingredients make eating and drinking more comfortable, which in turn helps prevent dehydration.

Some adult variations of this mouthwash contain a topical anesthetic such as lidocaine. When such an ingredient is included, the mouthwash should not be swallowed. For this reason, topical anesthetics are usually left out of the pediatric versions.

Here's my favorite recipe for magic mouthwash: Mix one part Maalox with one part Children's Benadryl Allergy Liquid (both available over the counter). You can mix a teaspoon of each, a cup of each, or two equal-size bottles of each. The key is to use an equal amount of each component. The amount you will give is based on your child's weight-appropriate Benadryl dose. You may repeat the dose every 2 to 4 hours as needed for pain. However, if you need to give it to your child more than four or five times in 24 hours, or if it is not helping, contact your doctor.

Weight in Pounds	Dose of Magic Mouthwash
<20	Speak with your doctor
20–24	½ tsp. (2.5 ml)
25–29	¾ tsp. (3.75 ml)
30–34	1 tsp. (5 ml)
35–39	1¼ tsp. (6.75 ml)
40–44	1½ tsp. (7.5 ml)
45–49	1¾ tsp. (8.75 ml)
50–60	2 tsp. (10 ml)

What are the possible complications?
Dehydration is the most common serious consequence of Cox-sackie. Dehydration is covered in detail in chapter 18.

Secondary skin infection is possible with any rash, but because hand-foot-mouth is typically not itchy, skin infections are very unusual.

In rare cases, Coxsackie can spread from the skin to other parts of the body. It can move through the bloodstream to the lungs (***pneumonia***) or heart (***carditis***). It can cause ***aseptic meningitis,*** during which the child will have a stiff neck, a severe headache, and a continuing fever. It can be hard to tell aseptic (or viral) meningitis from bacterial meningitis, the latter being a medical emergency. If you have any doubt that your child has meningitis, take him to the doctor right away. He may need to be admitted to the hospital.

> *Additional Resources:*
> http://www.cdc.gov/ncidod/diseases/ (Select letter "H" and scroll down to "hand-foot-mouth.")
> http://dermatlas.med.jhmi.edu/derm/ (Go to "search" and type in "hand-foot-mouth.")

DIAPER RASH

What is happening inside my child's body?
Diaper rashes are rashes on the skin of the groin and buttocks. Despite the name, these rashes can appear even when your child is out of diapers. The phrase has come to describe any rash that appears in the area covered by diapers, pull-ups, and even underpants. This includes the buttocks, the skin folds of the thighs, the penis or vagina, and around the anus.

There are four basic types of diaper rash: irritation rashes, chafing rashes, yeast infections, and bacterial infections. Many other types of rashes that appear in the diaper area also appear on other parts of the body. These rashes — including eczema, psoriasis, impetigo, and scabies — are not exclusive to the groin and buttocks area and therefore are not covered in this section.

An *irritation rash* is the most common diaper rash. Disposable diapers with strong absorbent chemicals or flowery perfumes sometimes cause these rashes. Cloth diapers that are washed in perfumed detergents or dried with a fabric softener also can be problematic. Other sources of irritation rashes are urine and stool that sit next to the skin. This problem is most common among diaper wearers but also occurs among underpants wearers who have accidents or don't wipe thoroughly. In fact, the simple act of covering the diaper area for long periods of time with tight-fitting diapers, pull-ups, or damp underpants can be enough to cause a rash.

Whatever the irritant, the rash looks basically the same: splotchy and pinkish red. Some children are not at all bothered by it; others protest with diaper changes or simple cleaning of the area.

A *chafing rash* results when the diaper rubs against the skin, causing redness where the rubbing takes place. Chafing is made worse when younger toddlers have healthy fat folds in the groin and thighs. These folds rub against each other and trap moisture, adding another source of irritation. Chafing can also occur when a child's thighs rub together as he walks or runs, especially if he is knock-kneed or flat-footed. Chafing rashes usually look redder than irritation rashes. Extreme rubbing can cause bleeding or blistering. The worst part of the rash is usually tucked between folds of skin where air does not circulate.

A *yeast infection* (typically caused by the fungus *candida*) is another source of rash in the groin area. Yeast is a normal inhabitant of the human body, but it is present in limited amounts. In areas that are warm, moist, and dark, yeast can grow quickly, sometimes out of control. The groin and buttocks are covered most of the day and night, providing the perfect breeding ground for yeast. This is especially problematic with toddlers who wear diapers or pull-ups, but even potty-trained children can get yeast rashes. If underpants are slightly damp from poor wiping or a little leakage, the environment mimics a humid diaper.

Most people expect yeast to look white, as it does in the mouth (in the form of *thrush*), but in the diaper area, it does not. A yeast diaper rash has irregularly shaped red patches with a shiny or leathery sheen. When a child has a yeast infection, wiping the diaper area usually stings. And to make matters worse, given the causes of yeast infections, these rashes can be harder to get rid of than many other diaper rashes unless you are willing to let your child run around without a diaper or underpants for much of the day.

Sometimes yeast rashes occur on their own, but often they exist in conjunction with another diaper rash. This double whammy occurs because irritated skin — regardless of the cause — breeds yeast easily. Therefore, the signs of yeast may appear all over the groin area or in isolated small patches, alone or on top of a pre-existing rash.

A **bacterial infection** in the diaper area occurs when bacteria that normally live on top of our skin in small numbers get beneath the skin and multiply. This can happen when the skin is dry or chapped and has small breaks in it. The result is a fiery red rash, sometimes oozing yellow liquid or white pus. Occasionally, the rash will scab over. Most bacterial rashes are warm to the touch and cause intense pain with wiping. They can appear as distinct spots all over the area or as a continuous swath of infected skin.

What can I do?

Air is the best initial treatment or preventive measure for any type of diaper rash. When a rash begins, keep your child out of diapers as much as possible. Leave him naked on the bottom for several minutes between diaper changes, or let him run around naked for as long as you can. Even if this doesn't solve the problem entirely, a rash will almost always improve with exposure to air.

Keep your child's bottom as clean and dry as possible. The longer he sits in a wet or dirty diaper (or pair of underpants), the more contact urine and stool have with the skin.

When you need to clean your child's bottom, use water and cotton instead of perfumed wipes, or even just dunk his bottom into a sink filled with lukewarm water. Prepackaged wipes can sting irritated skin and can even make a rash worse, so if you must use them, rinse them with water first. Alcohol-free, perfume-free wipes are another alternative.

Many rashes respond well to a small amount of cornstarch applied to the groin and buttocks between changes. (Cornstarch is generally recommended in lieu of baby powder made from talc because the baby powder can be inhaled deep into the lungs, causing irritation.) The cornstarch wicks away moisture, reducing the likelihood of yeast growth. You can apply the cornstarch directly, or you can mix it with a little Maalox to make a paste. Spread a thin film of this paste onto the area. A little exposure to air, followed by cornstarch, may be all that is needed to nip an early diaper rash in the bud.

Rashes that are getting worse may improve when treated with zinc. Zinc heals skin and provides a strong barrier against the irritants in urine and stool. There are many diaper creams on the market that contain zinc. Be aware, though, that zinc can sting irritated skin. Sometimes it helps to put a very thin layer of petroleum jelly (Vaseline) on the skin before applying a thin layer of zinc-containing cream. If you think yeast is starting to grow, add some antifungal cream. These and other medicinal creams are reviewed in the treatments section.

When does my doctor need to be involved?

You should call your doctor if the rash gets significantly worse or does not get better. Most rashes will improve within three or four days. After a week of no improvement — or at any point if the rash is worrisome to you — call your doctor.

If a rash develops signs of a bacterial infection (very red skin, pus or yellow liquid oozing, warm to the touch), your doctor should definitely take a look. If the rash is associated with a fever, or if the skin on the diaper area peels off in sheets, a visit to the doctor is necessary.

What tests need to be done, and what do the results mean?

Tests are rarely necessary. However, for a severe or persistent rash, a culture may help to determine the exact cause.

Some sources of diaper rash — such as eczema and psoriasis — also cause rashes on other parts of the body. When the diaper area is the first to be involved, it can seem like an average diaper rash that just won't go away. Sometimes a small skin biopsy (usually done by a dermatologist) can help make the diagnosis. Other times the rash will move to other parts of the body, and the cause will become obvious without any tests.

What are the treatments?
As described previously, cornstarch and creams that contain zinc often help diaper rashes. There are literally hundreds of diaper rash creams on the market, most of which promise to heal the skin. Look for these ingredients, which are proven to soothe irritating rashes and heal skin: allantoin, calamine, cod-liver oil, dimethicone, kaolin, lanolin, mineral oil, petroleum jelly, white petrolatum, and, of course, zinc.

Other additives, often advertised in creams but *not* proven to be effective, include cholecalciferol, peruvian balsam, bismuth subnitrate, and vitamin E.

Finally, avoid creams that have the following ingredients, because they may make the condition worse: boric acid, camphor, phenol, methyl salicylate, and benzoin tincture.

For a yeast diaper rash, an antifungal cream may stop, or at least slow, the growth of the yeast. It is important to remember that yeast thrives in warm, dark, moist environments. Therefore, antifungal creams will help, but they will work much better if they are used sparingly and in conjunction with exposing the diaper area to air. The most common antifungal creams contain nystatin, terbinafine, or an "-azole" compound (clotrimazole, ketoconazole, econazole, miconazole).

What are the possible complications?
One type of diaper rash often evolves into another rash over time. Therefore, the biggest complication of a diaper rash is another diaper rash! Other, less common complications include scarring, bleeding, and pain. Diaper rashes usually hurt most when the area is being cleaned or when urine and stool come into contact with the tender skin.

Additional Resources:
http://www.nlm.nih.gov/medlineplus/encyclopedia.html (Click on "D-Di," then scroll down to "diaper dermatitis.")

http://dermatlas.med.jhmi.edu/derm/ (Go to "search" and type in "diaper dermatitis.")

http://www.uspharmacist.com (Go to "search" in upper right-hand corner and type in "diaper rash.")

ECZEMA (DRY SKIN)

What is happening inside my child's body?

At some point, almost every child has dry skin. Sometimes it appears in small patches behind the knees or in the creases of the elbows. It can involve larger areas of skin, too, such as the fronts of the thighs. And sometimes the skin all over the body gets dry.

The medical term for dry skin is **eczema** or **atopic dermatitis.** In a toddler, eczema classically appears in the folds of the knees and elbows. It can also show up as dry or red patches on the cheeks, behind the ears, or on the wrists or ankles. Some children develop skin-colored bumps on their thighs, the backs of their arms, or their bellies. Eczema can range in color from normal skin tone to bright red.

There are two main causes of dry skin: air and irritation. The skin is designed to be air-dried. When we sweat, the moisture dries off the skin and helps to lower our body temperature. But if the skin is wet and dried too frequently, or if it is not moisturized enough, eventually it will dry out. If you bathe your child every night, you may find that his skin gradually becomes rougher. In dry climates (and when dry indoor heating systems are running in the winter), the skin may lose its moisture quickly. People who wash their hands several times a day, such as doctors, have to continually moisturize their hands, or the skin will become so dry that it will crack.

The other source of dry skin is irritation. Perfumes, detergents, dyes and colors, clothing materials, and even foods can cause the skin to become dry or inflamed. Whereas some children develop a noticeable rash, others simply get dry and flaky. You can usually tell if an irritant is causing your child's rash because the rash will break out only where the irritant comes into contact with the skin. For instance, if your detergent is to blame, the rash will occur only on skin covered by clothing. Nickel, which is found in belt buckles and pant snaps, is another common culprit. A nickel rash occurs only where the nickel touches the skin.

This rule of rash distribution doesn't hold true for food rashes. In fact, when eczema is caused by food, the rash can be localized to a very small area (such as just around the mouth), or it can cover the entire body.

What can I do?

If your child's skin is dry, try to reduce the frequency of baths or showers. This can be difficult if your toddler is adventurous and comes home covered with dirt almost every day. It's also important to use a hypoallergenic moisturizer to help return water to the skin, especially after bathing. As a rule, the thicker the moisturizer, the better. Dermatologists often recommend products such as petroleum jelly (Vaseline), Aquaphor, Aveeno, or even Crisco shortening (you know, the stuff you can cook with!).

In the summer, try to avoid chlorinated pools, or have your child rinse off after swimming in one. Chlorine is a common source of eczema exacerbation.

If your house is heated and the dry heat seems to be making the eczema worse, try using a humidifier or vaporizer. The goal is to return moisture to the air, helping to moisturize the skin. But be careful not to use a device that creates so much moisture that droplets of water collect on the walls or ceiling. This can cause mold to grow, which can mark the beginning of a new potential health problem. Also, make sure to wash out the humidifier often to prevent bacteria and mold buildup in the unit.

When something irritates the skin, remove the irritant. In fact, once the skin is irritated, you should try to use only color-free, perfume-free detergents, soaps, and lotions — even if you don't think that a detergent, soap, or lotion was the original culprit. Doing so will prevent further irritation, because perfumes and colors almost always exacerbate already irritated skin. Sometimes running the laundry through an extra rinse cycle to make sure all of the detergent is out of the wash can help speed healing.

And don't forget to trim your child's nails. Dry skin is itchy skin.

By keeping his fingernails short, you will minimize bleeding and other complications from scratching.

When does my doctor need to be involved?

If the skin is so dry that it bleeds, your child needs to be treated by a doctor: broken skin can become infected. Other reasons to call your doctor include eczema that appears to be spreading (despite attempts to control it) or is causing your child significant discomfort.

What tests need to be done, and what do the results mean?

Most of the time, children with eczema do not undergo any testing. Rather, irritants are removed, moisturizers or anti-inflammatory creams are applied, and the eczema resolves. However, if the eczema is severe and an underlying allergy is suspected, then testing may be done.

Allergy tests require either that the skin be pricked with several small needles or that blood be drawn from a vein. Given the discomfort to the child, you can see why allergy testing isn't automatically recommended. Furthermore, it is not very accurate in children younger than two years of age. And even when allergy testing is done, the source of the eczema is not always identified. For all of these reasons, it is often easier to use a trial-and-error approach, removing suspected allergens and then, if your child's skin improves, reintroducing them one at a time to see what happens.

The two main types of allergy testing are skin testing and RAST (blood) testing. Neither test is perfectly reliable.

A **skin test** involves pricking your child's skin with tiny needles, each coated with a specific allergen — cat dander, mold, egg, and so on. If the area around a needle stick becomes red and irritated, the test is positive. This test generally works well as long as someone can convince your child to participate. In children younger than two years, negative results do not mean much. For instance, if the skin around the egg needle stick does not react, the child may still have an allergy to egg, even though the test appears negative. Only a positive test proves an allergy. Among older toddlers, skin testing is much more reliable.

A **RAST** test is the most common blood test used to check for allergies. Blood is drawn from a vein (not a finger or heel stick), then checked for various allergies. Blood testing is helpful if the skin is so severely irritated that skin testing cannot be done or if there is concern that a skin test will cause a severe reaction. Like skin tests, RAST tests are not always reliable, especially in younger children.

It is important to remember that antihistamines such as diphenhydramine (Benadryl), loratadine (Claritin), fexofenadine (Allegra), and cetirizine (Zyrtec) can interfere with allergy test results. If your child is taking any medicines, discuss them with your doctor several days before allergy testing. A medicine might need to be stopped up to a week prior to testing.

What are the treatments?

The best treatments for eczema are moisturizing and removing the irritant. These treatments are reviewed earlier in this section.

Some cases of eczema may be treated with a steroid cream or a nonsteroidal anti-inflammatory cream. These are used in addition to moisturizers. Steroid creams come in a range of strengths. Over-the-counter creams contain either 0.5 percent or 1 percent steroid. Prescription creams can contain 2.5 percent steroid or more. These creams have some side effects if they are used too often or over too big an area, because the body absorbs the steroid. When too much is absorbed, side effects such as mood or appetite changes can result. However, it is important to emphasize that this is extremely rare. More commonly, steroid creams used in the same area over time can cause the skin to thin, changing the pigmentation. Among the steroid creams are the mild steroid hydrocortisone 1 percent (sold under a number of brand names, including Cortaid), the moderate steroid triamcinolone acetonide (Aristocort), and the strong steroids fluticasone propionate (Cutivate) and mometasone furoate (Elocon).

Nonsteroidal anti-inflammatory creams are an alternative to steroid creams. The two used with children are tacrolimus (Protopic) and pimecrolimus (Elidel). Both of these work well to calm inflamed skin. Initially, they were thought to have fewer side effects than steroids. However, in 2005 a warning was added to the label identifying a potential increased risk of cancer with use of these nonsteroidal creams. This issue is being studied, and the current recommendation is to avoid using these creams in young children, especially those under two years.

What are the possible complications?

When the skin becomes so dry that it cracks, it can easily become infected. Likewise, when a child scratches an irritated area, the skin can break, and a secondary infection may result. Skin infections may require antibiotic treatment.

Many other conditions are associated with eczema. These include **asthma,** rashes other than eczema (such as **hives**), **ear infections,** and **sinus infections.** Like eczema, these conditions occur because of inflammation somewhere in the body — lungs, skin, sinuses, and so on — making it difficult for that part of the body to work effectively. In the lungs, inflammation makes breathing difficult because it clogs the airways. In the skin, inflammation causes swelling, irritation, and itchiness. In the sinuses, inflammation causes congestion, creating an environment ripe for bacterial infections. Because inflammation lies at the core of all these problems, it is not uncommon to discover that a child with eczema also has other skin sensitivities, allergies, sinus problems, or asthma. In fact, one triad is so common — eczema, asthma, and allergy — that it has a name: **atopy.**

Additional Resources:
http://dermatlas.med.jhmi.edu/derm/ (Go to "search" at top and type in
   "eczema.")
http://www.nationaljewish.org/medfacts/testing.html
http://www.medic8.com/healthguide/articles/topicalsteroids.html

◈   ◈   ◈

FRECKLES AND MOLES

What is happening inside my child's body?

A freckle is a small pigmentation, usually no bigger than an eraser head, caused by exposure to the sun. A mole is a bigger version of a freckle and results from a combination of genetic predisposition and sun exposure. They both come from skin cells (called **melano-cytes**) that produce dark pigments. Whereas freckles usually show up in sun-exposed areas and in patches by the dozen, moles can appear anywhere on the body, ranging widely in shape and size. In medical terms, a mole is also known as a **nevus.**

Your doctor will examine any moles on your child's skin. A mole should be watched over time to determine whether it is changing in shape, size, color, or appearance. The general rule about moles is as follows: A mole that is perfectly circular and that has consistent color and texture throughout is typically benign. A mole that has an unusual shape, that is partially raised and partially flat, or that has multiple colors throughout will be followed more closely or even removed. If your child has several moles, or if he has one mole that looks worrisome to you, you may want to take him to a dermatologist for evaluation.

What can I do?

There is nothing you need to do about freckles or moles, except to point out to your doctor any that are changing or worrisome. If you are not sure whether a mole is changing, it may help to take a picture every few months to document any changes.

To prevent freckles and moles, use sunscreen. Sunscreens are rated by SPF, or sun protection factor. This number can range from 0 to 50. Pediatric sunscreens are formulated with high SPFs (never use a sunscreen with an SPF less than 15) and other kid-specific features, such as fun colors, easy-to-apply dispensers, and waterproofing to minimize the need for reapplication. Sunscreen should be used on any sun-exposed area. This generally includes the face, ears, forearms, and lower legs, although a child wearing a bathing suit will need more areas covered. If your child will not wear a hat and has thin or fair hair, you should apply sunscreen to the scalp as well. And be sure to apply sunscreen to the tops of your child's feet.

When does my doctor need to be involved?

When there is a significant change in the size, shape, color, or consistency of a mole, talk with your doctor. Moles that suddenly bleed, itch, or ulcerate should be evaluated by your pediatrician or by a dermatologist.

What tests need to be done, and what do the results mean?

In a young child, moles are rarely removed. However, a dermatologist may want to take a small **biopsy** — a sample of the tissue in the mole — to determine whether the mark is **benign** (not worrisome) or **malignant** (cancerous). This is a fairly uncommon occurrence among toddlers. The older the patient, the more likely it is that a mole will be biopsied.

What are the treatments?

If a mole is determined to be worrisome by a pediatrician or dermatologist, it may need to be biopsied or removed. This is the only treatment. Medications, creams, or lasers are not used in lieu of removal.

What are the possible complications?

It is possible for a birthmark or mole to become malignant over time. About 1 percent of newborns are born with one or more moles, most of which are quite small. The risk of a small mole becoming malignant is very low, and this usually occurs only during or after puberty.

The bigger a nevus is, the greater the chances that melanoma will develop in the mole. For example, in moles bigger than about half an inch (1.5 cm), the risk of malignancy is about 5 percent. It is estimated that the risk of developing melanoma is about the same for people born with moles and people who acquire them later in life.

Additional Resources:

http://www.nlm.nih.gov/medlineplus/encyclopedia.html (Click on "B-Bk," then scroll down to "birthmarks — pigmented.")

http://dermatlas.med.jhmi.edu/derm/ (Go to "search" and type in "nevus.")

http://www.dermatologychannel.net/moles/

IMPETIGO

What is happening inside my child's body?
Impetigo is an infection of the skin caused by bacteria. It usually appears first as a red mark, becomes flaky or pus filled, oozes, and eventually scabs over.

This rash is a result of bacteria that normally live on the skin, such as **staphylococcus** (staph) and **streptococcus** (strep). On top of the skin, these bacteria cause no problems. But if they get underneath the skin through small cuts, bug bites, or scratches, they can cause inflammation and local infection. The most common sites for impetigo are around the mouth and nose, but it can occur just about anywhere on the body.

Many cases of impetigo go away on their own within two to three weeks. However, some cases continue to spread, get worse rather than better, or seem never to go away. Children at the highest risk for impetigo are those who have had skin problems (such as eczema) in the past. Skin that has a tendency to become inflamed is also more susceptible to infection.

Impetigo is theoretically considered highly contagious, probably because a large number of bacteria are contained in a very small space. However, most of these bacteria are harmless on the surface of the skin. Therefore, when impetigo is passed from one person to another, the bacteria must find a way underneath the skin of the recipient, or the rash will not appear. This does not happen very often. A child with impetigo can spread it to other children or can spread it to other parts of her own body. The bacteria can live on sheets, towels, and clothing, providing other routes of spread. Impetigo is considered to be contagious until all of the lesions are gone or until a child has been on antibiotics for at least 24 hours.

What can I do?
If your child has impetigo, the most important first step is to explain to her the importance of keeping her hands off the rash. By minimizing touching and scratching, you can minimize spread.

Older toddlers can follow these directions, although they usually need to be reminded repeatedly; younger toddlers often cannot.

Trim your child's nails. Nails trap bacteria, facilitating spread. Also, the more your child picks at a scab, the slower the healing, and the greater the likelihood that the area will be further infected.

Keep dry skin moisturized. This prevents breakage and minimizes entry points for bacteria. Frequent bathing, use of drying soaps, and swimming in pools treated with chlorine can increase dry skin. Try to minimize baths and use moisturizing soaps. After your child has been swimming in a pool, rinse her off or bathe her. And after all baths, use a moisturizer.

When does my doctor need to be involved?
Your doctor should see your child if the impetigo is getting worse in one particular area, continuing to spread, or not getting better after two to three weeks. If your child is complaining of significant pain associated with the impetigo, have your doctor take a look. Anytime a child has a fever associated with impetigo, a doctor should evaluate the child.

What tests need to be done, and what do the results mean?
Tests rarely need to be done. It is quite obvious to most clinicians what is causing this distinct rash.

If there is concern that the bacteria have moved into the bloodstream, a complete blood count and a blood culture may be done. This is highly unusual with impetigo.

What are the treatments?
Impetigo will usually go away on its own. When it doesn't, antibiotics can be used to help kill the bacteria. For isolated spots of impetigo, you can use a topical antibiotic cream or ointment. Many different types are sold over the counter, including Neosporin, bacitracin, and triple antibiotic ointment. If one of these does not help, your doctor may prescribe a stronger topical antibiotic, such as mupirocin (Bactroban).

Generally speaking, antibiotic ointments work better than creams because the medicine penetrates more deeply. However, creams tend to be less greasy.

Oral antibiotics are used to treat impetigo that has spread to distant places on the body. Oral antibiotics also are used for impetigo that is located inside the nose or mouth, since these areas cannot be treated with topical antibiotics. Finally, oral antibiotics are used for rashes that are not improving — or that are getting worse — despite the use of topical antibiotics. The most common classes of oral antibiotics used to treat impetigo are penicillins, cephalosporins, and sulfa drugs.

What are the possible complications?

If treated appropriately, run-of-the-mill impetigo will not cause scarring. However, it can leave a scar, especially if your child scratches often. Generally speaking, the scars are very subtle.

Rarely, the bacteria causing impetigo spread to distant parts of the body. This can cause bigger problems, such as infection of the bloodstream (**bacteremia**), the lungs (**pneumonia**), or, in very rare cases, the entire body (**sepsis**). It should be emphasized that these types of spreading infections are uncommon with impetigo.

Additional Resources:
http://www.nlm.nih.gov/medlineplus/encyclopedia.html (Click on "I-In," then scroll down to "impetigo.")
http::/dermatlas.med.jhmi.edu/derm/ (Go to "search" and type in "impetigo.")

MOLLUSCUM CONTAGIOSUM

What is happening inside my child's body?

Molluscum contagiosum is a wartlike rash that is very common during childhood. It is caused by a virus that is a member of the pox family (the same family that includes chicken pox).

Molluscum has a distinct appearance in children. It consists of 1- to 5-millimeter bumps that are perfectly round, slightly raised, and opalescent pink or flesh-colored. If you look closely, you will usually see a small dimple in the middle of each bump. This dent (called the ***umbilicated center,*** as in umbilicus, or belly button) is the hallmark of molluscum. Sometimes molluscum bumps appear individually, but more often they appear in clusters of three or four on different parts of the body. The total number of molluscum lesions can be anywhere from 2 to 200. Sometimes the bumps itch.

The virus gets underneath the topmost layer of skin by entering through tiny breaks usually around hair follicles. It exists only on the skin and never affects other organs in the body because it does not travel through the blood.

As its name implies, molluscum contagiosum is considered quite contagious. For this reason, it usually appears on parts of the body that most often come into contact with other people: the arms and legs. It can also be spread in a swimming pool with direct person-to-person contact (it is not transmitted through the water), and it can be self-spread when a child touches the rash and then touches another part of the body.

The incubation period for molluscum ranges from two to seven weeks. This means that if your child is exposed to molluscum, the rash will usually appear within two months. There have been some reports of molluscum appearing as long as six months after initial exposure.

What can I do?
Not a lot. If your child is old enough, explain that it is important to avoid touching the bumps in order to limit spread. Homeopaths and herbalists may have some recommendations about how to treat molluscum, but there are no proven home remedies for parents to try on their own. Patience is the best cure, as molluscum always goes away over time.

When does my doctor need to be involved?
Generally speaking, molluscum does not need medical attention. However, if the number of molluscum bumps increases dramatically, or if the rash becomes itchy and you think there might be a secondary infection caused by your child's scratching, let your doctor know. Children with eczema may have more significant cases of molluscum requiring medical intervention.

What tests need to be done, and what do the results mean?
Occasionally, there is doubt as to the cause of a rash. If you and
your doctor are not sure that your child has molluscum, a lesion
may be scraped and examined under a microscope.

What are the treatments?
Molluscum will go away on its own, but this can take anywhere
from six months to five years. Sometimes schools or day care centers will bar entry to a child with obvious molluscum. Because it
takes so long for the rash to go away on its own, children in a
school or day care quandary may be candidates for more aggressive treatment.

Molluscum can be removed in a doctor's office in a number of
ways, including **cryotherapy** (freezing with liquid nitrogen or
dry ice); scooping out the lesion using a scalpel or other instrument to get rid of both the superficial bump and the virus underneath; treating with a liquid (such as podophyllin, cantharidin,
iodine, or salicylic acid) to burn or blister the area; or even tape
stripping (repeatedly applying and removing adhesive tape to
remove the top layer of skin). Lasers and electric needles (called
electrocautery) also can be effective. Regardless of which
approach is used, retreatment is usually required every four to six
weeks for several months. Because the treatments themselves can
be painful and leave scars, they are generally used on toddlers
only when absolutely necessary.

At-home medical treatments include creams, ointments, and
gels that help get rid of the underlying virus. One such treatment
is tretinoin, a form of vitamin A. This is the same ingredient that is
used to treat facial acne in teens and young adults and to reduce
wrinkles in older patients. Other topical treatments include potassium hydroxide and imiquimod. Although these therapies are significantly more comfortable than the more invasive techniques
listed above, none of them has a very impressive success rate.

Oral medications such as cimetidine also have been used to
treat molluscum. Cimetidine is normally used for the treatment of
stomach and intestinal ulcers. Again, the success rate with cimetidine is mixed at best.

What are the possible complications?

Molluscum can scar, especially when your child scratches the bumps and they become infected. Molluscum also can scar with treatment, as burning, lasering, scooping, and scraping can all leave marks.

Additional Resources:
http://www.aad.org/ (Go to "public resource center" and click on "dermatology A–Z." Click on "M," scroll down to "molluscum contagiosum," and click on "AAD pamphlet.")
http://dermatology.cdlib.org/92/reviews/molluscum/diven.html

◈   ◈   ◈

PARVOVIRUS B19 (FIFTH DISEASE)

What is happening inside my child's body?

Fifth disease is a mild illness with a classic rash caused by a virus called **parvovirus B19.** It tends to occur during the toddler years, although it can infect people of all ages.

The rash is often described as "slapped cheeks" because the cheeks get bright red, just as if they had been slapped. Its medical name is **erythema infectiosum.** The rash also appears on other parts of the body, notably the trunk, shoulders, and upper arms. Here it looks like red lace or sunburn. The rash is hard to miss, but it does not hurt at all. Occasionally, it itches just a little. It lasts anywhere from 3 to 10 days.

Generally speaking, once the rash is visible, your child will be happy and healthy. Prior to the appearance of the rash, he may experience a low-grade fever, some muscle or joint pain, and increased sleepiness. Often, however, kids with fifth disease feel great.

Probably the most frustrating aspect of fifth disease is that it is contagious before the rash appears. Because many children feel fine when they have it, parents don't know that their child is "sick," and so the illness is spread unwittingly. In fact, by the time the rash appears, the child likely isn't contagious anymore and can go to school or out on playdates. Regular hand washing is always a good way to minimize the spread of any infection, even when you think your child is well.

During the contagious period, parvovirus is spread by direct contact with saliva or nasal discharge. Young toddlers who are still mouthing toys are very effective spreaders of parvovirus. Older toddlers who wipe their noses with their hands and then reach for toys, doorknobs, and other objects also spread the infection rapidly. Sharing eating utensils, drinks, or food can pass parvovirus from one person to another.

The incubation period for fifth disease is anywhere from three or four days to three weeks. This means that the time from initial exposure to being contagious and ultimately breaking out in a rash can range widely. Once your child has had fifth disease, he is immune to it for the rest of his life.

If you have a pet, you may have heard of parvovirus among dogs and cats. This is a different type of parvovirus. Your pets and children cannot pass the illness back and forth.

What can I do?

There is not much to do for fifth disease because most kids feel fine. If your child has mild coldlike symptoms, treat fifth disease as you would any other mild illness: maximize clear liquids, minimize dairy products, use a fever reducer when necessary, and limit physical activity when possible. By the time you read this chapter, however, your child's symptoms will probably be gone and the rash will have appeared.

There really is nothing to do for the rash. If it itches significantly, try giving your child an oatmeal bath (either using actual oatmeal or an oatmeal-containing bath solution). When your child gets out of the tub, pat him dry, but try not to wipe off the film covering his skin. This film provides anti-itch properties.

It is worth noting that the rash can recur weeks or even months later. The triggers that tend to bring out the rash are fever and sun exposure.

When does my doctor need to be involved?

Because fifth disease tends to be so mild, your doctor usually doesn't need to be involved. But if you are unsure whether parvovirus is the cause of your child's rash, contact your doctor.

Call your doctor if your child has a history of chronic illness associated with anemia (such as sickle-cell anemia) or an immunodeficiency (such as HIV). Parvovirus can exaggerate preexisting anemia.

What tests need to be done, and what do the results mean?

The rash of fifth disease is so classic that the diagnosis can usually be made when your doctor looks at your child. Testing is generally unnecessary.

However, if your child has a chronic illness associated with anemia, your doctor may suggest checking a complete blood count and parvovirus antibody levels. The blood count will determine whether the anemia has been made worse by the viral infection. The antibody titers look for evidence of current or recent parvovirus infection.

What are the treatments?

Parvovirus is a self-limited disease. This means that it runs its course and gets better on its own. Medications are not necessary.

In the rare case that the rash itches significantly, you can give your child an antihistamine, such as the over-the-counter diphenhydramine (Benadryl) or loratadine (Claritin), or the prescription hydroxyzine (Atarax) or cetirizine (Zyrtec). Diphenhydramine is available in both creams and oral preparations. The oral form works significantly better than the cream.

For children with severe chronic anemia who are infected with parvovirus, a blood transfusion may be necessary. Healthy children without chronic illnesses do not face this risk.

What are the possible complications?

The most significant complication of parvovirus is **anemia.** The virus can reduce the production of red blood cells by the bone marrow, causing anemia. This is why parvovirus is more worrisome among children with chronic illnesses associated with anemia (such as sickle-cell anemia, immunodeficiency, and cancer). If the number of red blood cells is already low and a child contracts parvovirus, the blood level can drop so low that it can pose a serious health risk. Severe anemia causes a child to be pale and weak and to have trouble with some organ function.

Adults who get parvovirus from their children may have the rash along with coldlike symptoms, including joint pain. It is not uncommon for adults to complain of sore wrists and knees.

Among pregnant women who are infected with parvovirus, the fetus is at a theoretically increased risk. Fetal anemia can cause rare complications such as miscarriage. The risk of complications during pregnancy is stated as less than 5 percent, but in clinical practice most obstetricians say the risk is much lower than that. Remember, most adult women already have antibodies to parvovirus, and even if they don't, just because someone is exposed does not mean she will become infected with the virus.

Additional Resources:
http://www.cdc.gov/ncidod/diseases/ (Select "P" and scroll down to
    "parvovirus B19 infection.")
http://www.nlm.nih.gov/medlineplus/ency/article/000977.htm
http://dermatlas.med.jhmi.edu/derm/ (Go to "search" and type in
    "parvovirus.")

RINGWORM

What is happening inside my child's body?

Ringworm (also known as ***tinea***) is not caused by a worm at all. Rather, it is an infection caused by a fungus. The infection can actually appear anywhere on the body, and depending on where it is, it is given different names. Ringworm on the feet is called ***tinea pedis*** (athlete's foot), on the scalp ***tinea capitis,*** and on the rest of the body ***tinea corporis.***

Tinea on the majority of the body looks like a perfect circle with central flaking and sometimes some mild redness. If you look closely at the edges, you may be able to see tiny pinpoint blisters forming the perimeter. Dark skin may appear lighter where there is ringworm.

Between the toes, tinea doesn't look nearly so circular, and the perimeter is often more flaky than blistery.

Tinea on the scalp looks perfectly round but doesn't always have associated central flaking. Instead, the area can be almost bald, with short stubs of broken hair extending 1 to 2 millimeters above the scalp. The presence of broken hairs within the patch helps to distinguish ringworm from **alopecia** (hair loss).

Sometimes the area with tinea itches; other times it is hardly noticeable. If your child scratches the rash, the central area can become very red, bloody, or even scabby.

It is important to remember that many different organisms live on our skin. Bacteria, viruses, and fungi are all normal inhabitants. When these invaders grow rapidly or penetrate under the skin surface, they can cause an infection. But it is a safe bet that most of the time, we all have a little bit of fungus or bacteria somewhere on our bodies, and we don't need to worry.

Fungi like to live in places that are warm, wet, and dark. Therefore, tinea thrives in parts of the body that meet these criteria — the groin, skin folds, and armpits. Yet it is not uncommon to see a patch of ringworm on an arm or leg, in an area that is airy and dry.

Ringworm is reportedly contagious, passed from one child to another when there is skin-to-skin contact or sharing of brushes, combs, towels, clothes, and so on. However, given that we all have various organisms living on our skin at all times, just because your child comes into contact with someone who has ringworm does not mean that she will develop the infection.

Dogs and cats commonly carry ringworm. This type of infection is slightly different from the one typically seen in humans, but it can be passed back and forth between pet and owner. Small pets, such as hamsters and gerbils, also can carry and transmit ringworm. In fact, transmission from these animals is actually more common than from cats and dogs.

What can I do?

There is not much you can do to prevent tinea except minimize the environment in which it likes to grow. If your child has ringworm in an area that is warm, dark, and moist, try to make the area cool, light, and dry.

For rash in the diaper area, let the area air out. Keep your child naked between diaper changes or let her run around the house naked for as long as possible. If your child is already wearing underpants, make sure they are loose fitting, allowing air to get in and out. And if the underpants get wet, put on a dry pair as soon as possible.

For the feet, classic athlete's foot occurs when the feet are sweaty and do not air out regularly. Try to take off your child's socks after a long period of play, especially on hot days. After a bath, be careful to dry between the toes to prevent moisture from collecting there.

There are many over-the-counter creams available to treat ring-worm. They generally contain either medicinal antifungals or other ingredients that help reduce the number of fungi and make the environment less conducive to the growth of fungi. In general, apply only a thin layer of cream. Remember that the wetter the area, the more likely it is that fungi will continue to grow, even if the moisture comes from an antifungal cream. These creams are described in detail in the treatments section.

When does my doctor need to be involved?
Your doctor does not need to see your child if she has a garden-variety ringworm rash. However, if the rash spreads, persists for a long time (weeks), causes significant discomfort such as itching or burning, or begins to look as though it is secondarily infected with bacteria (it becomes red, warm, and inflamed), your doctor should take a look.

What tests need to be done, and what do the results mean?
Tinea is fairly easy for a doctor to diagnose by sight, making tests unnecessary most of the time. However, if there is uncertainty, the rash can be scraped so that a few cells can be inspected under a microscope. If a microscope is not readily available, the sample can be sent to a laboratory, where the fungi can grow in a culture.

What are the treatments?
The home remedy — air, air, and more air — is the best way to begin to eradicate tinea. However, sometimes it is not enough, or the rash appears in an area that is already fairly clean and dry. In these cases, antifungal creams can be beneficial. The most com-

mon creams contain nystatin, terbinafine, or an "-azole" compound (clotrimazole, ketoconazole, econazole, miconazole). Usually the cream must be used for four to six weeks before the rash resolves. Remember to use a thin film rather than a thick layer of cream. The tinea will respond to the medication in the cream, but air continues to be an important part of the treatment.

Ringworm on the scalp requires oral medication. Topical treatments do not work, probably because they do not penetrate deep enough into the scalp. The most common medicine used is griseofulvin. It must be taken daily for at least four to six weeks to eradicate the tinea.

What are the possible complications?

Ringworm on the scalp can cause significant hair loss. However, once the infection has resolved, the hair should grow again, and the bald patch should fill in.

Skin infected with tinea can become secondarily infected with bacteria, as broken, inflamed skin is fertile ground for bacteria to grow.

Tinea can spread from one part of the body to another. Most commonly, ringworm appears on the scalp, on the feet, and in the groin, although it can appear just about anywhere.

Additional Resources:
http://www.nlm.nih.gov/medlineplus/encyclopedia.html (Click on "R," then scroll down to "ringworm.")
http://dermatlas.med.jhmi.edu/derm/ (Go to "search" and type in "tinea corporis.")

SCABIES

What is happening inside my child's body?

Scabies is a skin infestation caused by a tiny insect called a mite. Its scientific name is *Sarcoptes scabiei*. The female mite lands on the skin and slowly burrows underneath to lay her eggs. The mite moves about a quarter inch per day, leaving a trail of eggs and feces. About a month after entering the skin, the mite dies. The eggs hatch two to four weeks after being laid, and the young larvae return to the surface of the skin, where they mature into adult mites. They mate, and then the females begin the process of burrowing down all over again.

The burrowing accounts for the classic scabies rash: narrow, vertical lines an inch or two long near an area of bumps, pimples, or simply irritated skin. The mites and their eggs eventually cause an allergic reaction, resulting in intense itching, especially at night. The rash and itching usually appear about four weeks after initial infestation.

The rash appears most often in warm parts of the body such as skin folds (wrists, elbows, and knees), the webbed areas between fingers, the buttocks, and the belt line. In an infant or young toddler, the most common place to see a scabies rash is on the upper chest around the nipples. In fact, if you don't see it around the nipples, it probably isn't scabies.

It is not uncommon to mistake another rash for scabies. Among the conditions most commonly confused with scabies are patches of multiple mosquito bites or rashes resulting from allergic reactions. Both of these conditions can cause little bumps that look to the untrained eye like scabies.

Scabies is contagious by direct skin-to-skin contact. The longer the skin contact, the more likely it is that transmission will occur. The mites can also live on sheets, towels, and clothing for up to 72 hours, so sharing these items can spread the infection. After 72 hours, however, the mites do not survive away from the human body.

It can take a month or two for symptoms of scabies to appear, especially the first time someone is infected. Once you have had scabies, itching may occur only a few days after your next exposure. It is important to realize that a person can be reinfected with scabies several times; there is no immunity to this mite.

Scabies can infest people from all walks of life: rich and poor, black and white, young and old. It is spread more easily in crowded living conditions.

Pets can get scabies, but it is a different form called ***mange.*** Although this mite can spread to humans and cause some itching, it dies quickly on human skin. This form of scabies does not require any treatment (for the human) because it is always short-lived. Your pet, however, may need medication.

What can I do?

Wash everything! Remember that mites live on sheets, towels, and clothing for up to three days. Wash your laundry in hot water and dry it in a hot dryer for one hour to maximize effectiveness. Washable toys should be washed. Nonwashable stuffed animals, dolls, and toys made of cloth should be put in a garbage bag and sealed for two weeks. Vacuum all your carpets, especially in high-traffic areas.

Keep your child's nails short. This is important because scabies causes intense itching, even after it has been treated. By cutting the nails, you will prevent related problems such as breaking the skin and secondary bacterial infection.

When does my doctor need to be involved?

Although the rash will need to be treated, if you know what it is, your doctor does not necessarily need to take a look. If you are not sure whether the rash is actually scabies, call your doctor and ask whether you should bring your child in.

If you think your child's skin has become secondarily infected from scratching, take your child to the doctor.

What tests need to be done, and what do the results mean?

If your doctor is unsure whether your child has scabies, a skin scraping can be done to look for the mites and their eggs. In the area of rash, a thin layer of skin cells is scraped using a blunt instrument such as a dull blade or the edge of a microscope slide. The scraping is then viewed under a microscope.

This is the only test that can be done to find scabies, and it is far from perfect. Infections can be missed because it takes very few mites to cause a rash. In fact, it is not uncommon for someone who has scabies to have fewer than a dozen mites altogether. So the chances that mites will actually be scraped in the sample are low.

What are the treatments?

There are a number of creams that treat scabies. In general, the principle is the same for all of them. The cream must be applied from the hairline down to the toes and left on overnight — a minimum of 8 hours but up to 14 hours. The entire surface of the body needs to be covered, including between the fingers and toes, under the fingernails, and in the crease of the buttocks. The only places that do not get covered with cream are the center of the face, the scalp, and the female genitals (the penis and scrotum should be treated). In the morning, bathe your child to clean off all the cream. Do not limit the cream to the areas with the rash because the mites can crawl elsewhere. Sometimes the treatment is repeated after 7 to 10 days.

The most commonly used medication is 5 percent permethrin (Nix or Elimite). This cream is generally very well tolerated, although it may cause some stinging or burning. In the past, lindane was a commonly used alternative. However, lindane has been found to have neurological side effects, specifically seizures, when overapplied, so it has been pulled off the market in some states. In extreme cases, an oral medicine such as ivermectin may be used for severe cases of scabies. Oral medication is generally not used to treat scabies in young children.

Everyone who has had close contact with an infected person should be treated for scabies. This means that the entire family will probably be sleeping slathered in cream for at least one night. Be sure to treat the family and implement all household cleaning measures at the same time. This will minimize the risk that one person will continue to be infested.

To help control the itching, antihistamines such as diphenhydramine (Benadryl), loratadine (Claritin), cetirizine (Zyrtec), or hydroxyzine (Atarax) can be given. It is safe to give these medications at the same time you are using permethrin. Diphenhydramine is available in both creams and oral preparations. The oral form should be used because it is much more effective and it won't physically interfere with the actual scabies treatment.

What are the possible complications?

Itching often lasts for weeks after treatment. This is normal — it does not mean that the mites are still alive. Unless a new rash appears, do not worry that treatment was ineffective.

Additional Resources:

http://www.cdc.gov/ncidod/diseases (Click on "S" and scroll down to "scabies.")

http://www.aad.org/ (Go to "Public Resource Center" and select "Dermatology A–Z," then click on "S" and scroll down to "scabies.")

http://dermatlas.med.jhmi.edu/derm/ (Go to "search" and type in "scabies burrow.")

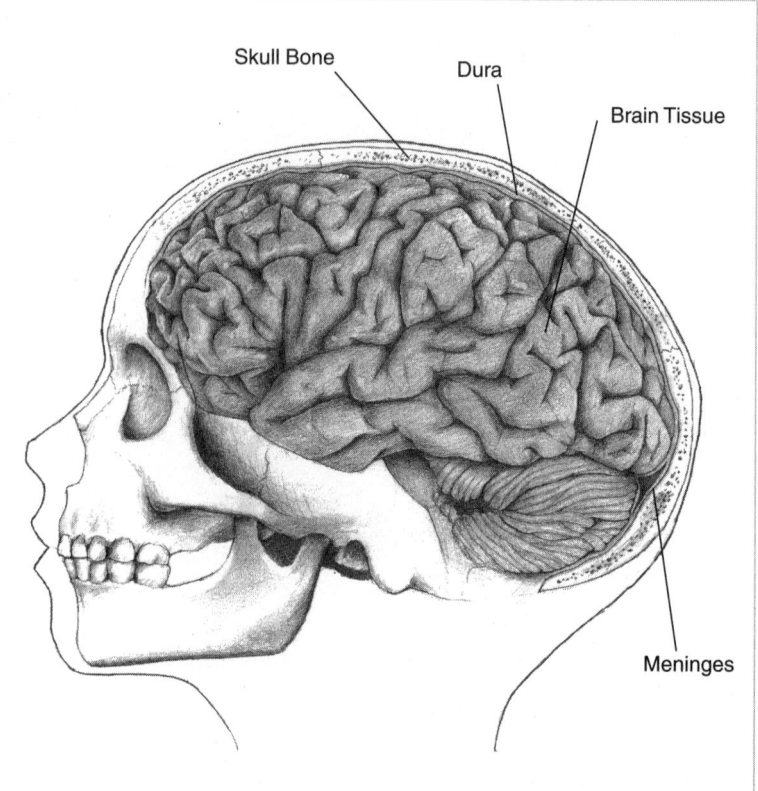

The brain is protected by three layers of insulation:
a cushion of fluid (meninges); a thick, fibrous tissue
coating (dura); and a resilient shell (skull bone).

2

Head

HEAD TRAUMA

What is happening inside my child's body?
Toddlers hit their heads often. They fall, trip, roll, and stumble. The sound of a head hitting the floor or wall can be a gut-wrenching noise. Before you panic, thinking that your child may have done serious damage, look at her. The best sign that there is nothing to worry about is that your child cries immediately, then calms down and goes back to her usual activity. Even if a big lump (often referred to as a "goose egg") emerges within minutes, her head is probably fine. In fact, goose eggs tend to be reassuring, because the swelling is heading outward onto the scalp and not inward toward the brain.

Trauma is the leading cause of injury and death in children younger than 16 years of age. Children have a higher risk of head injury in accidents than adults. This is partly because they have larger heads (relative to their body size) and underdeveloped neck muscles.

Head trauma, in the most general terms, is classified as mild, moderate, or severe. One type of mild to moderate head injury is called **concussive injury** or **concussion**. A concussion is defined as a head injury associated with any of the following: loss of consciousness, amnesia, seizure, or altered mental status. If your child has a concussion, she may complain of a headache, visual changes, dizziness, or ringing in the ears. She might have poor balance, confusion, or difficulty concentrating.

A child who has had a concussive injury is at increased risk of more significant damage with a second head trauma in the initial six months following the first event. This is why a child who sustains a concussion should not be involved in activities that put her at risk of another head injury for the next six months, including sports such as soccer, football, and gymnastics.

A severe head injury can result in bleeding inside the skull. When the bleeding occurs between the covering of the brain (called the **dura**) and the brain itself, the injury is called a **subdural hematoma** (a hematoma is a blood collection). Most frequently, the bleeding occurs here when there is a tear in a vein along the surface of the brain. The subdural bleeding that follows head trauma may be sudden and large, or it may be slow and chronic.

Another type of bleed is an **epidural hematoma.** Here bleeding occurs between the dura surrounding the brain and the skull bones, causing blood to collect around the outside of the brain. This is notably different from a subdural hematoma because it cannot cause bleeding within the tissue of the brain. And unlike a subdural hematoma, which is caused by a broken vein, an epidural hematoma usually (but not always) results from a torn artery. Because arteries carry "high-pressure" blood, these bleeds tend to be sudden and large.

Finally, there is an **intraparenchymal hemorrhage** (or **cerebral contusion**). This is bleeding in the brain tissue itself — not near the skull, but deep in the brain. Think of it as a bruise in the brain tissue. The degree of intraparenchymal hemorrhage can range from a mild bruise to a large clot or hematoma.

Most signs that a head trauma might have caused a concussion or a bleeding injury appear within six hours of the injury. (In rare cases, they can appear 24 to 48 hours later.) These include loss of consciousness immediately after the trauma, seizure, abnormal behavior, vomiting, or inappropriate sleepiness. The sleep issue can be difficult to assess because most toddlers are due for a nap or bedtime within six hours of an injury. Appropriate sleepiness according to your child's regular schedule is *not* cause for concern unless it is coupled with other signs.

What can I do?

If your child has just hit her head, check for the signs that go along with a concussion or bleed.

If she has started to cry, console her. Sometimes a child will cry so hard that she will vomit, and it becomes difficult to tell whether the head trauma or the crying caused the vomiting.

If a big goose egg appears, try to ice the area. Bags of ice can be uncomfortable because ice cubes often have sharp edges. Crush the ice or, better yet, use a bag of frozen corn or peas that will mold to the shape of the head. An ice pack that is completely frozen can be too cold, so if that's all you have, wrap it in a towel. It is nearly impossible to convince a toddler to comply with putting on an ice pack. Sometimes wetting a washcloth, ringing out the excess water, and freezing it for a few minutes to cool it down is the only source of cool a toddler will accept. Do the best you

---

**HOW TO ASSESS FOR CONCUSSION
AFTER A HEAD TRAUMA**

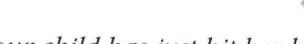

If your child has just hit her head and your answers to the following questions are no, your child probably does not have a concussion. Call your doctor if you have any doubt.

- *Did the child lose consciousness or become sleepy after hitting her head?*
- *Did the child vomit after the head trauma?*
- *Did the child's behavior change dramatically so that she is not acting like her usual self? (Is she confused, speaking with slurred speech, or extremely unsteady?)*
- *Is the child having a seizure?*
- *Is there bleeding that will not stop?*

can — even a couple of minutes with a cool compress will help minimize swelling. If your child has a large goose egg or if the lump continues to grow, call your doctor.

Children often hit their heads just before it is time to take a nap or go to bed at night because as they become tired, they are either clumsier or more wound up than usual. As long as you can establish that after the fall, your child resumed her normal demeanor and she did not vomit, you can let her go to sleep. Wake her up about an hour later, and if it is nighttime, again three to four hours later. Make sure she is appropriately annoyed that you are interrupting her sleep.

Some parents like to check their child's pupils. When a child is in a dark or dimly lit room and you shine a flashlight in one eye, the pupil should shrink down rapidly. When the room is bright, the pupils will already be small, and they should be relatively equal in size. I don't find the pupil check all that helpful because a child with unequal pupils is likely one who will have other, more obvious symptoms of a concussion or bleeding.

If your child has broken the skin during the head trauma, apply gentle pressure to the injured area with a dry or damp washcloth. You can try to wash the area with soap if the wound looks dirty. If the skin is split or the bleeding does not stop, your child may need stitches.

When does my doctor need to be involved?

If your child loses consciousness immediately after a head trauma or begins seizing, call 911. If she becomes increasingly sleepy (and it is not naptime or bedtime), vomits, or begins to behave in an inappropriate or unusual manner following a head trauma, call your doctor right away. If you are not sure whether your child is okay, it is best to check with a doctor.

If the skin on the face or scalp is split, or if there is a significant amount of bleeding, your child may need stitches. Call your doctor or, if the bleeding continues despite gentle pressure, consider going to the emergency room. Also, if she has not had a tetanus shot, she may need one.

Call your doctor if there is a noticeable dent in the forehead or if your child is complaining of impaired or altered eyesight. You should also call your doctor if there is any clear liquid coming from your child's nose or ears when she is not crying. If your child has a goose egg that seems to be growing in size, call your doctor.

What tests need to be done, and what do the results mean?
In most cases of head trauma, no tests need to be done. However, if your child has lost consciousness, vomited, seized, or experienced a change in behavior following the trauma, she will likely need an X ray or CT scan.

An X ray of the head is called a **skull film.** It will show whether there is a fracture of the skull but generally will not show if there is any associated bleeding. Sometimes it will show bleeding around the skull bones, either on top of them or underneath.

CT scans provide better images of the bones, brain, and bleeding. Most emergency rooms have spiral CT scanners, machines that can take the CT pictures in 30 to 120 seconds. This is valuable because a toddler will rarely lie still for an extended period of time. If a CT scan is necessary, and if it takes several minutes to complete, the child will need sedation with anesthetic drugs. However, if the image can be captured very quickly, no sedation will be necessary. This removes the risks of sedating medicines and the need for a pediatric anesthesiologist to be involved.

A CT scan can show collections of blood around the skull or within the brain tissue and fractures of the skull bones.

What are the treatments?
For an uncomplicated head trauma — when your child cries immediately after the trauma and then resumes normal activity with no vomiting, behavior change, or inappropriate sleepiness — no specific medical treatment is necessary. It is still important to observe your child over the next several hours.

If the head trauma is complicated by a skull fracture or concussion, your child will likely need to be observed in the hospital overnight. Often a CT scan is repeated 6 to 12 hours after the initial scan to make sure the internal bleeding has stopped. Many times the bleeding is self-contained, and no intervention is necessary.

In rare cases, the bleeding around the skull or within the brain is significant enough to exert pressure on the brain tissue. In such an instance, the blood must be removed. A neurosurgeon will become involved in the care of the child, often drilling a small hole in the skull to help drain the blood and relieve the pressure. This is a very rare consequence of toddler head injuries. In extremely unusual circumstances, a child may need brain surgery to remove a large blood clot or to stop ongoing bleeding.

What are the possible complications?

Serious head trauma can be associated with a number of complications. Probably the most common — and most benign — is a headache. Using an over-the-counter pain reliever such as acetaminophen (Tylenol) will usually solve the problem. Rarely, a child will develop chronic headaches after a head injury. This is more common in a child who has a family history of migraines. These headaches usually get better within a few months of the injury. However, if your child develops recurrent headaches, you should let your doctor know.

Most concussions are small, and symptoms last only a few minutes or hours. They are generally not associated with any permanent brain damage. However, repeated concussions can cause permanent damage. This is an especially important issue for young athletes whose sports injuries involve the head.

Additional Resources:
http://www.packardchildrenshospital.org (Go to "search" in upper right-hand corner and type in "head trauma.")
http://www.aafp.org/ (Go to "search" in upper right-hand corner and type in "head trauma.")
http://www.mayoclinic.com (Go to "search" in upper right-hand corner and type in "head trauma.")

HEADACHES

What is happening inside my child's body?

Children get headaches, just like adults. However, a child is not always able to communicate that he has a headache either because of limited language skills or an inability to express what he is feeling in his body.

Because it can be so difficult for a toddler to describe a headache, he will often simply resort to holding his head or ears. Sometimes a toddler with a headache will bang his head against the wall, a stimulus that may counteract the pain. Other cues that your child is experiencing a headache include complaints of eye pain, cheek pain, or pain with chewing.

There are three general types of headaches: structural (something in the brain is causing the pain), secondary (headaches caused by some other underlying problem, often somewhere else in the body), and benign (all of the rest).

Structural headaches are the most worrisome. Here a mass — such as a tumor or a collection of blood — somewhere in the brain causes the headache. Most structural headaches are worst in the morning and get better as the day goes on. They increase with pressure from sneezing, coughing, or vomiting. They tend to get progressively worse in both intensity and frequency over time.

Structural headaches can also result from a head trauma that involves bleeding in or around the brain. A concussion or hemorrhage causes significant pain. Most older children and adults describe this pain as "the worst headache of my life." If your toddler has a head trauma and does not complain of a headache, but instead has a big bruise that looks like a goose egg, you can usually be reassured that there is no associated bleeding. Goose eggs represent swelling of the tissue outside the skull and are not associated in any way with brain injury. Head trauma is covered in detail in the preceding section.

Secondary headaches are caused by some underlying problem. Among toddlers, headaches are often associated with infections. An ear infection may cause a child to bang his head, or he may hold the side or top of his head to communicate his pain. A sinus infection can cause discomfort around the cheeks or in the middle of the forehead. In extremely rare circumstances, a headache may be the result of an infection of the brain itself (called **encephalitis**) or the fluid surrounding the brain (called **meningitis**). A child with one of these infections will look very ill and may have a high fever, have a significantly depressed energy level, or exhibit unusual behavior.

Even an infection far from the top of the head may cause a secondary headache. A classic example is strep throat: it is not uncommon for a child with strep throat to complain of a headache, even sometimes in lieu of a sore throat. Viral infections such as mononucleosis (Epstein-Barr virus) and influenza are also associated with headaches.

The last category of headaches is **benign headache.** This category encompasses all other headaches. As with adults, children can have headaches without any associated problems. They can also have recurrent headaches, such as migraines and tension headaches. In families with a history of chronic headaches, young children who have inherited this tendency may begin to experience their headaches as early as the toddler years.

Classic **migraines** are exceptionally bad headaches that can be accompanied by an **aura** — visual changes such as flashing lights (**scatomas**) that obscure the visual field and precede the headache. Most toddlers cannot report these. Almost all children with migraines have sensitivity to light or noise. Migraines can be difficult to appreciate in a toddler who does not have the language to describe them. However, almost all children who suffer from migraines also experience nausea, stomach pain, or vomiting. These symptoms may result from the headache or the visual changes, but they also may be separate manifestations called **abdominal migraines.**

What can I do?

If your child complains of a headache but is otherwise well, you can use acetaminophen (Tylenol) or ibuprofen (Motrin or Advil) to help relieve the pain. Also try dimming the lights and quieting the room. Turn off any music and put away loud toys. If the house is especially busy at the time, shut the door to the child's room to keep the noise to a minimum.

Sleep is probably the best treatment for a benign headache. Although no parent can make a child sleep, encouraging rest and creating an environment conducive to sleep can help.

If your child has associated symptoms, address those as well. For fever, both acetaminophen and ibuprofen will help. A lukewarm bath can bring down the fever as well. For ear pain, drops of garlic-mullein oil (or even olive oil) dripped directly into the affected ear can temporarily relieve the pain.

When does my doctor need to be involved?

Call your doctor anytime your child has an incapacitating headache. When the headache is accompanied by persistent vomiting, visual symptoms, loss of balance, neck pain or stiffness, lethargy, or behavioral changes, let your doctor know right away. If your child has a fever with the headache and you don't have an explanation for the fever (such as a cold), you should call your doctor.

If your child's headache follows a head trauma, you should contact your doctor.

If your child has ear pain or sinus pressure in association with a headache, he should be checked by a physician.

What tests need to be done, and what do the results mean?

Most headaches do not require testing beyond a good physical exam. However, there are some scenarios in which tests will be recommended.

If your doctor suspects strep throat, a strep test will be done. This test is described in detail in chapter 7.

If there is concern that the headache is caused by a structural problem, imaging will be considered. MRI is the most sensitive form of brain imaging. However, it takes time (about an hour, if not more) to do an MRI, and most toddlers require sedation to cooperate. A CT scan can be done much more quickly — often without any sedation — but the imaging is not nearly as detailed. For certain problems, such as bleeding in the brain, a CT scan is as good as (if not better than) an MRI.

In rare cases, when meningitis or another serious illness is suspected, a spinal tap (also called a lumbar puncture) will be done.
More often than not, a CT scan will be performed before the
spinal tap. A spinal tap can demonstrate whether there is an
infection, blood, or other unusual products in the fluid around
the brain. Spinal taps are reviewed in more detail in chapter 19.

What are the treatments?

The treatment really depends on the cause. For a structural headache, the treatment is often surgery. Your pediatrician will recommend that you consult a neurosurgeon who specializes in the
brain.

When the headache is secondary, treating the underlying problem will fix the headache. If an ear infection or sinus infection is
causing the pain, antibiotics should eradicate the infection, thus
relieving the headache.

Benign headaches are the most difficult to treat. Over-the-
counter pain relievers such as acetaminophen and ibuprofen
often help. But many of the stronger medications available for
older children and adults are not approved for use in young children. These medications include the migraine remedies sumatrip-
tan (Imitrex) and isometheptene (Midrin).

One reason benign headaches are difficult to treat is that children rarely identify the problem early on. They would rather continue playing than stop to take medicine. The longer the
headache has been going on before treatment begins, the more
difficult it often is to treat.

What are the possible complications?

Most headaches go away, either with treatment or with time.
However, benign headaches generally recur. The greatest frustration of people who have recurrent headaches is the knowledge
that they will come back again and again. Alternatively, it is reassuring to know that there is no long-term brain damage associated with benign headaches.

The complications of treating headaches depend on the treatment. Neurosurgery to remove a mass or blood clot has an array

of possible complications, including bleeding and infection. When antibiotics are given to treat ear, sinus, or throat infections, a child can have an allergic reaction to the medication. In general, a specific treatment will be offered only if the benefits of the therapy are deemed to outweigh the risks.

Additional Resources:
http://www.clevelandclinic.org/ (Go to "search" in upper right-hand corner and type in "headache.")
http://www.emedicine.com/neuro/topic528.htm
http://www.mayoclinic.com (Go to "search" in upper right-hand corner and type in "headache.")

◆   ◆   ◆

HEAD BANGING

What is happening inside my child's body?

It is not uncommon to see a child walk over to the wall and bang his head repeatedly. Such banging is usually rhythmic and deliberate. This behavior is simply called head banging.

There is no consensus on why some children bang their heads, but one theory is that the behavior stimulates the vestibular system, the same mechanism in the inner ear that controls balance. Other rhythmic behaviors, such as body rocking and head rolling, are thought to be similar because they, too, stimulate the vestibular system. Alternative explanations for head banging range from boredom to self-stimulation (similar, in fact, to masturbation).

Head banging can occur in isolation, or it can be accompanied by other soothing behaviors such as thumb sucking. Often the banging is rapid. Children tend to pick hard surfaces, such as a wall or crib, on which to bang their heads.

A completely different type of head banging occurs when a toddler is having a temper tantrum. Sometimes, out of frustration or anger, a child will bang his head. If your child does this and then sees you react with a wince or an expression of concern, he is more likely to repeat the behavior. In this instance, the head banging is entirely volitional and will continue if it attracts attention. Your reaction — even if it is negative and you try to get him to stop the behavior — provides attention and therefore reinforces the head banging.

Many parents worry that head banging is a sign of developmental problems. In fact, head banging is seen in all types of children. Yes, the behavior can be present among children with developmental delays. But it also appears among developmentally normal children. It alone should not be considered a diagnostic sign of developmental issues.

The other concern related to head banging is injury. Because head bangers tend to bang hard and fast, you may worry that your child is going to injure himself. It is actually quite rare for head bangers to cause serious injury. Although the behavior looks painful, a child will actually limit himself if he experiences pain. It is highly unlikely that a child will bang his head to the point of a concussion.

Head banging is more common in younger toddlers (under age two) than in older ones. The behavior should go away by the time a child is two to three years old.

What can I do?

If your child is banging his head while in a crib, pull the crib away from the wall. Often a child will stand in the crib and bang his head on the wall. Sometimes, however, a child will bang on the crib itself.

Place the crib on a thick rug. This will reduce the noise associated with the banging and immobilize the crib, making it harder for your child to rock the crib back to the wall, where he can bang some more.

Crib bumpers are controversial. They may be helpful to minimize head banging, but your child may use them to climb out of the crib as well. If you use crib bumpers, tie them securely to the railings. Use thin bumpers with the least amount of cushioning possible to minimize the area on which your child can climb. In general, bumpers are not recommended because the risks associated with your child's climbing out of the crib outweigh the risks associated with head banging.

Some people recommend playing rhythmic music to help moderate head banging. This may substitute for the banging altogether, or it may provide a slower rhythm to which the child can bang his head.

For normal head banging, the best thing you can do is to maximize your child's safety and ignore the behavior.

When does my doctor need to be involved?

Call your doctor if your child has injured himself by head banging. If the behavior is escalating and seems to be interrupting normal daily activities such as sleep and play, you should speak with your doctor.

You should also speak with your doctor if you are concerned that your child has signs of developmental delay or poor social skills. Remember, though, that head banging can appear in all types of children. It does not necessarily indicate developmental problems.

What tests need to be done, and what do the results mean?

Isolated head banging requires no testing. If there are other developmental or behavioral concerns, developmental testing may be appropriate.

No imaging studies, such as X rays or CT scans, are necessary with head banging.

What are the treatments?

There are no medical treatments for head banging in an otherwise healthy child. In some children with neurological issues, head banging can be minimized with medication, although these cases are relatively rare.

What are the possible complications?

The most significant complication from head banging is head injury. Banging against a blunt object can cause bruising or abrasions. Although superficial injury is possible, more serious head injury (such as concussion) is nearly unheard-of.

Additional Resources:
http://www.findarticles.com/ (Go to "find" in center and type in "head banging.")
http://www.med.umich.edu/1libr/yourchild/badhabit.htm (Click on "head banging / body rocking" along right-hand margin.)

LICE

What is happening inside my child's body?

A louse is a small (0.08-inch) insect that lives on the human body. Its official name is *Pediculus humanus*. But a louse never lives alone, which is why infestation with this organism is referred to in the plural: lice.

There are actually two distinct types of lice: head lice and clothing or pubic lice. These two different parasites thrive in separate environments and tend not to interbreed.

Lice have a very predictable life cycle. A live louse lays small, oval eggs called **nits** 1 to 2 centimeters above the scalp on a hair shaft. Within 7 to 10 days, the eggs hatch, and within another 7 to 10 days, the female lice mature and lay up to 100 eggs each. Just after hatching, the lice are translucent, but a week later they are reddish brown because they feed on human blood. The average louse lives 30 days.

Lice are contagious, but this does not mean that they can leap from person to person. In fact, they cannot jump, and they do not have wings. They can only crawl. This means that to pass lice, people must have physical contact or share combs, towels, pillows, or any other objects onto which a louse can crawl. A head louse can live for only 24 hours away from the scalp. And pets, even though they have hair, are not reservoirs of lice. Lice need human blood to survive.

Infestation with head lice has often been assumed to be a sign of poor hygiene, but one has very little to do with the other. In fact, many studies have shown that head lice are increasing in populations with good hygiene.

What can I do?

Getting rid of lice can be difficult. Treatment requires two steps. The first step is to kill all of the live lice. This can be achieved either by smothering the scalp with petroleum jelly (Vaseline), mayonnaise, or oil to suffocate the lice or by washing with a medicated shampoo. If you choose to use a suffocant, leave it on the scalp overnight. A shower cap will keep the pillow clean and makes the process a little more manageable. Even the shampoo should be left on for 1 to 8 hours, rather than the 10 minutes recommended in the directions, for best results.

Given the life cycle of a louse, it is clear that a single attempt to kill all of the live lice does not get rid of the infestation. Hundreds of unhatched eggs can survive the initial treatment. So a treatment designed to kill live lice must be repeated a week later to address the previously unhatched eggs. In addition, topical treatments are rarely left on long enough to kill all of the existing lice. The survivors can become resistant to the treatment, eventually creating a bigger problem.

The second step in lice treatment is physical removal. This is done using a fine-tooth comb. By combing through each hair, the nits can be plucked off the hair shafts and the eggs weeded out of the scalp. Some lice will remain affixed to the shafts, but the comb can damage the insects' legs, thus reducing their ability to hold on to the hair.

Each and every nit and egg needs to be removed to prevent reinfestation. That means that *each hair* must be combed through. Just a few shafts retaining nits or unhatched eggs will result in a new round of infestation. The removal process can be very time-consuming in children with thick or coarse hair. There are products available to help loosen eggs and nits that adhere to the shafts. There is also the option of simply cutting off the hair.

When does my doctor need to be involved?

Call your doctor if your child has recurrent visible lice or incessant itching despite attempts to treat the condition with combing and over-the-counter topical therapies.

If your child has scratched his scalp so much that the area is red, swollen, crusty, or tender, you should show your doctor.

What tests need to be done, and what do the results mean?
The presence of lice is a clinical diagnosis: when someone sees the lice or nits, the diagnosis is made. No tests need to be done.

What are the treatments?
As described, the most effective treatment for lice is a combination of treating the hair and scalp and combing out the lice. Treatments are available as both over-the-counter and prescription-only shampoos and creams.

Lice-eradicating treatments are called ***pediculicides.*** They fall under the general category of antiparasitic medications. The most common brands include permethrin (Nix or Elimite), pyrethrin (Rid), and malathion (Ovide). There are stronger drugs available that actually target the nervous system of the louse. Lindane (Kwell) was once the most commonly used, but it has since been associated with seizures and other neurological side effects. Today it is rarely used for the treatment of lice and has even been banned in some states.

A new product currently being studied is applied to wet hair and then blow-dried to make a shrink-wrap over the hair and scalp to suffocate the lice. It is rinsed off after a minimum of eight hours, and the treatment is repeated weekly for three weeks. This product is currently under review by the FDA.

What are the possible complications?
One of the most frustrating consequences of lice is more lice. As mentioned previously, lice infestations often recur because of the nature of their life cycle and the number of treatments necessary to get rid of them. ***Persistent lice*** is defined as a minimum of three incidents over six weeks.

Lice cause itching of the scalp, which in turn can cause scalp injury. Cuts or scalp infections can result. Even with fully treated lice, itching can linger for some time.

There are also complications related to the treatment of lice. Neurotoxins aimed at killing the lice can cause neurological problems (such as seizures) in a child. This is why neurotoxic drugs such as lindane are not commonly used. The potential for complications is described in the package insert for each medicine.

Additional Resources:
http://www.headlice.org
http://www.nlm.nih.gov/medlineplus/encyclopedia.html (Click on "H-Hf,"
    then scroll down to "head lice.")
http://dermatlas.med.jhmi.edu/derm/ (Go to "search" and type in "lice.")

◆   ◆   ◆

ALOPECIA (HAIR LOSS)

What is happening inside my child's body?

Alopecia means "hair loss." Also known as *alopecia areata,* this disorder generally causes hair loss on the scalp but can affect hair anywhere on the body. In toddlers, isolated or patchy hair loss in one or two small areas of the scalp is by far the most common.

Classic alopecia causes patches of bald skin with almost no visible broken hairs. The patches are generally round or oval. The skin sometimes looks a little pink in the area of hair loss.

The underlying cause is not well understood, but there seems to be a genetic predisposition, with a 10 to 20 percent chance that one family member will get alopecia if another family member has it. There is also a significant amount of evidence that something that triggers inflammation is involved. These inflammatory processes include viral infection, drugs, stress, and autoimmune responses in which the body essentially sees itself as foreign.

In general, alopecia occurs when the hair follicle becomes inflamed, swells, and loses its grip on the hair. This form of hair loss is referred to as "shedding," because entire strands fall out, often in significant numbers. But the shedding effect is not at all immediate. Rather, the hair loss appears three to six months after the triggering event or illness, and then it typically lasts another three or four months. (This is the same reason many new mothers experience hair thinning three to four months after a baby is born.)

There are other causes of isolated hair loss in children. Mechanical force is the most common. Rubbing, tugging, and pulling can all result in hair loss. When a rubber band is repeatedly placed in the same spot near the scalp, or when a ponytail is tied too tight, the hair will break or pull out from the root. This is known as **traction alopecia.** Unlike classic alopecia, which produces patches of completely bald skin, traction alopecia results in visibly broken hairs, and the patches tend to be irregularly shaped.

Other forms of mechanical causes of hair loss include vigorous combing or brushing of the hair or rubbing the scalp repeatedly in the same place. Some children have the habit of pulling on their hair, which causes patches of alopecia. In its most extreme form, this condition is called **trichotillomania.**

Alopecia can be temporary or long-lasting. The majority of children will have hair regrowth within weeks or months. If the alopecia is caused by traction or pulling, as soon as the cause is removed, the problem will go away. In children who have alopecia, however, future episodes of hair loss are not uncommon.

What can I do?

If the cause of the hair loss is mechanical, you can usually fix the problem. If rubber bands are breaking the hair, stop using them. If brushing vigorously is causing the hair to fall out, brush gently and occasionally. If your child has become a hair puller, talk to your doctor about strategies for changing this behavior. One approach is to cut the hair short enough that there isn't much to grab.

If the alopecia is spontaneous, there is nothing you can do to minimize the hair loss. In time, the hair will likely grow back. If the hair loss is significant, hats, hairpieces, or wigs are all worth considering. Most toddlers are not self-conscious, but some will mention that the hair loss bothers them.

When does my doctor need to be involved?

Involve your doctor if your child's scalp is irritated, itchy, or painful, or if it looks infected. If your child is pulling her hair, your doctor may be able to help you change the behavior.

If your child is experiencing long-lasting or recurrent alopecia, you will definitely want your doctor involved.

What tests need to be done, and what do the results mean?
A ***positive pull test*** proves that a child has active alopecia. This test is very simple: if hairs fall out easily with gentle traction at the border of the bald spot, more hair loss can be expected.

Sometimes your doctor will examine the hair to see if it is shaped like an exclamation point, with narrowing just before the root. This is typical of classic alopecia, but it does not always occur when alopecia is present.

What are the treatments?
Generally speaking, time is the best treatment for alopecia. In the vast majority of children, the hair will eventually grow back.

There are some treatments that may help stimulate hair growth, but these are rarely used in children and never in mild cases of alopecia. They include topical steroids, oral steroids, minoxidil (Rogaine), and nonsteroidal anti-inflammatory medications.

What are the possible complications?
There are really no medical complications of alopecia, but the cosmetic consequences and self-esteem issues that may arise are significant. Although toddlers tend to handle alopecia quite well, school-age children may have a harder time, as their peers can be insensitive to the problem.

In some patients with alopecia, the nails also become pitted. This usually occurs in the fingernails but not the toenails.

Additional Resources:
http://www.emedicine.com/DERM/topic14.htm
http://www.naaf.org
http://www.umm.edu/ (Go to "search" in upper right-hand corner and type in "alopecia.")

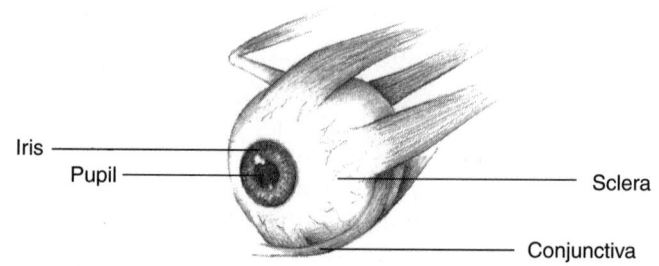

Iris
Pupil
Sclera
Conjunctiva

The eye's pupil and iris are covered by a thin protective coating called the cornea. The conjunctiva protects the white of the eye (sclera) all the way to the lids. The movements of the eye are coordinated by a series of six muscles that surround it, turning the eye in various directions.

3

Eyes

◆

CONJUNCTIVITIS (PINKEYE) AND OTHER EYE INFECTIONS

What is happening inside my child's body?
An infected eye can look pink or red, glassy or goopy, swollen or even a little bit black-and-blue. Many of these infections in the eye fall under the general umbrella of **conjunctivitis.** This term comes from the **conjunctiva,** which is the mucous membrane on the inside of the eyelid. Although the infection often shows up on the white part of the eye (the **sclera**), the real site of irritation is usually underneath the lid.

Not all eye infections are conjunctivitis. The conjunctiva has to be inflamed for the label to apply.

Conjunctivitis is typically very contagious. It is passed when a child with the infection rubs his eyes and then touches something else — a toy, a door handle, or your mouth. Infections that cause pinkeye can also cause other forms of illness, such as an ear infection or a classic "cold" (also known as an ***upper respiratory infection,*** or ***URI,*** with its runny nose, cough, and general malaise). Therefore, from the same underlying infection, one child may develop pinkeye and another may get a cough and a runny nose.

Conjunctivitis can be caused by either a virus or bacteria. With both types of infection, the eyes may look pink or red, making it difficult to tell which is the underlying cause: bacteria or virus.

There are, however, some classic features that distinguish viral from bacterial conjunctivitis. Eyes with viral conjunctivitis typically stream clear, watery tears. Eyes with bacterial conjunctivitis often have a thick yellow or green discharge. Viral conjunctivitis tends to be accompanied by a clear runny nose and a mild cough. Bacterial conjunctivitis is usually either an isolated infection or is accompanied by a green runny nose, sinus pain, a thick or deep cough, or swollen and itchy lids.

Why does the distinction matter? The treatments for viral and bacterial conjunctivitis are different, as are the potential complications. Sometimes an eye infection is not isolated to the eyes. For instance, bacterial conjunctivitis often occurs together with an ear infection. Because the eyes and ears are connected via the sinuses, an infection in one place can spread to the other.

There are certainly many causes of pink eyes that are *not* conjunctivitis. Allergies can cause the whites of the eyes to look pink while the conjunctivas look normal. An eye injury, such as having been hit in the eye, can cause discoloration, although this is more often in the form of a bright red spot from a broken blood vessel. Irritants that come into contact with the eyes can cause watering and a pink discoloration. Soap, shampoo, pollen, lemon juice, and other acidic liquids also can result in pink eyes. None of these is conjunctivitis.

What can I do?

To get rid of the discharge, wipe the eyes gently with a damp washcloth when the lids are closed. Wipe from the corner nearest the nose toward the corner nearest the ear.

With some infections, the discharge is very thick and tenacious. You may need to apply a lukewarm compress to your child's closed eyes for a few minutes so that you can wipe away the discharge more easily.

To help prevent a sticky discharge from repeatedly collecting around the eyes, it may help to gently wash the eyelids with baby shampoo mixed with warm water. Although baby shampoo is generally very gentle and does not cause stinging, you should still try not to get the shampoo under the eyelids.

For itchy eyes, lubricating drops can be very effective. These over-the-counter drops are chemically similar to tears, so they gently bathe the irritated eyes. However, the battle to get drops into a toddler's eyes may not be worth the relief he experiences once they are in.

When does my doctor need to be involved?

Call the doctor if there is a persistent yellow or green discharge from the eyes or if your child has other symptoms, such as a fever or ear pain.

A doctor needs to see your child if his eyelid becomes increasingly swollen or red, or if redness appears in the skin surrounding the eye. This unusual circumstance can mean that the infection has moved into the skin, and from the skin it can spread quite rapidly.

You also need to contact your doctor if the discharge in the eyes is not improving despite antibiotic eyedrops. This can signal that the infection has moved into the sinuses or ears. When this happens, no matter how many eyedrops are used, the eyes will continue to be infected, because the ears or sinuses are a reservoir of bacteria.

What tests need to be done, and what do the results mean?

Sometimes a culture of the discharge can determine what type of infection is causing the pinkeye. If your doctor can pinpoint the infection, treating it becomes relatively easy.

That said, it is usually not that important to do a culture to determine precisely what kind of bacteria is causing the infection. Remember that bacteria normally inhabit the skin, including the area surrounding the eyes. Therefore, when a sample of a discharge is tested, the results often show normal skin bacteria. This is not very helpful in determining a course of action, because it can be very hard to tell whether the normal bacteria are contaminating the culture (masking the true source of the infection) or whether they have actually infected the eyes. Normal bacteria can indeed cause conjunctivitis, but almost all antibiotic treatments used for conjunctivitis are effective against these bacteria. If your child is started on antibiotics, you can be fairly certain that the medicine will treat an infection caused by the bacteria that normally live on the skin. So unless the eye continues to get worse despite treatment, a culture is generally not needed.

If your child's eyelid swells and becomes infected, a CT scan or an MRI may be necessary. These pictures determine where the infection is located — on the outer skin only or behind the eye. Infections within and behind the eye are extremely rare and require significantly stronger medicines. If left untreated, these infections can lead to blindness.

What are the treatments?
Whether conjunctivitis requires medication depends on the underlying cause. Bacterial conjunctivitis can be treated directly with antibiotic drops or gels. Oral antibiotics also are used to treat bacterial pinkeye because the medicine gets to the eye via the bloodstream.

Viral conjunctivitis will not improve with antibiotics. This is because viruses are not killed by antibiotic medications. Viral pinkeye usually causes a watery drainage, but it also can cause a thicker discharge. In this case, all you can do to help your child is to clean his eyelids carefully when the discharge accumulates. The virus will resolve on its own over time.

When the source of pink eyes is an allergy and the allergy is severe, antihistamines or steroids (in the form of eyedrops or oral medications) may be used. This is covered in chapter 5.

What are the possible complications?
Most eye infections are uncomplicated. However, if the infection moves deep into the surrounding skin or behind the eyeball — rather than remaining on the lid — it can spread rapidly. This secondary infection is called **cellulitis,** meaning that there is inflammation of the skin and deeper tissues. Two of the most worrisome complications of conjunctivitis are periorbital cellulitis (*peri* means "around"; *orbital* means "of or relating to the socket") and orbital cellulitis (infections within the socket behind the eye).

Periorbital cellulitis (also known as ***preseptal cellulitis***) usually starts as a sinus infection rather than as conjunctivitis. The infection moves to the skin around the eye, typically causing the top and/or bottom eyelid to swell. A red rim can also appear where the infection is spreading. Periorbital cellulitis is far less serious than orbital cellulitis, but in some cases a periorbital infection can move behind the eye, causing orbital cellulitis.

Orbital cellulitis is far more worrisome than periorbital cellulitis. This infection exists within the eye socket — behind the eyeball — involving the muscles, fat, nerves, or bones. Signs of orbital cellulitis include pain with movement of the eye, severe swelling, or high fever. Whenever there is a concern about orbital cellulitis, a CT scan or MRI should be done. Untreated orbital cellulitis can travel along the optic nerve to the brain, causing blindness or ***meningitis*** (infection of the fluid around the brain). Therefore, children with these infections must be treated in the hospital using IV antibiotics.

Additional Resources:
http://www.nlm.nih.gov/medlineplus/encyclopedia.html (Click on "Ch-Co," then scroll down to "conjunctivitis.")
http://www.emedicine.com/emerg/topic110.htm
http://www.clevelandclinic.org/health/ (Go to "search" in upper right-hand corner and type in "conjunctivitis.")

◆ ◆ ◆

CORNEAL ABRASION (SCRATCHED EYE)

What is happening inside my child's body?
The ***cornea*** is a clear layer of tissue covering the front of the eye. It protects the eye from irritants and minor damage. When this tissue is scratched or damaged, the result is called a ***corneal abrasion.***

Anything that swipes across the eye, such as sand, a fingernail, or a piece of paper, plastic, or metal, can cause a corneal abrasion. Because a corneal abrasion is caused by physical damage, it is not contagious.

A scratch on the cornea usually causes acute pain. Bright lights become uncomfortable, and so a child with a corneal abrasion will likely close her eyes in the daylight or in a well-lit room. Her eye will tear frequently, and she will likely blink more often than usual. The eye may look red and irritated, but it also may look completely normal. In some cases, your child may be in so much pain that it is difficult for you to inspect her eye.

What can I do?

You could patch the eye temporarily using a piece of gauze or other material to make your child more comfortable in bright light. Often, though, the patch is more irritating than soothing, especially a makeshift patch placed by a parent. Therefore, it is better to let a health care provider patch the eye than to attempt to do it yourself.

When does my doctor need to be involved?

Anytime you suspect that the eye has been injured, you should consult your doctor immediately.

What tests need to be done, and what do the results mean?

The entire eye — including the eyeball and the area underneath the lid — will be checked for tears, scratches, and foreign bodies (such as pieces of sand or glass). Many doctors will use ***fluorescein*** — a fluorescent eyedrop — along with a handheld light, to try to detect any abrasion. The fluorescein lasts for only a few seconds, is harmless, and does not cause any additional pain.

If a health care provider is unable to examine the eye thoroughly, or if a more detailed exam is necessary, an ophthalmologist (eye doctor) should be called to do an extensive exam. During this ***slit lamp exam,*** your child will sit in a chair, resting her chin on a stable surface. The ophthalmologist will be able to see all layers of the eye, from the cornea to the retina in the back of the eye, and can check for various types of injury. Toddlers are generally able to cooperate with slit lamp exams because they do not hurt.

What are the treatments?

If your child's cornea is scratched, your doctor will likely prescribe an antibiotic to prevent a secondary infection. The scratch itself is probably sterile, unless it was caused by a dirty piece of metal or glass. But a broken corneal surface can attract numerous bacteria, complicating the healing of the abrasion. The antibiotic may be in the form of a drop, an ointment, or an oral preparation.

Your doctor may suggest an eye patch to help make the eye more comfortable. The patch will minimize rapid blinking, which in turn will speed the healing of the abrasion. The most important part of this treatment is to leave the patch in place for as long as directed. If your child removes the patch, she will likely blink more, squint in light, and have more pain because of these automatic responses. All of this movement will delay healing.

Patching the eye is controversial because many children, especially toddlers, find it bothersome. But it really can make your child more comfortable. Most patches are used for only 24 hours. The larger the abrasion, the more likely it is that your doctor will suggest a patch.

What are the possible complications?

The cornea typically heals within a few days. However, a deep abrasion may become infected, especially if prophylactic antibiotics are not used. Abrasions can also scar. Poorly healed corneal abrasions may develop recurrent erosion. Scars and erosions in the eye can cause a range of symptoms, including tearing, mild discomfort, and blurry vision.

In the most extreme cases, the cornea may be so damaged that your child will eventually need a new one. This is accomplished through ***corneal transplantation.*** Although this procedure is exceedingly rare, the prospect of needing such surgery highlights the importance of detecting and treating a corneal abrasion.

Additional Resources:
http://www.packardchildrenshospital.org (Go to "health library," then go to "search" in upper right-hand corner and type in "corneal abrasion.")
http://www.mayoclinic.com/ (Go to "search" in upper right-hand corner and type in "corneal abrasion.")

LAZY EYE

What is happening inside my child's body?
A lazy eye is an eye that wanders in toward the nose or out toward the ear. This laziness can occur constantly, but more often it happens intermittently. In fact, the most common time you will notice it is when your child is tired.

A lazy eye is usually the result of weakness in one of the muscles that control eye movement. There are 6 muscles attached to each eyeball — so 12 in all — that must coordinate to make the two eyes move in sync. If one of those muscles is either too strong or too weak, it will pull (or fail to pull) the eye in a certain direction. This is called **strabismus.** Although laziness could certainly happen in both eyes at the same time, it is far more likely that it will occur in just one eye.

When both eyes seem to point in toward the nose, a child will appear cross-eyed. This can be a result of unbalanced muscles in both eyes, but more often it is simply an optical illusion. The illusion may be caused by a wide space between the eyes, a flat nasal bridge, or a thickening of the upper eyelids where they meet the skin near the nose (called the **epicanthal folds**). In each of these circumstances, the child may appear to have crossed eyes because the whites of the eyes closest to the nose seem smaller than the whites of the eyes closest to the ears. This phenomenon is called **pseudostrabismus.** It is normal in children of many ethnic backgrounds, especially Asians.

The best way to tell whether your child has true strabismus or pseudostrabismus is to look at the way light reflects on the eyes. When your child is looking straight ahead and the light shines in the same place on both eyes, the eyes are aligned. When it reflects in different spots on the two eyes, the eyes are not aligned. Even though this test looks for how light "reflects," doctors refer to it as the light "reflex."

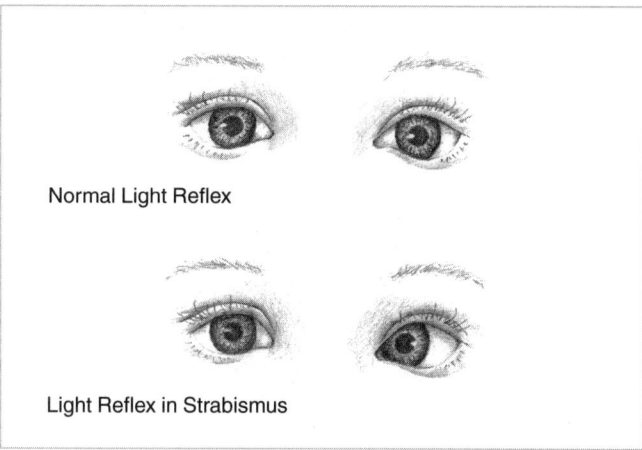

Normal Light Reflex

Light Reflex in Strabismus

The light reflex test can be done only when the person is looking straight ahead. On normally aligned eyes, light reflects at the same point on the left and right pupil or iris. In the case of strabismus, light reflects at different spots on each eye.

What can I do?

If you think your child has a lazy eye, tell your doctor. If it is only intermittent and you catch it because you have seen it in photographs or late at night before bed, let your doctor know. Often lazy eyes are not apparent during a doctor's visit.

If the crossing is an optical illusion and your child has pseudostrabismus, there is nothing you can (or should) do. If you are not sure, ask your doctor to check. As your child grows, the eyes will probably come to look less crossed.

If your child is diagnosed with strabismus, you may need to have him do eye-strengthening exercises. Other medical treatments for strabismus are described in the treatments section.

When does my doctor need to be involved?

If your pediatrician is not sure whether there is a problem, you will likely be referred to an ophthalmologist (eye doctor), who will thoroughly evaluate your child. It is important to address eye

problems early because the brain relies on eye alignment to integrate the information from both eyes and produce a single normal image. If the eyes are not aligned, this can lead to blurry
vision, double vision, or worse. When in doubt, speak with your
doctor.

What tests need to be done, and what do the results mean?

Your pediatrician or ophthalmologist may do a **cover/uncover
test.** This test checks eye alignment and identifies strabismus. In
this test, while an attention-getting object is held in your child's
line of vision, a cover is placed over one eye for at least two seconds and then removed. A normal eye will continue to focus on
the target when the cover is on and off. An eye that is truly lazy
will move slightly when the other (normal) eye is covered. This
lazy eye is trying to maintain focus on the object.

This test is far more reliable when done in an older child or an
adult who can cooperate with the test. In toddlers, sometimes the
only way to determine that the eyes are misaligned is to look at
the light reflex or have an ophthalmologist do a more intensive
exam. Bear in mind that when the laziness is intermittent, the
exam can look normal.

What are the treatments?

When strabismus is diagnosed early (before six years of age,
although this is certainly not an absolute), it can usually be corrected with glasses. The glasses work by keeping the eyes
aligned — converged on a single focal point. The glasses essentially exercise the lazy eye, helping to strengthen weak muscles
and relax overused ones. The strabismus will resolve when the
glasses force a new balance among the muscles surrounding the
eyes. If the balance can be maintained without the glasses, the eyes
will look straight, and the glasses may no longer be necessary.

When strabismus is diagnosed too late, the brain has already
learned to see with misaligned eyes. The brain actually sup-
presses images from the lazy eye because the information coming
in is so unpredictable. In these cases, even with glasses, the eye
will continue to wander. A child whose strabismus is diagnosed

too late may require eye muscle surgery and will likely continue to need glasses after the surgery.

What are the possible complications?

The worst complication of untreated strabismus is **amblyopia,** which means functional blindness in the lazy eye. This happens because the brain is designed to integrate the images from both eyes "in stereo." If one eye is misaligned or wandering randomly, the brain cannot integrate the input from both eyes, and it will categorically reject or suppress the input from the misaligned eye. If the brain accepts the input only from the dominant eye, the nondominant eye will behave as if it were blind. Even though the eye itself is normal, the brain will treat it as though it does not exist.

Amblyopia can be caused by strabismus, but it can also result from a number of other sources. If something blocks or blurs the vision from one eye for a long enough time, amblyopia can result. Examples include cataracts or improperly formed eyelids, both of which can obstruct a child's view. Whatever the underlying cause, when the brain cannot integrate the input from one eye with the input from the other, the eventual result is functional blindness in one eye.

Sometimes amblyopia can be treated by patching the dominant eye, which encourages use of the nondominant eye. But if it is not treated in early childhood, even glasses and patching will not improve the condition.

Whereas most doctors and parents can easily detect strabismus, only an eye doctor comfortable examining young children can diagnose amblyopia without strabismus.

Additional Resources:
http://www.nlm.nih.gov/medlineplus/encyclopedia.html (Click on "Sq-Sz," then scroll down to "strabismus," or click on "Ah-Ap," then scroll down to "amblyopia.")
http://www.hopkinsmedicine.org/wilmer/ (Go to "search" in upper right-hand corner and type in "strabismus.")

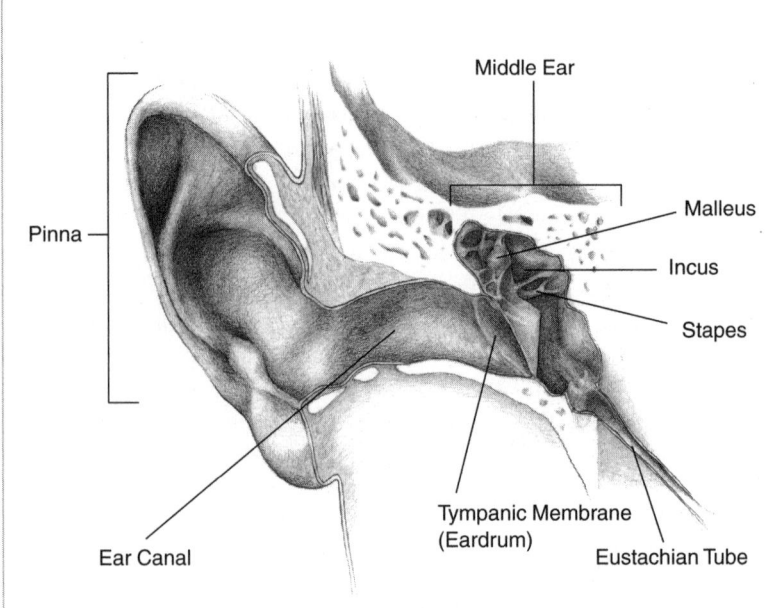

The outer ear includes the pinna and the ear canal.
The middle ear begins at the eardrum and is filled
with an intricate collection of bones responsible
for the transmission of sound. The eustachian tube
drains fluid that collects in the middle ear.

4

Ears

OTITIS MEDIA (EAR INFECTION)

What is happening inside my child's body?
Toddlers often complain of ear pain. But just because your toddler tells you his ear hurts doesn't mean he has an infection. The opposite also is true: some toddlers are so stoic that they aren't bothered by the pain resulting from an infection. Thus, determining whether your toddler has an ear infection can be a challenge.

Ears hurt for a number of reasons, but certainly middle-ear infections are the primary cause. This is especially true if a child has cold symptoms. The term "ear infection" really refers to fluid in the middle ear, located directly behind the eardrum. The medical term for this condition is *otitis media.*

The ear is made up of several distinct parts. The most visible part is the external ear, which includes the firm, folded upper ear, called the *pinna;* the earlobe hanging below it; and the ear canal leading from the visible part of the ear down to the eardrum (or *tympanic membrane*). The middle and inner ear are the parts behind the eardrum. The middle ear houses the three bones — the *malleus, incus,* and *stapes* — that conduct sounds from the middle ear toward the brain. The **eustachian tube** is responsible for draining fluid that may collect in the middle and inner ear.

When fluid fills the area behind the eardrum, a number of things can happen. The bones of the middle ear have difficulty conducting sound when they are bathed in fluid, so a child with an ear infection may have difficulty hearing. The fluid may also put pressure on the eardrum from the inside, causing a feeling of fullness or pain. Sometimes air bubbles will collect, and these are felt as popping in the ear.

Different types of fluid can collect behind the eardrum. The most common is a clear or pinkish fluid associated with a viral infection. In fact, viruses cause about 85 percent of all infections in the ear. But thick, white, pussy fluid also can collect — the sign of a bacterial infection. Sometimes bacteria will appear a few days after clear viral fluid is seen. This is called a **secondary infection** because the fluid generated by the virus provides a breeding ground for the bacteria.

Another type of ear infection occurs in a different part of the ear. Swimmer's ear, or **otitis externa,** is an infection along the ear canal in the external ear (see the next section). It does not involve the eardrum or the middle or inner ear. When doctors or parents talk about a child having an ear infection, however, they are almost always referring to otitis media.

There are many reasons why a child may have ear pain without an infection. These include teething (those molars and eyeteeth hurt when they come in), impacted earwax, and a foreign body in the ear (like that Barbie shoe that's been missing for a few days). Some infections cause ear pain without directly infecting the ear. Strep throat can result in ear pain because the pain in the throat is referred to the ear — that is, it is felt in the ear even though the infection is actually in the neighboring throat. A sinus infection can also cause ear pain for similar reasons.

So how can you tell if your child's ear is infected? If your child is telling you his ear hurts, suspect that it is infected. True ear infections are usually accompanied or preceded by a fever and cold symptoms, but not always. The ear itself or the area around the ear may look red, but this is unusual. If you see fluid coming out of the ear, that is a strong indicator of an infection.

What can I do?

If your child is complaining of ear pain, take his temperature. Impacted earwax will not cause a fever, but teething, ear infections, or neighboring infections in the throat or sinuses may. You can give your child a fever reducer to help him feel more comfortable.

Look inside the mouth. If the gums are swollen and teeth are erupting, the ear pain may be due to teething. However, teething pain felt in the ear is not always associated with visible teething because the pain can be caused by the movement of teeth deep in the gums (not visible when your child opens his mouth). Therefore, looking inside the mouth is not a perfect way to judge whether the pain is related to teething.

If your child has had wax impacted in his ear before and you think this may be the problem, you can try putting a few drops of oil in the ear. Any type of vegetable oil — olive, garlic, you name it — will relieve the pain after a few days of use. You can use the oil at room temperature or run the bottle under warm water so that the oil becomes lukewarm. Two or three drops in each ear every night will help soften the wax. This also makes it easier for your doctor to clean the wax out.

Hydrogen peroxide is another home remedy for softening wax. It can be used the same way that oil is used.

You can clean the wax on the outside of the ear canal, but never attempt to stick a Q-Tip or other narrow object deep into the ear. There are two reasons for this. First, you can inadvertently push the wax farther inside. And second, if your child jerks his head while the Q-Tip is in his ear, you can inflict trauma to the ear canal or even the eardrum.

Although these general tips can help, nothing beats having a doctor look inside the ear to determine whether there is an infection.

When does my doctor need to be involved?
If your child is complaining of ear pain, your doctor should take a look. If his fever is higher than 101°F or he has had a recent cold, if the ear itself is red or swollen, or if you see liquid draining from the ear, you should see your doctor.

What tests need to be done, and what do the results mean?
Tests rarely need to be done when your child has ear pain. Looking inside the ear with a special light called an **otoscope** is usually all that is necessary.

Sometimes doctors will suggest a test called a **tympanogram.** Here a device that looks like an ear thermometer is inserted into the ear and emits sound waves. The sound waves bounce off the eardrum and are recorded on a slip of paper in the form of a bell-shaped curve. The flatter the curve, the more fluid there is behind the drum. Tympanograms are especially useful when a child has had recurrent ear infections and a doctor is trying to confirm whether the fluid is still there.

Tympanograms do not work when there is wax obstructing the canal. Remember that the sound waves need to be able to bounce off the eardrum. If wax is in the way, the curve will look similar to a curve demonstrating fluid behind the drum. For this reason, a doctor should always look in the ear before doing a tympanogram to make sure the canal is clear.

What are the treatments?
Ear infections do not always need to be treated. Remember that viruses cause the vast majority of ear infections, and these cannot be treated with antibiotics (antibiotics treat only bacterial infections). Instead, viral ear infections need to run their course. The pain can be treated with a pain reliever such as acetaminophen (Tylenol) or ibuprofen (Advil or Motrin). These infections almost always go away on their own, but sometimes they leave behind excess fluid that sits indefinitely in the middle ear.

Bacterial ear infections, on the other hand, generally require antibiotics. It should be noted that the approach to treating such infections varies throughout the world. In Europe, for example, doctors will often watch ear infections for a few days before prescribing antibiotics, giving the infections a chance to resolve on their own. This approach has recently been adopted in the United States, although large or symptomatic bacterial infections continue to be treated with antibiotics as soon as they are diagnosed. The goal is to minimize the use of antibiotics.

When an infection is caused by stagnant fluid sitting in the middle ear, as soon as the fluid drains, the infection will go away. However, most bacterial ear infections in infants and toddlers do not get better on their own because the eustachian tubes in young children are flat, and drainage is poor. By contrast, fluid in older children and adults drains more effectively because their eustachian tubes are oriented downward. Based on this anatomical difference, you and your doctor can discuss whether your child needs an antibiotic or not.

Sometimes doctors recommend **tympanocentesis,** a procedure performed in a pediatrician's or ear specialist's office. During the procedure, a small needle is passed down the ear canal and inserted into the eardrum. The pressure behind the drum is immediately relieved, and the fluid drains out the canal. Most children who have had tympanocentesis say that the pain went away the moment the needle punctured the eardrum and that the procedure itself was not painful. However, this procedure takes special training and a compliant child.

When a child has had recurrent ear infections, has not been able to clear the fluid from his middle ear for months, or has associated hearing loss or speech difficulties, **tympanostomy tubes** are an option. These small plastic or metal tubes are inserted into the eardrum by an otolaryngologist (also called an ear, nose, and throat doctor, or ENT). The tubes provide a vent for pressure and a drain for fluid. The procedure requires sedation so that the child will lie still, which is probably the most controversial part of tympanostomy tube placement. Once placed, the tubes stay in the eardrum until they fall out — anywhere from three months to a couple of years after insertion. Sometimes, especially if the tubes fall out relatively quickly, a child will need a second set.

But for the most part, one pair of tubes ends the vicious cycle of recurrent ear infections and antibiotic use.

When your child's ear pain is caused not by infection but by impacted earwax, a doctor or nurse can usually remove the wax. The techniques range from using a tiny Q-Tip to scoop out the wax to irrigating the ear canal with warm water. If the wax is very hard, your doctor may have you use drops for a couple of days to soften the wax, then return for another round of cleaning.

When the cause of your child's ear pain is teething, treatments such as gum rubbing, teething rings, and pain relief medicines can be effective. These treatments are covered in chapter 6.

What are the possible complications?

An untreated bacterial infection can spread to other parts of the body. **Mastoiditis** is a bacterial infection of the mastoid air spaces in the bones directly behind the ear. When the infection moves into these bones, the area becomes red, hot, and swollen, pushing the ear forward. Sometimes the ear itself becomes red and swollen as well. The physical change is dramatic — mastoiditis is hard to miss. This infection is severe and requires strong antibiotics and sometimes even surgery. If your child's ear looks red or swollen, you should contact your doctor.

Ear infections can be associated with eye infections because the bacteria that are growing behind the eardrum can move through the sinuses and up into the eyes. This combination is called *otitis-conjunctivitis.*

Ear infections also can spread into the fluid surrounding the brain. Infection of this fluid is called *meningitis.* This is a very rare complication of ear infections, but when a child with an ear infection travels on an airplane, the risk of developing meningitis increases. For this reason, if your child is complaining of ear pain prior to flying, you should call the doctor.

Multiple ear infections, untreated ear infections, or persistent fluid behind the eardrum can eventually cause hearing loss, with associated attentional and language problems. To avoid this result, doctors often suggest that you bring your child back to the office for an examination after an ear infection is treated with antibiotics. As described earlier, tympanostomy tubes are another means of minimizing hearing loss and speech delay.

Neither teething nor impacted earwax has any long-term effects on the ears. Wax is often a lifelong problem, and many adults continue to need to have their ears cleaned by a doctor.

Additional Resources:
http://www.emedicine.com/emerg/topic351.htm
http://www.mayoclinic.com (Go to "search" in upper right-hand corner, type in "ear infection," and scroll down to "ear infection guide.")
http://www.nlm.nih.gov/medlineplus/encyclopedia.html (Click on "W," then scroll down to "wax blockage.")

◈   ◈   ◈

OTITIS EXTERNA (SWIMMER'S EAR)

What is happening inside my child's body?
The ear has a long canal leading to the eardrum, and behind the drum are the bones that help conduct sound. The term "ear infection" usually refers to an infection in the area behind the drum. This is called **otitis media.** However, the canal itself also can become inflamed or infected. This is called **otitis externa** (or **swimmer's ear**).

There are two main causes of otitis externa: mechanical injury and humidity. Mechanical injury can be inflicted with fingernails, Q-Tips, or anything that scrapes the inside of the canal (such as small toys). Scratches allow bacteria that normally live on top of the skin to get underneath it, causing infection and inflammation.

In fact, this is why our ears make wax. Wax lines the ear canal, preventing it from losing its top protective layer. In most cases, wax minimizes the chances that bacteria will enter through tiny breaks in the skin. However, too much wax can do just the opposite. Large amounts of wax can trap bacteria, increasing the number of bacteria living in the canal. This in turn can cause otitis externa.

The other cause of otitis externa is moisture. This is where the infection gets the name "swimmer's ear." Moisture causes otitis externa by eroding the protective layer lining the ear canal, which in turn makes the skin more susceptible to inflammation. Inflammation causes microscopic breaks in the skin, providing entry points for bacteria.

It is important to note that although water entering the ear (during a bath or shower, for instance) can cause otitis externa, it cannot cause otitis media. And otitis externa caused by bathing is extremely rare. Think about how many baths and showers you have taken over a lifetime. Did you get repeated (or any) otitis externa infections from these? The point here is that parents often worry that they will cause ear infections during routine bathing. In this situation, otitis externa is theoretically possible, but it is very unlikely.

Regardless of the mechanism, when bacteria get under the skin in the ear canal, they multiply, causing swelling, itching, or tenderness. In some cases, the canal may smell bad or produce a yellow or white discharge. It often hurts to touch or pull on any part of the ear, or even to move it as when chewing. Otitis externa also may cause temporary difficulty with hearing.

What can I do?

The best way to prevent otitis externa is to keep the ear canal dry. After a bath or shower, gently wipe the ear with a towel. Frequent swimmers should use a drying agent — such as hydrogen peroxide or rubbing alcohol — after swimming. Earplugs worn during swimming do not seem to reduce the risk of otitis externa.

If your child has otitis externa, some data suggest that acetic acid (vinegar) drops help reduce bacteria in the canal. The recommended regimen is five drops of acetic acid given three times a day for one week. This may be a reasonable thing to try, but if the symptoms get worse, or if your child does not improve with the drops, you should contact your doctor.

There are also many swimmer's ear drops sold over the counter. These are reviewed in the treatments section.

When does my doctor need to be involved?

Call your doctor if the ear appears red or if liquid is draining from the canal. If your child is in significant pain anytime the ear is touched, let your doctor know.

If your child has symptoms of otitis externa along with a fever, you should call your doctor, as the two don't generally go together.

What tests need to be done, and what do the results mean?

Most of the time, tests are unnecessary with otitis externa. However, if the condition becomes chronic, or if it fails to improve with treatment, a culture may be performed. This can help determine precisely what type of bacteria is causing the problem and what antibiotic will be most effective.

The culture is very easy to do: a sterile Q-Tip–like device is used to swab the lining of the canal. But it is usually not that important to do a culture to determine precisely what kind of bacteria is causing the infection. Remember that bacteria normally inhabit the skin, including the skin in the ear canal. Therefore, when a sample is taken, the results often show normal skin bacteria. This is not very helpful in determining a course of action, because it can be very hard to tell whether the normal bacteria are contaminating the culture (masking the true source of the infection) or they have actually infected the ear canal. Normal bacteria can cause otitis externa, but almost all antibiotic treatments used for otitis externa are effective against these bacteria. If your child is started on antibiotics, you can be fairly certain that the medicine will treat an infection caused by the bacteria that normally live on the skin. So unless the ear continues to get worse despite treatment, a culture usually is not needed.

What are the treatments?

Antibiotic drops are almost always used in otitis externa. The drops are inserted directly into the ear, minimizing any systemic (whole-body) absorption of the medication. They typically work quickly and painlessly, although some children continue to have pain for several days after starting the drops. Dozens of antibiotic drops are available. Some are sold as single antibiotics, some as combinations, and some are mixed with steroids to help reduce swelling in the canal. Some ear drops are sold over the counter, while others are available by prescription only.

An *ear wick* may be helpful to mop up the fluid in the canal and increase the delivery of antibiotic drops. Wicks are sold in many pharmacies and drugstores. They are made of foam or gauze and are placed in the ear, remaining there through an entire course of antibiotic drops. The drops travel down the wick, causing it to expand and bring the drops into contact with the infected skin.

For complicated otitis externa infections — such as those that involve surrounding tissues or are associated with fever — an oral antibiotic is often necessary. The downside to this is that oral antibiotics are absorbed systemically and can have consequences for other organs. One of the most common side effects of oral antibiotics is stomach upset.

There is a significant effort among doctors to avoid the use of oral antibiotics in order to minimize the growing problem of antibiotic-resistant bacteria. Resistance is more likely to appear with oral antibiotics than with local (topical) antibiotics.

Because otitis externa can be quite uncomfortable, pain management is important. Numbing drops, such as benzocaine/ antipyrine (Auralgan), can ease the pain for two to four hours at a time. Oral medications such as acetaminophen (Tylenol) and ibuprofen (Motrin or Advil) also work well to reduce pain.

If your child is in extreme pain, your doctor may suggest a stronger pain reliever such as codeine until the infection is more under control. This type of pain is highly unusual with otitis externa.

What are the possible complications?

Untreated otitis externa can spread to the external ear, and even to the tissues surrounding the ear. In very rare cases, namely among immunocompromised people, the infection can spread to the temporal bone located near the ear. This is called *malignant* or *necrotizing otitis externa.*

Additional Resources:
http://healthlink.mcw.edu/article/991235533.html
http://www.mayoclinic.com (Go to "search" in upper right-hand corner
and type in "swimmer's ear.")

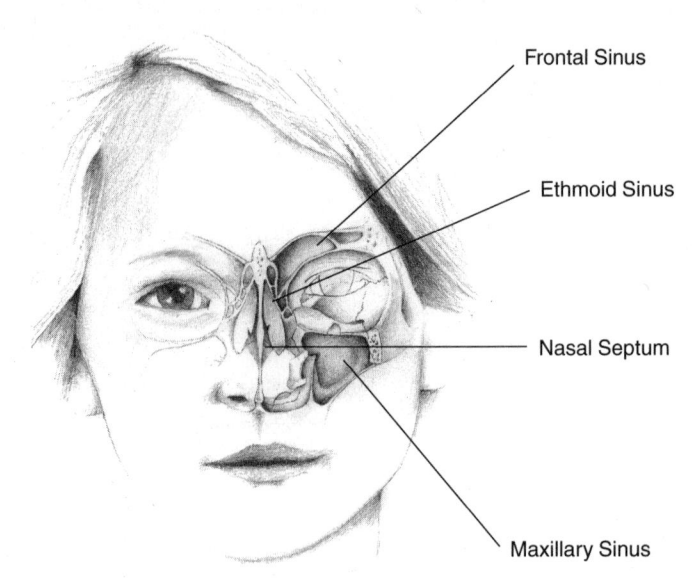

Frontal Sinus

Ethmoid Sinus

Nasal Septum

Maxillary Sinus

The sinuses are actually air spaces within the bones
that surround the eyes and nose. These air pockets develop
over time and are only partly formed in toddlers.

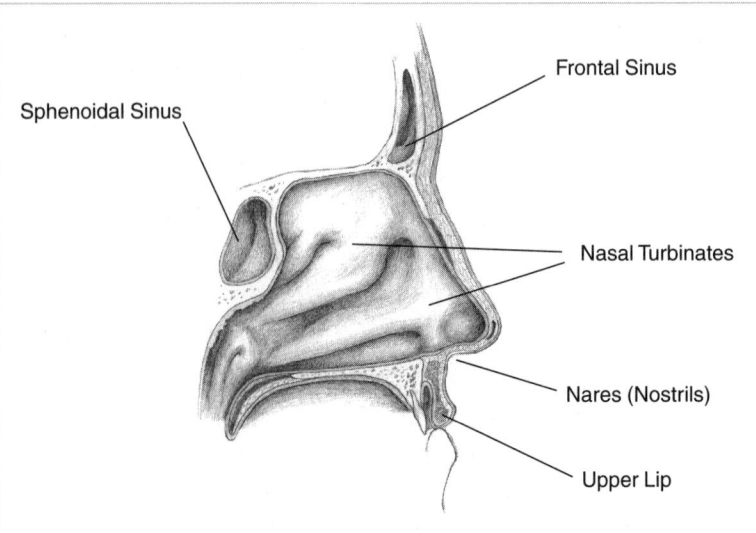

Sphenoidal Sinus

Frontal Sinus

Nasal Turbinates

Nares (Nostrils)

Upper Lip

The nose is surrounded by the sinuses, allowing fluid
or congestion in one area to flow into another.

5

Nose and Sinuses

◆

CONGESTION AND NOISY BREATHING

What is happening inside my child's body?
Congestion describes that rumbly or thick fluid caught in the back passages of the nose. When it drips out the nose or down the back of the throat, it is often called ***mucus.***

Any irritant in the nose can cause congestion: infection (whether viral or bacterial), airborne pollen, dust, mold, or perfume. Teething, with its associated increased mucus production in the upper respiratory passages (including lots of drooling), can cause congestion because the extra fluid gets trapped in the back of the nose.

A congested nose is often described as "stuffed up" or "plugged." The fluid is trapped in the back of the nose near the sinuses, which causes wet, thick, or even musical ("wheezy") breathing sounds.

The opposite of nasal congestion is ***rhinorrhea,*** or a runny nose. With rhinorrhea, mucus drains out the nostrils. From a medical standpoint, a runny nose is preferable to a congested nose because trapped fluid can serve as a reservoir for secondary bacterial infections whereas draining fluid cannot.

Both congestion and rhinorrhea are often associated with a cough because the fluid in the nose drips down the back of the throat. This type of drainage is called **postnasal drip.** It stimulates the gag reflex, causing a cough.

What can I do?

If your child is congested, you want her nose to drain. The easiest way to make this happen is to go into a steam shower or steamy bathroom. (Make sure to prevent the hot water from coming into direct contact with you or your child.) The old-fashioned trick of putting a towel over the face and leaning over a pot of boiling water also works. However, this can be dangerous with a toddler: the water can spill, and the steam can be extremely hot, both of which are capable of burning your child. Another way to get steam up the nose is to have your child drink soup or other warm liquids.

Regardless of your steaming approach, the steam will work its way up the nose within minutes. Once the steam has helped to break up the congestion, an older child can usually blow her nose. Younger toddlers, however, have difficulty mastering nose blowing. You can try using a **bulb syringe** (also called a **nasal aspirator**). This plastic handheld nose and mouth sucker can be used to suck out the mucus, but most toddlers won't let you near their noses with an aspirator. When neither nose blowing nor suction is an option, you are left with waiting to see whether the congestion starts to drain on its own. Although steam is fairly safe, do not stay in a steamy environment for too long. Five to 15 minutes should be plenty.

Humidifiers and vaporizers sometimes help. They work like steam, providing moisture to help break up congestion, but they are significantly less intense. Moisturized air can make a congested child more comfortable, but it doesn't always help the nose to drain. Make sure the humidifier is not running for too long or on too high a setting. When droplets of moisture collect on the walls or ceiling, mold can easily grow. Also, clean and disinfect the humidifier regularly.

If you are really adventurous, or if you have an extremely patient and compliant child, you can help treat congestion by

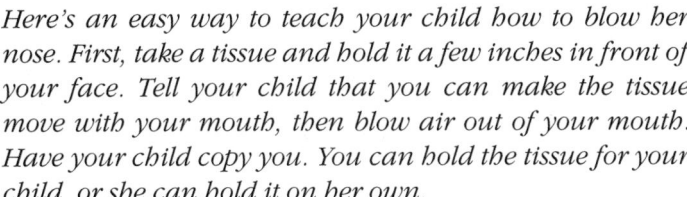

TEACHING A CHILD HOW TO BLOW HER NOSE

Here's an easy way to teach your child how to blow her nose. First, take a tissue and hold it a few inches in front of your face. Tell your child that you can make the tissue move with your mouth, then blow air out of your mouth. Have your child copy you. You can hold the tissue for your child, or she can hold it on her own.

Then tell your child that you can also make the tissue move using your nose. Hold the tissue in one hand (again, a few inches from your face) and cover your mouth with your other hand. Then blow air out of your nose, making the tissue move. Have your child copy you. You can hold the tissue for your child, or she can hold it herself, but either way she should be the one to cover her mouth with one hand.

The first few times, the nose blowing may not be very productive. But your child will have the sensation of moving mucus out — rather than sniffing it back in — and in no time will be an effective nose blower.

squirting saline solution (salt water) up her nose. The key is for your child to sit upright looking straight ahead or tilting her head down slightly. This allows the fluid to be squirted as high up into her nose as possible. If the head is cocked back, the liquid will squirt through her nose and directly into the back of her throat.

Congestion often gets worse with lying flat, so try to prop your child up for sleep. This prevents mucus from pooling at the back of the nose where it meets the throat. Sometimes propping a child up during sleep is nearly impossible, especially if your child moves a lot during the night or naturally scoots down to a flatter part of the bed. But it is worth a try. A child who sleeps facedown on her tummy will generally have less postnasal drip because the mucus can drain out of the nostrils during the night.

When does my doctor need to be involved?

If your child's congestion is associated with difficulty breathing, you need to contact your doctor. Sometimes it is difficult to tell the difference between noisy, congested breathing and labored breathing.

There are some objective ways to determine whether your child is having difficulty breathing. Call your doctor if your child displays two or more of these symptoms or if you have any doubt.

Flaring the nostrils with each breath. This allows more air to flow into the airway and lungs.

Visible flexing or contracting of the long muscles at the neck, between the jaw and shoulders. This pulls on the tops of the lungs, increasing the size of the lungs and the amount of air they can hold. The notch between the collarbones, called the sternal notch, may also be pulling in with each breath.

Visible flexing or contracting of the muscles between the ribs. This pulls on the lungs to open them horizontally. It also increases lung size and capacity. To see these muscles pulling, draw an imaginary line from your child's armpit to her hip. Halfway along that line, look for the ribs moving with each breath. They will look like a row of bucket handles moving up and down.

Moving the belly up and down in an exaggerated way with each breath. This forces the diaphragm down, increasing the depth of the lungs and their air capacity.

Breathing fast. This increases the flow of air into the lungs simply by speeding it up. Remember that a child who has a fever will breathe fast to "blow off" the fever. This is a very good way to help cool down the body; it is *not* a sign that she is having difficulty breathing. In the absence of a fever, the normal rate of breathing is age dependent: young toddlers may breathe 25 to 35 times a minute, while children over two years old breathe 20 to 30 times a minute. (Adults typically breathe 12 to 14 times per minute.) If your child has a fever, give her a fever-reducing medicine. When her temperature has returned to normal, recheck her respiratory rate.

These symptoms are helpful in evaluating a (relatively) calm child. However, if your child is crying, they are not necessarily accurate indicators of difficulty breathing. This is because a crying child will flare her nostrils, open her mouth, and breathe fast, and the muscles between her ribs will pull, as part of crying. Breathing is discussed in detail in chapter 8.

What tests need to be done, and what do the results mean?

Figuring out the root cause of congestion rarely requires any tests. An **upper respiratory infection (URI)** — in which a virus causes congestion, cough, and postnasal drip — is probably the most common culprit among toddlers. Environmental irritants such as pollen and dust are also very common causes of congestion. One way to tell the difference between an infection and an allergy is to have your doctor do a physical exam. Another way is trial and error. If you suspect an allergy, remove your child from the presumed irritant. If the congestion goes away, you have proven an association. If the congestion returns when your child is reexposed, you can be certain that you have found the cause.

Foods also can cause congestion. Sometimes a food causes an allergic response; removing suspicious foods and then reintroducing them may help you identify the cause of congestion. Other times a food is not so much an allergen as a source of increased mucus production. Cow's milk and dairy products can fall into this category. Certainly, when a child has a URI, cow's milk is known to increase mucus thickness and congestion.

What are the treatments?

A number of medicines are used to help treat congestion. These include antihistamines, decongestants, and anti-inflammatories. Which medicine to choose depends on the underlying cause of the congestion.

An **antihistamine** helps reduce the body's response to allergens. When a child is allergic to something — carpeting, cats, cigarette smoke, and so on — the body releases chemicals called histamines upon exposure to the allergen. Histamines produce a classic allergic response: sneezing, watery eyes, and runny nose. Antihistamines blunt this response so that even with exposure, the histamine effect is reduced. Remember, though, that removing the irritant is the best treatment.

Decongestants are medicines that help dry up the fluid and mucus produced by the nose and sinuses. They are designed to treat congestion, but they are really best at mopping up fluid. Therefore, if the mucus is thin and clear, they tend to be very effective. But if the mucus is thick and yellow or green, a decongestant can dry up the fluid but leave behind thick gobs of mucus blocking the back of the nose and the sinuses. This can actually make the congestion worse. Decongestants also may have a stimulatory effect on some children. Be careful when you use one for the first time, because there is a chance that your child will become quite active for a few hours following the dose.

Anti-inflammatories target inflammation in the body. Infections and allergies often stimulate inflammation in the nose and sinuses. Inflammation increases mucus production and thickens the mucus. Using an anti-inflammatory reduces mucus volume and thins the mucus so that it can drain more easily. Remember that a draining nose is always better than a congested one, and this is where an anti-inflammatory may help your child.

What are the possible complications?

It is rare for nasal congestion to become seriously complicated. If it lingers for too long, the mucus congesting the nose can back up through the sinuses — the spaces in the bones above the cheeks, next to the nose, and surrounding the eyes. Children have small and underdeveloped sinuses that can easily get clogged with mucus. From there, a child can go on to develop a **sinus infection** or **ear infection.** These secondary infections are often accompanied by a fever, irritability, and a thick nasal discharge. In rare cases, postnasal drip can drain into the lungs, leading to **bronchitis** or **pneumonia.**

DRUG TABLE: ANTIHISTAMINES, DECONGESTANTS, AND ANTI-INFLAMMATORIES

Class of Drug	Mechanism	Active Ingredients	Common Pediatric Brands
Antihistamine	Blocks histamine, which in turn stops itching, sneezing, runny nose, and watery eyes	promethazine, diphenhydramine	Benadryl Claritin Zyrtec Allegra
Decongestant	Narrows blood vessels, which in turn reduces nose, sinus, and ear congestion	pseudoephedrine, phenylephrine	Dimetapp PediaCare Sudafed Triaminic
Anti-inflammatory	Blocks the chemical chain that leads to swelling and inflammation	NSAIDs such as ibuprofen	Advil Motrin

Additional Resources:
http://www.nlm.nih.gov/medlineplus/encyclopedia.html (Click on "N," then scroll down to "nasal congestion.")
http://www.mayoclinic.com/ (Go to "search" in upper right-hand corner and type in "nasal congestion.")

ALLERGIES AND HAY FEVER

What is happening inside my child's body?

An allergy can do many things in the body. On the skin, it can cause a rash or hives. In the intestine, it can manifest as diarrhea. And in the nose and sinuses, it can result in classic **hay fever,** with watery eyes and a drippy nose.

Allergies are caused by an immune response to some irritant, such as pollen, food, perfume, animal dander, dust mites, or mold. When your child is exposed to the irritant, his body releases a chemical called **histamine** from special cells called

mast cells. Histamines, along with other components of mast cells, cause tissues to become swollen and irritated and to release fluid. Mast cells are most numerous in the skin, mouth, nose, lungs, and intestinal tract, and histamine release in these parts of the body causes the wateriness associated with allergies.

What can I do?

The best way to manage an allergy is to remove the offending agent. If you know what your child is sensitive to, this should be easy. But often you have no idea. In such circumstances, you can begin by trying to minimize exposure to the most common allergens. Here are some good initial steps.

- Vacuum your child's room daily or every other day (if it has carpeting) to reduce the number of dust mites.

- Try running an air purifier such as a HEPA (high-efficiency particulate air) filter in the corner of your child's room to pick up additional dust mites and dander.

- If there is a flowering tree outside one of your windows, try to keep that window closed to minimize pollen entry into the house.

- If your child sleeps with a down pillow or down comforter, try hypoallergenic covers to seal in the feathers.

- If you have a family pet and you suspect that he is the cause of the allergy, make sure the pet is limited to one part of the house away from your child's bedroom.

- If you see mold growing along ceiling, walls, or floor, clean it or have it removed professionally.

- If your child comes home from school with allergy symptoms and her condition improves once she gets home, consider visiting the classroom to see if an obvious allergen — such as a class pet or aging carpeting — is present.

Of course, if the problem is something in the environment, such as pollen, it is almost impossible to minimize exposure. Substances in the air that cause allergies are ubiquitous. But when the seasons change, the allergens in the air change, too, and your child's symptoms should get better.

If your child is just beginning to have a runny nose and the mucus is still fairly clear, you will want to minimize further congestion. Some people feel that it helps to limit your child's intake of milk, cheese, yogurt, and other dairy products. Soy or rice milk products can be used as alternatives.

When does my doctor need to be involved?

Call your doctor if this is the first time your child has allergies and you are having trouble controlling the symptoms. Classic allergy symptoms involve a clear, watery discharge. If the nose runs green or you notice a discharge from the eyes, your child may have a secondary infection, and you should contact your doctor.

Also call your doctor if the symptoms seem to be getting worse or are simply not getting better. If your child is having trouble participating in her usual activities or is having difficulty sleeping, let your doctor know.

What tests need to be done, and what do the results mean?

Whether your child needs testing depends on the severity of her symptoms. A runny nose and an occasional dry cough or sneeze, even if they last a few weeks, don't warrant allergy tests. But congestion and a cough that interrupt normal activity or sleep may prompt testing. Likewise, if your child has associated allergic symptoms, such as hives, you will probably want to find the underlying cause.

There are two main types of allergy tests — a skin test and a RAST test. The RAST test may be a bit more sensitive, but it also is more invasive. Neither test is extremely reliable in children under two years of age.

A **skin test** involves pricking the child's skin with tiny needles, each coated with a specific allergen — cat dander, mold, egg, and so on. If the area around a specific needle stick becomes red and irritated, the test is positive. This test generally works well as long as someone can convince the child to participate. In children younger than two years old, negative results do not mean much — in other words, if the skin around the mold needle stick does not react, the child may still have an allergy to mold. Only a positive result is helpful because it proves an allergy.

A **RAST test** is the most common blood test used to check for allergies. Blood is drawn from a vein (not a finger or heel stick), then checked for evidence of various allergies. Blood testing is helpful if the skin is so severely irritated that skin testing cannot be done or if there is concern that a skin test will cause a severe reaction. Like skin tests, RAST tests are not always reliable, especially in younger children.

Both skin and RAST tests give a range of responses. When a test is positive, the degree of positivity will vary. Therefore, it is possible to distinguish mild from severe allergies using either test.

It is important to remember that antihistamines can interfere with allergy test results. If your child is taking any medicines, discuss this with your doctor several days before allergy testing. The medicine may need to be stopped prior to testing.

What are the treatments?

The most common treatment for allergies is an **antihistamine.** This medicine blocks the histamines that are released from mast cells, aborting their ability to wreak havoc in the nose, eyes, lungs, and so on.

Antihistamines are available in a number of preparations. The over-the-counter brands include diphenhydramine (Benadryl) and loratadine (Claritin). Diphenhydramine appears in some combination medications as well. Antihistamines requiring a doctor's prescription include fexofenadine (Allegra), hydroxyzine (Atarax), and cetirizine (Zyrtec). Most of these are available in liquid form.

In some extreme cases, an antihistamine will not be sufficient to control the symptoms. When this happens, a **corticosteroid** may be used instead. Steroids are potent anti-inflammatory medications that can quickly blunt allergic reactions. However, they tend to have more side effects than antihistamines, which is why they are not generally used as first-line drugs.

Steroids come in the form of nasal sprays, inhalants, syrups, tablets, and even injectables. Nasal sprays and inhalants work locally in the areas where they are received. Therefore, a nasal spray reduces nasal symptoms, while an inhalant targets the lungs and breathing. All of the other forms affect the entire body, exposing the child to higher doses and subsequently more side effects.

What are the possible complications?

The most severe manifestation of an allergic reaction is called **anaphylaxis.** This is a whole-body allergic reaction. It can be associated with hives, swelling (of the lips, mouth, or lung tissue), low blood pressure, and even shock. These reactions range from mild to life threatening.

When an allergy causes an itchy rash, a toddler may scratch at the skin incessantly. This can cause bleeding and a secondary infection. Skin that is scratched repeatedly and is never given the chance to heal can scar.

Allergic reactions in the upper respiratory tract result in the pooling of mucus, which can lead to viral and bacterial infections. **Sinus infections** and **ear infections** are not uncommon consequences of chronic allergies in toddlers.

Additional Resources:
http://www.nationaljewish.org/medfacts/allergic_rhinitis.html
http://www.cchs.net (Go to "search" in upper right-hand corner and type in "allergy.")

GREEN RUNNY NOSE AND SINUSITIS

What is happening inside my child's body?

Toddlers always seem to have runny noses. So when do you need to worry about it? When it is draining clear? Or yellow? Or green? When it has been dripping for a week? A month?

A clear runny nose is commonplace for a toddler. It may represent teething or allergies, or it may just come out of the blue. Most parents — and certainly most pediatricians — don't pay much attention to a clear runny nose unless it has persisted for many weeks or is associated with other symptoms.

But when that clear runny nose turns yellow and then green, there tends to be more concern. A yellow discharge can mean just about anything from a mild viral infection to some irritation in the nose. Yellow usually does not indicate a serious or a bacterial infection.

A green discharge, however, can signify a bacterial infection. A green discharge also can be caused by dried blood. The blood usually results from irritation inside the nose. When the blood is exposed to oxygen and mixed with mucus, it can look green rather than red. Green stuff coming out of your child's nose should not cause you to panic, but it is worth keeping an eye on. It alone does not necessarily mean there is a sinus infection.

A diagnosis of **sinusitis** (or **sinus infection**) requires that your child have at least one of the following symptoms: persistent upper respiratory symptoms, such as congestion, cough, and runny nose lasting more than 10 to 14 days or getting significantly worse after 7 days; increasing headache, especially at the forehead or around the nose; persistent daytime cough; fever; ear pain; or just plain fussiness.

Many of these symptoms are nonspecific, so the bigger picture becomes important. For instance, a child with a fever may have any number of things going on, but a child with a fever, green nasal discharge, and headache on one side of the forehead or face is fairly likely to have sinusitis.

Remember that sinusitis is usually a secondary infection. First the nose gets congested, then the mucus and fluid plugging the nose filter back into the neighboring sinuses. Or the nose is plugged, and the mucus that forms in the neighboring areas cannot drain properly. Either way, congestion has backed up into the sinuses.

It is estimated that 5 to 10 percent of upper respiratory infections (URIs) are followed by a sinus infection. This range represents an average for people of all ages. The sinuses are very small and underdeveloped at birth. They grow through the childhood years, maturing by adolescence. The bigger the sinuses, the more likely they are to become infected. Therefore, even though toddlers get an average of six URIs per year, most never have a sinus infection.

Certain medical issues predispose a child to sinusitis. ***Allergic rhinitis*** — an allergy present in the nose — can cause mucus pooling. ***Gastroesophageal reflux disease (GERD)*** is another predisposing factor. And immunodeficiency can certainly lead to a sinus infection. If the immune system cannot fight viruses or bacteria efficiently, there is a greater chance that infections will occur.

What can I do?

If your child is just beginning to have a clear runny nose, you will want to minimize further congestion. Some people feel that reducing the intake of dairy products (milk, cheese, yogurt, and the like) can help accomplish this. Soy or rice milk products can be used as alternatives.

You may also want to try to dry up the nose by using an over-the-counter decongestant. This class of medications is described in greater detail in the treatments section. The benefit of using a decongestant early on is that it may prevent the accumulation of fluid in the sinuses.

When the nose gets stuffy and doesn't drain very well, steam can help keep things moving. The easiest way to create a steamy environment is to go into a steam shower or steamy bathroom. (Make sure to prevent the hot water from coming into direct contact with you or your child.) The old-fashioned trick of putting a towel over the face and leaning over a pot of boiling water also works. However, this can be dangerous with a toddler: the water can spill, and the steam can be extremely hot, both of which are capable of burning your child. Another way to get steam up the nose is to have your child drink soup or other warm liquids.

Regardless of your steaming approach, the steam will work its way up the nose within minutes. An older child can usually blow her nose, but a young toddler is often unable to do this. (For tips on how to teach a toddler to blow her nose, see page 87.) You can try using a ***bulb syringe*** (also called a ***nasal aspirator***) to suck out the draining fluid, but most toddlers won't let you near their noses with an aspirator. When neither nose blowing nor suction is an option, you are left with waiting to see whether the congestion starts to drain on its own. Although steam is fairly safe, do not stay in a steamy environment for too long. Five to 15 minutes should be plenty.

Nasal sprays can be used to treat congestion, but they are diffi-cult to get into most toddlers. With this technique, saline solution (salt water) or some other liquid is squirted up the nose. The spray helps unclog the nasal passages and stimulates the body's natural mechanisms for clearing infection. It also physically removes bacteria living in the nose, minimizing the risk that they will further infect the sinuses. Irrigation can be performed using lukewarm water, a saline nasal spray, or a special medicated solu-tion. Some medicated sprays contain ingredients to reduce blood flow in the lining of the nose, which in turn reduces mucus production. Other medicated sprays contain steroids that treat nasal inflammation. Steroid sprays are discussed in the treatments section.

Sometimes an anti-inflammatory medicine such as ibuprofen (Motrin or Advil) can help a congested nose to drain by reducing swelling in the nose and sinuses.

When does my doctor need to be involved?
Call your doctor if your child's symptoms have persisted for more than three weeks or if they are getting significantly worse. You also should contact your doctor if your child has an intense headache or a high fever.

What tests need to be done, and what do the results mean?
Sinusitis is usually easy to diagnose based on the course of the ill-ness and the physical exam. However, in some borderline or per-sistent cases, testing may be helpful.

An X ray can show whether there is fluid in the sinuses. The head is held in a particular position so that the sinuses can be visualized optimally. Radiologists call this a **Waters' view.**

Over the past several years, CT scans have become the pre-ferred method for imaging the sinuses. CT scans are much more accurate than X rays when it comes to looking at the sinuses, and they also are fast. It can take as little as 30 to 60 seconds to cap-ture the images necessary to evaluate the sinuses.

One important note: among children who have CT scans for reasons other than possible sinusitis, almost half have swelling or fluid in their sinuses. Because these children do not complain of any symptoms related to sinus infection, it is clear that swelling or fluid in the sinuses can happen incidentally. In other words, seeing fluid in your child's sinuses does not mean that your child has sinusitis.

What are the treatments?

Half of the time, sinusitis resolves on its own. This is why most doctors will not treat sinusitis with antibiotics until the symptoms are increasing (profuse cough, green runny nose, or bad headache) or have persisted for two to three weeks. Furthermore, the course of antibiotics is long. To treat sinusitis completely, antibiotics must be given for 10 to 14 days, sometimes longer.

A broad range of **antibiotics** can be used for sinus infections. Penicillins, cephalosporins, and macrolides (such as erythromycin) are among the most commonly used antibiotics. Your doctor's choice will depend on how recently your child has been on an antibiotic, how sensitive the bacteria in the community are to various drugs, and whether your child is allergic to any medications.

There are many treatments for sinusitis other than antibiotics. **Decongestants** can help drain the sinuses quickly and effectively. These medicines are generally very safe and may be worth trying. They work best when the nasal drainage is clear or thin. If they are not helping the situation, however, they should be discontinued. Decongestants are available in many forms. They can be sprayed up the nose or taken by mouth as a liquid, a chewable tablet, or a melt-away tablet.

Nasal spray steroids can be very effective in reducing swelling and inflammation in the nose. This in turn enhances drainage of the sinuses. In children with large tonsils or adenoids in the neck, nasal steroids may drip down the back of the nose and into the throat, shrinking these tissues as well. This, too, helps with sinus drainage. Many parents wish to avoid steroids because they are worried about the side effects. However, nasal steroids work directly in the nose, with very little medicine being absorbed by the rest of the body. Therefore, there is limited risk of the side effects seen with oral steroids.

In some cases, **oral steroids** are necessary to treat sinusitis. When the sinuses are severely impacted, oral steroids may be the only way to reduce the inflammation enough to allow drainage. In such circumstances, steroids can be an important adjunct to antibiotics — without them, the antibiotics may not be able to penetrate the infected sinuses. When used to treat sinusitis, steroids are generally given for no more than a few days. The risk of long-term side effects is very low, especially if the steroids are used for fewer than 14 days (in a single course) or less than twice per year.

What are the possible complications?

Chronic sinusitis lasts for three months or longer. The symptoms are usually low-grade, but they never resolve completely. They are the same as for acute sinusitis, although a nighttime cough may be more noticeable. Chronic sinusitis is not dangerous, but it can be frustrating for children and their parents.

Occasionally, sinus infections will evolve into ear infections. This happens when the same mechanism that causes congestion in the sinuses also causes poor drainage from the middle ear. Generally speaking, the bacteria causing simultaneous ear and sinus infections will be the same. Thus the antibiotics used to treat one should treat the other.

Additional Resources:
http://www.emedicine.com/ent/topic612.htm
http://www.aaaai.org/ (Go to "search" in upper right-hand corner and
    type in "sinusitis.")

FOREIGN BODY UP THE NOSE

What is happening inside my child's body?

A **foreign body** is anything not organic to the human body: a toy, a piece of wadded-up newspaper, or a bead. Even something technically organic, such as a pea, is considered a foreign body since it's not supposed to be lodged in the nose.

Toddlers put all sorts of things up their noses. Even if your child does not seem bothered, these objects can eventually cause problems and must be removed.

Sometimes objects end up in the nose accidentally. For instance, an object can become lodged in the nose after a fall.

Objects can also wind up in the nose thanks to friends or siblings. As a result, the answer to the question "Did you put something up your nose?" may be a truthful "No," even though an object is stuck in there.

What can I do?

The best way to remove a foreign body from the nose simply and painlessly is to make your child sneeze. Small objects that are not too far up the nose will come flying out.

Do *not* stick anything up your child's nose in an effort to remove the object. More often than not, you will end up injuring your child or pushing the object in even farther. This could make it harder for the doctor to remove the object later.

If you can see the object, you can try to force it out with a mouth-to-mouth breath. Tell your child what you are going to do. If he is too young to understand, explain that you are going to give him a big kiss. Then put your finger over the nostril that does *not* have the foreign body in it. Cover your child's mouth with your mouth and, keeping your finger against the nostril without the foreign body, blow into your child's mouth with great force. You can repeat this once or twice, if needed. If you are unsuccessful after three attempts, you should call your doctor.

When does my doctor need to be involved?

If your child has a foreign body lodged up her nose, your doctor will have to take a look. Certainly, if there is significant pain or bleeding, call your doctor. Even if you don't see anything up there, if your child tells you she has put something up her nose, it is worthwhile to have your doctor check it out. Children rarely say this without meaning it.

What tests need to be done, and what do the results mean?
Tests are generally not done when an object is stuck up the nose. Looking with a special light and magnifier is usually all that is needed.

What are the treatments?
The first step in removing a foreign body from the nose is to look and see where it is. An object that is so far up it is barely visible may need to be removed by a surgeon. In these cases, special tools and numbing medicines are often necessary.

However, if the object is visible and relatively accessible, it can be removed using a very narrow Q-Tip called a **Calgiswab** or a special tool called an **alligator forceps.** An alligator forceps looks like a pair of scissors, but its tip has a very small and narrow clamp. Your child will need to hold still for the removal. If holding still presents a big challenge — and for some toddlers it is simply impossible — your child will need to be held in an immobile position. A light is shone up the nostril and the swab or forceps is inserted into the nostril until the object is retrievable. If your child holds still, she will feel no pain as the object is fished out of the nostril.

What are the possible complications?
There are two types of potential complications: complications of the foreign body being in the nose and complications of removing it.

When an object is stuck in the nose, it can cause swelling, pain, and a foul-smelling nasal discharge. In fact, the area around the object may swell, making the object more difficult to retrieve. The main issue with having a foreign body in the nose is the potential for infection. Any foreign object anywhere in the body can — and eventually will — cause an infection.

The risk of removing a foreign body is the risk of pushing it farther up the nose or damaging the tissues during removal. A foreign body can be lodged so high up in the nose that removing it can require surgery. It can also get pushed all the way into the back of the throat, creating the potential for choking.

Additional Resources:

http://www.emedicine.com/aaem/topic200.htm

http://www.nlm.nih.gov/medlineplus/encyclopedia.html (Click on "F,"
then scroll down to "foreign body in the nose.")

http://www.chop.edu (Click on "your child's health" along left-hand
margin, then go to "search" in upper right-hand corner and type in
"foreign body nose.")

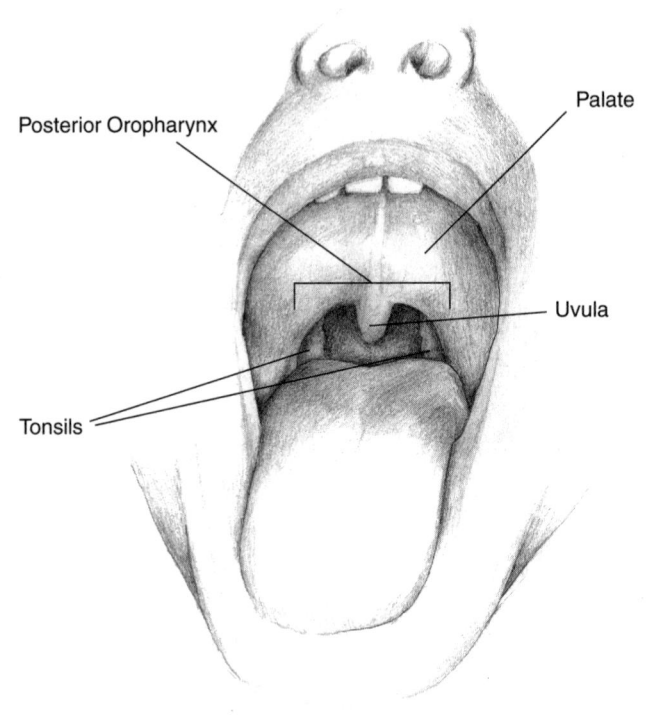

Posterior Oropharynx

Palate

Uvula

Tonsils

The back of the mouth (called the posterior oropharynx)
is a common site of infection among toddlers. Often,
the tonsils become inflamed and swell, sometimes growing
to two or three times their normal size.

6

Mouth

CANKER SORES AND FEVER BLISTERS

What is happening inside my child's body?
Canker sores are small ulcers that appear inside the mouth where there is loose tissue: on the inner surface of the cheeks or lips, on or below the tongue, or at the back of the throat near the soft palate and tonsils. Canker sores are oval or round, and they gradually change from red spots to white or grayish shallow ulcers. The neighboring tissue looks pink and healthy. The medical name for a canker sore is an ***aphthous ulcer.***

Canker sores have a variety of causes. Most are thought to be an immune reaction to something inside the mouth. They can also occur after mechanical trauma, such as self-inflicted biting or eating something sharp. Allergies to foods or products that go into the mouth can cause canker sores. Certain nutritional deficiencies also have been associated with canker sores, especially deficiencies in vitamin B_{12}, folic acid, and iron. In some studies, canker sores have been linked with deficiencies in vitamins B_1, B_2, B_6, and C, as well as zinc, selenium, and calcium. Canker sores can be a side effect of medication. Among children, the most common medications to have this effect are nonsteroidal anti-inflammatory drugs, such as ibuprofen (Motrin or Advil).

Even toothpaste can lead to canker sore formation because sodium lauryl sulfate (SLS), a common ingredient that causes foaming, can dry the inside of the mouth, reducing the level of protection along the mucous membranes.

Canker sores can also be associated with other illnesses. Infections can cause sores directly, by penetrating the mucous membranes, or indirectly, by causing stress on the body. Problems of the immune system are also associated with canker sores. When the immune system is weak and cannot provide an adequate barrier in the mouth, sores may result.

Fever blisters are quite different from canker sores. These blisters appear on or around the outside of the mouth. They generally look like small, round blisters sitting on a red base. They often become crusty after a few days as the normal bacteria that live on the skin infect the surface of the blisters.

Fever blisters are usually caused by the **herpes simplex virus.** This is why the term "herpes" is often used to describe a fever blister outbreak. There are two types of herpes — type 1 and type 2. Historically, it was thought that type 1 herpes caused sores around the mouth, and type 2 herpes resulted in sores on the genitals. Today it is well accepted that either type can appear in either location.

The herpesvirus is highly contagious when a lesion is present. This means that a parent with a fever blister can pass the virus to her child by direct contact such as kissing. If a child touches the sore and then touches his own skin, the virus can spread, too. In most cases (85 percent), you won't know that your child has been infected because there is no immediate visible evidence. However, in about 15 percent of cases, a child will break out with multiple blisters on or around his mouth within three to five days of acquiring the virus. Over several days, the blisters will coalesce, crust, and then heal without scarring. After exposure, with or without visible sores, a child will build antibodies to the virus, protecting against future herpes infection.

Once someone has herpes sores, the infection never goes away completely. Instead, a small group of viruses live in an area underneath the cheek called the **nerve root** or **ganglion.** During times of stress or illness (or sometimes even with too much sun exposure), the virus may become reactivated, and it may move from the nerve root back out to the surface of the skin around the mouth. This is known as a **recurrence.**

Both canker sores and fever blisters last anywhere from 4 to 14 days. While the sores are visible, both conditions can be painful. Children with canker sores or fever blisters don't complain of any other symptoms. In fact, in both cases, they tend to be healthy and robust.

What can I do?

Whether your child has fever blisters or canker sores, the first thing to do is to make him comfortable. For sores inside the mouth, try to avoid foods that are sharp and crunchy, such as potato chips. Small, sharp pieces of food will chronically reinjure the sores. Also avoid acidic, spicy, and salty foods. This will help reduce pain during eating. And check that your toothpaste does not contain SLS. If it does, use another type.

For sores around the mouth, try to minimize stretching or chapping of the skin. Toddlers with fever blisters will often lick the sores — sometimes multiple times a minute — to relieve the pain. The moisture of the saliva temporarily soothes the area, but as soon as the air dries it, the skin becomes drier and more irritated. Eventually, the skin will crack, making it prone to secondary infection by bacteria.

In older children, cleaning the surface of the ulcer and removing excess debris can sometimes speed healing. Hydrogen peroxide is commonly used for cleaning, but this is generally not advised in younger children, because it can be uncomfortable. Look out: a toddler who fights you during the application of hydrogen peroxide may bite you.

One of the easiest and best remedies to minimize pain is "magic mouthwash." This mixture of Children's Benadryl Allergy Liquid and Maalox coats the sores, reducing inflammation and protecting them from saliva and other contents of the mouth (see page 11).

To prevent future canker sores, **lactobacillus acidophilus** may be helpful. This **probiotic** protects the mucous membranes in the body, helping to ward off secondary bacterial infections.

Acidophilus can be found in yogurt, but make sure that the label reads "with live cultures."

When does my doctor need to be involved?
Call your doctor if the sores are causing so much pain that they are limiting eating or drinking. If you think the area around the sores is infected with bacteria, let your doctor know. In this case, you may notice bright red skin and sometimes even pus.

What tests need to be done, and what do the results mean?
Generally speaking, tests are unnecessary with canker sores and fever blisters. If an associated illness is suspected, your doctor may do tests to look for evidence of that illness. But canker sores and fever blisters themselves can be diagnosed just by inspection.

What are the treatments?
Many over-the-counter medications help minimize the pain of canker sores. Some work by providing a barrier between the sore and the rest of the mouth, while others work by numbing the area. These contain active ingredients such as benzocaine, benzoin tincture, lidocaine, camphor, and phenol. Other over-the-counter treatments contain antibacterial ingredients such as copper sulfate and iodine, which help reduce the likelihood of a secondary bacterial infection in the sores.

Prescription medications for toddlers with oral sores are rarely used. Topical steroids can help reduce the inflammation around canker sores, but very few are approved for children. Sometimes adults are given chlorhexidine to use as a swish-and-spit mouthwash, but this is not approved for use in children — and certainly not in children who are too young to understand how to spit effectively.

If your child has herpes and the infection is significant enough that he cannot eat or drink well, your doctor may recommend acyclovir (Zovirax). This antiviral medication stops the multiplication of the herpesvirus, shortening the course of the outbreak and minimizing the number of sores. It can be given in an oral form (liquid) or topically applied directly to the site of the sores. Other antiviral medicines effective against herpes, such as valacyclovir

(Valtrex) and famciclovir (Famvir), are not approved for use in young children.

What are the possible complications?

Canker sores can become infected with the bacteria that normally live in the mouth. Although this is usually not serious, infection will increase the pain associated with the sores and delay healing time.

Fever blisters can become infected with normal skin bacteria. This can delay healing, create itching, and even cause scarring if your child picks at the area regularly.

Additional Resources:
http://www.pueblo.gsa.gov/cic_text/health/fever-blister/fever-canker.html
http://www.nidcr.nih.gov (Go to "health information" in upper left-hand corner; click on "diseases and conditions," then "children's oral health.")

TEETHING

What is happening inside my child's body?

By the time your child has hit the toddler years, she has probably cut several teeth. There are certainly children with no teeth at 15 or even 18 months, but the vast majority of children get some teeth before their first birthdays. Some children don't even wince when a tooth is coming in, but most have discomfort somewhere along the way. By the toddler years, the bigger teeth are emerging, causing more pain. A molar, for instance, is twice as big as an incisor, so it can hurt twice as much coming in.

A total of 20 teeth must emerge before all of the primary teeth are in. Contrary to popular belief, there is no "correct" order of the emergence of teeth. Some children get one tooth at a time; others get four. Sometimes the lowers come in first; other times the uppers, the molars, or even all of the teeth on one side of the mouth are the first to appear.

Despite what the term implies, **teething** does not necessarily mean that a tooth is ready to erupt through the gum. The process of teething refers to the entire journey of a tooth within the gum

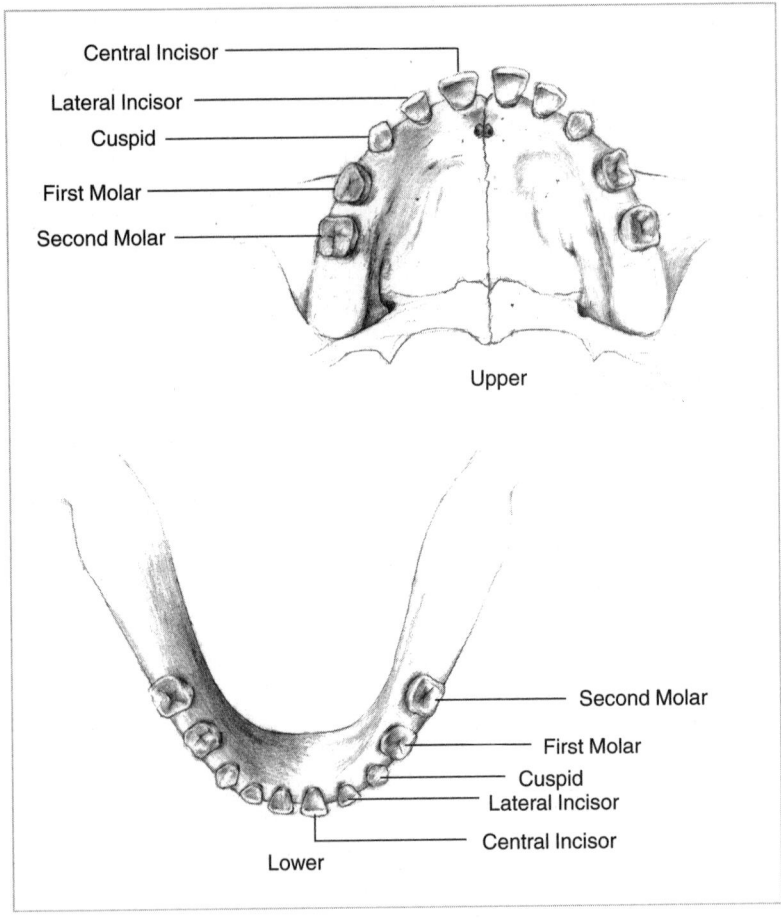

When teething is complete, a toddler will have 20 teeth. There is, however, no absolute order in which the teeth will appear.

and then through its surface. As the tooth moves within the gum, it cuts through nerves and tissue, sometimes resulting in hidden swelling and inflammation. This deep movement may be more painful than a tooth visibly erupting through the topmost layer of gum.

Teething pain is thought to be most acute when a child is lying down because in this position, tenderness in the gum is felt back by the ears as well. With sitting or standing, or even lying at an incline, the pain in the ears is usually less severe.

The excessive drooling associated with teething results in swallowed saliva, which can fill the stomach and reduce your child's appetite. The saliva must pass out of the stomach and through the intestine, resulting in loose or mucus-containing stools or even diarrhea.

What can I do?
Some toddlers will soothe themselves. They will suck on their fingers or gnaw on a toy or a cold spoon. Older kids may rub their fingers or tongues along their gums to massage the area.

If your child is having teething pain and cannot soothe herself, you can rub her gum or offer something cool to help reduce the inflammation. But be careful: your toddler's mouth already has many teeth, and with teething pain, she may inadvertently bite down to find relief.

A variety of medicines is available for extreme teething pain. These are covered in the treatments section.

When does my doctor need to be involved?
Doctors rarely need to be involved in a child's teething. However, it may be difficult for you to determine whether your child's discomfort is from teething or from something else going on. Problems that may imitate teething include infections at the back of the throat and ear infections.

If your toddler tells you that she is having pain but refuses to let you look in her mouth, you will likely wind up seeing the doctor. Although it may be frustrating to be told "It's just teething," better safe than sorry.

A few clear signs suggest that your child's pain may be due to an infection rather than teething. These include a fever higher than 101°F, complaints of ear pain or repeated ear tugging, decreased appetite, or complaints of tremendous discomfort. When these symptoms are present, you should take your child to the doctor.

Drooling is often a sign of teething, but if the drooling is excessive, or if it seems that your child is having difficulty swallowing her saliva, you should see your doctor.

What tests need to be done, and what do the results mean?

A good physical exam is the only "test" needed in the case of teething. If the exam turns up nothing at the back of the throat, no ear infection, and no other source of pain or infection, teething is the default diagnosis. Your doctor might mention that the gums look swollen, but remember that gums don't have to swell visibly for there to be teething pain.

What are the treatments?

There are three types of medical treatments for teething: topical medications, oral medications, and alternative remedies.

Topical treatments for teething are liquids or gels rubbed on the gums to soothe them. Their ingredients — such as salicylic acid, lignocaine, tannic acid, menthol, thymol, glycerol, and ethanol — reportedly reduce swelling and pain. However, there is little data about how well these treatments work. In addition, they work only for a very short time, and it is probably the act of massaging them on the gums that helps the most.

Oral pain relievers come in two main types: acetaminophen (Tylenol) and ibuprofen (Advil or Motrin). "Baby aspirin" is a misnomer and should *never* be given to infants or children. It has been associated with **Reye's syndrome,** an illness involving liver failure and brain disease. There are certainly stronger prescription pain relievers (such as codeine), but teething pain never warrants anything so potent.

Acetaminophen and ibuprofen are dosed according to weight. They are both fever reducers and pain relievers. Ibuprofen is also an anti-inflammatory. Both of these medicines are generally considered safe. For children who refuse to take the liquid form of these medicines, they are also available as chewable tablets and even as rectal suppositories. Ask your doctor for more information.

There are many alternative remedies to treat teething pain. They come in drops, tablets, gels, and solutions. Many herbal

ACETAMINOPHEN VERSUS IBUPROFEN

Acetaminophen *is the active ingredient in Tylenol. It is also used as an ingredient in more than 100 different products sold over the counter and by prescription because it works as both a pain reliever and a fever reducer. It is dosed by weight in children and can be given every four to six hours.*

Acetaminophen is broken down by the liver, and in large doses it can cause liver toxicity or even liver failure. However, to reach a toxic level, you would have to give your child five to ten times the recommended dose in a single sitting, or more than two times the recommended dose every four hours around the clock. For this reason, accidental acetaminophen overdosing is quite unusual. Make sure to check the ingredients when you give your child an over-the-counter cold medication. If you give Tylenol and another acetaminophen-containing medication, you could be giving her an excessive dose.

Ibuprofen *is the active ingredient in Advil and Motrin. It belongs to a class of drugs called **NSAIDs,** or non-steroidal anti-inflammatory drugs. Ibuprofen acts as a fever reducer and pain reliever (like acetaminophen), but it also helps reduce inflammation. Ibuprofen is associated with slightly more side effects than acetaminophen, particularly stomach upset. In extreme cases, high doses can cause stomach ulcers and gastrointestinal bleeding.*

Ibuprofen is cleared by the kidneys. Therefore, it is not recommended for use in patients with kidney disease. Because it is not broken down by the liver, it does not have the same potential for liver toxicity that acetaminophen has.

remedies work because they have active ingredients that are potent anti-inflammatories, reducing the swelling and pain in the gums much the same way ibuprofen does. Remember that even though these are nonprescription remedies, they are drugs and therefore need to be mentioned when your doctor asks what medication you are giving your child.

What are the possible complications?

Teething is generally uncomplicated. The drool that accompanies it may decrease your child's appetite because it physically fills the stomach. When it passes through the intestine, it may also make her stools loose. Sometimes excessive drool will cause a rash to break out around the mouth.

Teething can be associated with a fever of 100° to 101°F. This fever occurs when the body releases natural chemicals as the tooth moves through the gum.

Occasionally, teething will cause bleeding. This happens when the gum is very swollen and the tooth erupts through, breaking some tiny blood vessels. The bleeding usually lasts only a few seconds. Blood can also collect underneath the swollen gum and look blue, like a bruise. When the tooth erupts, the blood is released, and the gum returns to normal. Excessive bleeding or oozing that does not stop on its own requires medical attention.

Additional Resources:

http://www.medem.com (Go to "search" in upper left-hand corner, type in "teething," and scroll down to "teething and dental hygiene.")

http://www.dentistry.uiowa.edu/public/oral/infants.html

http://www.nlm.nih.gov/medlineplus/encyclopedia.html (Click on "T-Tn," then scroll down to "teething.")

http://www.nlm.nih.gov/medlineplus/ency/imagepages/1138.htm

http://www.chop.edu/ (Click on "your child's health" along left-hand margin, then go to "search" in upper right-hand corner and type in "teething.")

◆　　◆　　◆

DISCOLORED TEETH

What is happening inside my child's body?

Healthy teeth look pearly white. If your child's teeth are discolored, there are only a few reasons this is happening.

If your child's teeth are yellowish, especially along the base of the tooth near the gum, the discoloration is likely caused by a thick layer of plaque. Inadequate brushing or excessive sugar in the diet are the sources of plaque.

If your child's teeth look grayish brown, the cause may be a past injury that led to nerve damage or compromised blood flow. In some cases of trauma, there is actually bleeding within a tooth, and the collected blood results in a brown or gray stain.

A much less common source of tooth discoloration is antibiotic use. For this reason, pediatricians generally do not prescribe antibiotics known to affect tooth color. Whereas trauma can cause one tooth or a few teeth to be discolored, antibiotics can stain the entire set.

Finally, there are rare genetic causes of brown or gray teeth.

If your child has teeth with bright white spots, he may have fluoride staining. This is called ***fluorosis,*** and it occurs when the teeth are exposed to too much fluoride. Sources of fluoride include toothpaste, tap water, and multivitamins with fluoride. Fluorosis is an example of too much of a good thing: when fluoride is used in moderation, it protects the teeth; when it is used in excess, it can damage them. Severe fluorosis can cause so much damage to the enamel that the teeth can look dark and have a rough or pitted texture.

If your child has tooth decay, his teeth may look yellow or brown, but often they are perfectly white. Sadly, 17 percent of American children have tooth decay by the time they reach the toddler years. By third grade, more than 50 percent have decay.

What can I do?

Brushing and flossing are the best preventive measures. Even toddlers should brush their teeth twice daily. And as soon as your child can tolerate flossing, this should be introduced into the routine as well.

It can be difficult to convince a toddler to brush his teeth and to do it effectively. Talk to your dentist about strategies you can use. Battery-operated toothbrushes may offer novelty and make the process more fun. They also generally feel good in the mouth. Toothpaste that tastes good can make brushing more appealing. The most important factor is that you help your child with brushing as often as possible. Left to their own devices, toddlers will do a poor job of cleaning their teeth.

When does my doctor need to be involved?
If your child's teeth are discolored, you should see a dentist. Many adult dentists are happy to examine children, so if you don't already have a pediatric dentist, you can start by calling your own dentist's office and asking whether someone will see your child. Otherwise, ask your pediatrician for a referral.

What tests need to be done, and what do the results mean?
Tests are generally unnecessary with discolored teeth. A thorough exam is all that is needed. If tooth decay is suspected, your dentist will recommend X rays to look for deep cavities. X rays are discussed in chapter 19.

What are the treatments?
The treatment depends on the source of the discoloration. Plaque can be removed during a professional cleaning. Future buildup can be prevented with regular and effective brushing.

A tooth that has been injured and is discolored because of bleeding or nerve damage is generally left alone. However, if the tooth and its root die, an infection may develop. Therefore, in some cases, your dentist may recommend removal of the tooth.

When tooth decay causes discoloration, the underlying decay must be addressed. Treatment may involve filling a cavity in a tooth or other dental procedures. The thought of filling a tooth may cause you apprehension, but treating cavities today is much less invasive than it used to be.

Fluorosis never disappears, but it can often be treated cosmetically. This is generally done on permanent teeth only. There is no reason to subject a child to cosmetic dental procedures on teeth that will eventually fall out, especially when the child may not be able to tolerate sitting in the dentist's chair or cooperate with the exam.

What are the possible complications?

The most worrisome complication of tooth discoloration is that sometimes the underlying cause — such as nerve damage or tooth decay — will cause permanent tooth damage. If the nerve root is destroyed, the tooth will die. Again, this isn't usually a major problem with a primary tooth, because a normal permanent tooth should emerge later on.

An **abscess** is a walled-off infection. Abscesses can form in the gums near the nerve roots and can cause significant pain. If left untreated, an abscess can lead to long-term damage to the tooth, or the infection can spread elsewhere in the body.

Additional Resources:
http://www.cdc.gov/oralhealth/topics/child.htm
http://www.nlm.nih.gov/medlineplus/ency/imagepages/1138.htm
http://www.aapd.org/publications/brochures/fluorosis.asp

BROKEN TEETH

What is happening inside my child's body?

Many toddlers have chipped or broken teeth. Usually the tooth gets chipped or broken accidentally during play. Just about anything can cause a tooth injury: falling and landing face-first, running into something, being hit in the mouth by a toy, and so on.

Unlike adult teeth, toddler teeth need not — and often cannot — be fixed. Even if a tooth is knocked out entirely, most dentists will leave a hole until the permanent tooth fills in the gap. The reason for this is that young children do not need all of their teeth to maintain the shape and integrity of the jaw. When an adult loses a tooth, the jaw shape will change over time. But when a child loses a tooth, the jaw almost always continues to grow normally despite the missing tooth, and eventually a permanent tooth will come in to fill its place.

What can I do?

Following a mouth injury, check to see whether your child has lost all or part of a tooth. If the tooth is chipped, look for the piece that has broken off to ensure that your child hasn't swallowed or aspirated it. If your child is able to cooperate, have her rinse her mouth with lukewarm water, spitting out instead of swallowing the water.

If the entire tooth has been knocked out, you will want to take it with you to the dentist just in case it can be replaced. Find the tooth and rinse it off with saline solution or milk rather than tap water. Don't scrub the tooth, even if it has dirt on it. On your way to the dentist, travel with the tooth submerged in milk. If you don't have any milk, tuck the tooth in your own mouth, between your cheek and gum. Although this sounds crazy, if there is a chance that the dentist can reinsert the tooth, milk or saliva are the only two preservatives that can sustain it. In the meantime, have your child hold a piece of wet gauze or a damp washcloth in her mouth at the site of the missing tooth. A toddler can be instructed to simply bite down on the towel.

If the injured area is bleeding, soak a washcloth or a piece of gauze in cold water and apply gentle pressure to the area. See if your child wants to suck on a Popsicle to help minimize swelling.

When does my doctor need to be involved?

Call your dentist if your child has had a traumatic tooth injury. If you don't have a dentist, call your doctor.

What tests need to be done, and what do the results mean?

Tests generally do not have to be done in the case of a broken tooth. Your dentist should be able to see everything simply by inspecting the mouth. In some cases, X rays are necessary at the dentist's office. X rays are described in chapter 19.

What are the treatments?

The treatment depends on the amount of damage to the tooth and the surrounding gum.

A tooth that is loose presents a potential choking hazard. This is why many dentists will pull a loose tooth rather than wait to see what happens.

In a few cases, the space left by a missing tooth can cause the jaw shape to change. If this is a risk, your dentist may recommend a **spacer.** This device will help keep the rest of the teeth and the jaw in normal alignment.

What are the possible complications?

A tooth that has been knocked out is a **choking hazard.** Most children will spit out the tooth. In some cases, they will swallow it immediately. However, if your child has a traumatic injury, loses a tooth, and immediately begins coughing, the tooth may be lodged somewhere in the airway, and you should call for help immediately.

The same holds true for a loose tooth. If the tooth comes out on its own, your child does not spit it out, and then she starts coughing repeatedly, the tooth may be stuck in the airway, and medical attention is necessary.

After trauma to a tooth, the adjacent gum often becomes swollen, and there may be bleeding around the site of the tooth. When this blood collects as a stagnant puddle, it is called a **hematoma.** The area of swelling and bleeding is prone to infection. If it becomes infected, it can cause severe pain and a high fever. This type of infection is called an **abscess.**

Additional Resources:
http://www.nlm.nih.gov/medlineplus/ency/article/000058.htm
http://www.emedicine.com/emerg/topic127.htm
http://www.chop.edu/ (Click on "your child's health" along left-hand margin, then go to "search" in upper right-hand corner and type in "dental emergencies.")

◆   ◆   ◆

THUMB SUCKING AND PACIFIER TEETH

What is happening inside my child's body?
If your child sucks on something throughout the day or night, her teeth will eventually conform to the shape of the item that is being sucked. The most common sucking items are thumbs, fingers, and pacifiers. Bottles can also be a source of crooked teeth, but by the toddler years most children have moved on to drinking from cups.

By the time a child is three years old, the orientation of the teeth changes as a result of thumb, finger, or pacifier sucking. The teeth will jut outward toward the lips. Normally, the upper teeth protrude slightly over the lower teeth. With excessive sucking, the cheeks exercise much more than usual, pulling in the upper jaw. Over time, the upper jaw becomes narrower, while the lower jaw widens. When this happens, the front teeth on the top and bottom may not be able to overlap when the mouth is closed and the molars are opposed. This is especially true for pacifier and bottle suckers.

Finger and thumb suckers usually have more subtle changes in their teeth. The pressure of the fingers against the teeth pushes them forward. The result is an exaggerated overbite, with the central incisors protruding out.

Rest assured, this is all temporary. Most dentists say that as long as the behavior that is causing the changes in the mouth stops by age four (and some say as late as seven), the teeth will return to their intended positions. After age four, though, all bets are off. The behavior may cause permanent changes in the structure of the jaw, leading to misalignment of the adult teeth.

This is why helping to wean your child off a bottle or a pacifier early in the toddler years (if not before) minimizes long-term complications. Remember that the older and more willful a child gets, the harder it is to explain why the bottle or pacifier needs to go.

What can I do?

Pacifiers and bottles: First, take a deep breath and realize that this habit may stop on its own. If you want to be proactive, often the easiest way to minimize sucking is simply to restrict access. Limiting the pacifier to the crib or bed is one way to cut down on its use. If your child asks for it, tell her she needs to be in her bed when she uses it. Some toddlers will ask to go to their beds in order to have a little time with their pacifiers.

To cut down on bottle use, slowly scale back until you are giving only one bottle per day. Make this the bottle that your child is most attached to — usually the one that she drinks from early in the morning or before bed at night. Let her know that she can have milk out of a bottle during that one time, but the rest of the day she must drink it out of a cup.

Some very strong-willed toddlers will find the pacifiers or bottles in the house and insist on using them. If your child does this, the clearest solution is to cut her off cold turkey and remove the pacifiers or bottles from the house.

A gentler solution is to help your child choose to give up the habit. For instance, pacifier weaning often happens more quickly when the pacifier is trimmed. Cut 1 millimeter off the end of every pacifier in the house. Some parents tell their child that the pacifiers are "getting old" or are "broken" or that "the pacifier bugs are eating them." Every few days, trim another millimeter off, until your child chooses to give up the pacifier or only a stump is left.

An alternative to cutting the pacifiers is to ceremoniously give them away. This can also be done with bottles. Pick a baby that you know and suggest to your child that the baby needs the pacifiers or bottles now. You can wrap them up in a box and mail them or give them to the recipient family. Make sure those parents know that you are trying to wean your child off the pacifier or bottle and that they should throw away the old pacifiers or bottles once your child is out of sight.

Thumb or fingers: Although you can get rid of (or trim) pacifiers and bottles, you can't get rid of (or trim) thumbs. Minimizing thumb or finger sucking is a bit more difficult because thumbs (or fingers, whichever is the case) are permanently attached to your child. However, you can ask your toddler if she is ready to give up the thumb, and if she is, you can help by applying a strong-tasting nail polish to the nail. The taste is a bitter reminder that the thumb is supposed to be out of the mouth. This technique works only if your child is a participant. If you try to surprise her and put on the polish without her agreeing to the plan, you may be equally surprised when she licks it off and even learns to like the taste.

Some of these strategies are better at certain ages. Younger toddlers tend to respond to removing or limiting access better than older toddlers do. By the time your child is three, she can clearly understand (and respond to) positive reinforcement. You can reward the elimination of pacifier or thumb sucking by using a star chart or some visual reminder. But make sure you simply ignore the thumb or pacifier sucking when your child chooses to do it. Remember that both positive and negative reinforcement can encourage a behavior. If you chastise your child for thumb or pacifier sucking, she will recognize that you want her to stop the behavior, and she may continue it just to spite you. This is a normal dynamic. Often the best way to minimize a behavior is to ignore it.

Once your child is four, your desire to stop the behavior will have increased significantly. Don't let your child know this, though. The more you care, often the less likely your child will be to comply with what you want. Try to make your child a participant in the process. Explain why it is important to stop the behavior and ask her what techniques she thinks will work. Let her choose the positive reinforcer, but try your best not to offer a material reward. It is always better to reward with an activity than with a toy.

When does my doctor need to be involved?

Alert your doctor or your dentist if you start to notice dramatic changes in the shape of the jaw or the orientation of the teeth. If your child begins to have speech difficulties, you should mention this to your doctor as well.

Particularly in the case of prolonged bottle use, the front teeth may become discolored or may appear to be thinning. Let your doctor or dentist know if this is the case.

What tests need to be done, and what do the results mean?
Testing is generally unnecessary.

What are the treatments?
Obviously, the main treatment is to remove the source of the problem: no more thumb, finger, bottle, or pacifier sucking. However, when the changes become more permanent, even removing the source of the problem won't help. At this point, an orthodontist should become involved. Braces, retainers, expanders, or spacers are often necessary to help reorient the teeth and expand the jaw.

What are the possible complications?
The most common complication is cosmetic: it doesn't look great to have teeth that jut out.

With bottle sucking, the front teeth can decay because of the repeated and extended exposure to sugar on the rubber nipple. Classic **bottle rot** affects the top teeth, often the incisors and cuspids. This condition is a function of how long the teeth are exposed to a sugar-coated nipple, so toddlers who drink a bottle quickly and put it down when they are done are generally not at risk for bottle rot. But children who insist on keeping a bottle in their mouths indefinitely may develop decay. For this reason, some parents substitute water for milk, minimizing the risk of bottle rot by reducing the sugar load on the teeth. Getting rid of the bottle altogether, however, is a much better solution.

Additional Resources:
http://www.chop.edu/ (Click on "your child's health" along left-hand margin, then go to "search" in upper right-hand corner and type in "thumb sucking.")

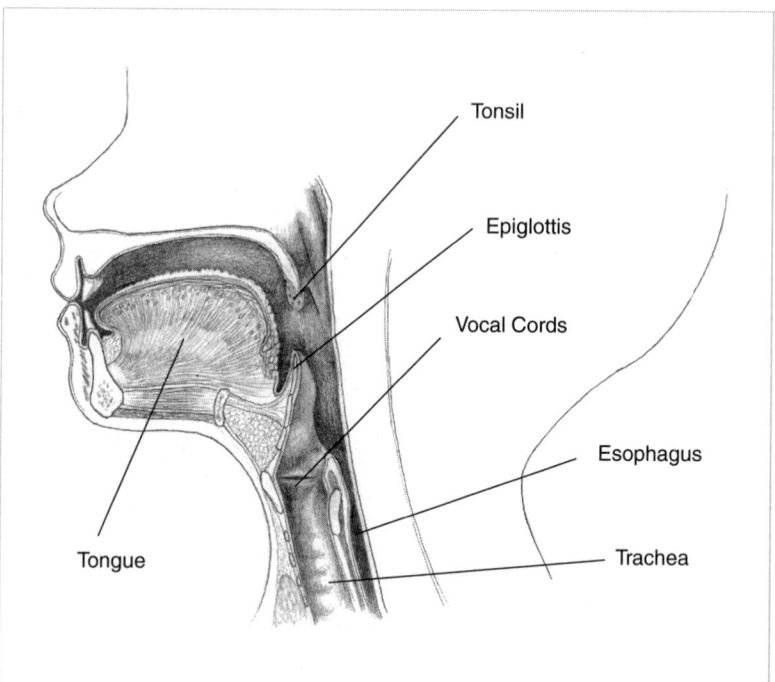

Within the neck, air must be directed one way (into the trachea) while food must go another (into the esophagus).

7

Neck and Throat

SORE THROAT

What is happening inside my child's body?
A sore throat is just that. Some toddlers will identify it clearly, with a perfunctory "My throat hurts." Others will complain of mouth pain, itching in the neck, or a spicy taste. Most will be fussy. Some sore throats are so mild that they cause little pain and eating and drinking are not affected. But other sore throats are severe, limiting the amount a toddler can eat or drink.

The most common cause of a sore throat in a toddler is infection. The infection may be caused by either a bacteria or a virus. Among bacteria, ***Group A beta-hemolytic streptococcus*** (***GABHS,*** more commonly known as ***strep throat***) is the number one culprit. GABHS is one particular type of streptococcal infection. Other types of strep can also be found in the mouth and throat, but they generally don't cause illness.

Strep throat can cause any or all of the following: sore throat, swollen glands in the neck, fever, abdominal pain, nausea, vomiting, headache, and rash. The rash has a distinct appearance and texture, looking and feeling like fine red sandpaper. When a child has strep throat with the accompanying rash, the illness is called ***scarlet fever.***

Many parents assume that a sore throat automatically means a strep infection. This is far from the truth. In fact, only 20 percent of sore throats are caused by GABHS. In other words, antibiotics are appropriate in only one out of every five cases of sore throat.

Viruses are much more likely to cause sore throat than are bacteria. Seasonal viruses that may result in a sore throat also tend to be associated with upper respiratory symptoms, such as runny nose, congestion, and cough. These viruses include the **Coxsackie virus.** One form of Coxsackie causes the painful **hand-foot-mouth disease,** which has as its hallmark blistering of the hands, feet, and back of the throat. Another form of Coxsackie causes **herpangina,** with blisters and ulcers in the front half of the mouth. Fever is not uncommon in children with Coxsackie. **Epstein-Barr virus** (also known as **mononucleosis** or **mono**) and **cytomegalovirus (CMV)** also cause a sore throat, along with swollen lymph nodes in the neck, fatigue, and usually headache. **Adenovirus** causes a sore throat and watery, red eyes.

It can be hard to tell when a bacterial infection is the cause of a sore throat and when a virus is to blame. In general, if your child has hoarseness, diarrhea, pinkeye, or blisters and sores in the front half of his mouth along with a sore throat, he probably has a virus. Strep throat rarely causes any of these symptoms.

A sore throat can be caused by things other than an infection. Injury to the throat happens when a sharp-edged piece of food (such as a tortilla chip) scrapes the tissue at the back of the mouth and down the esophagus. The pain will continue until the tissue heals, which can take a few days. Sometimes a foreign object (such as a fish bone) becomes lodged in the back of the throat. Discomfort will continue until it is swallowed or removed. Swallowing hot food also can cause local injury, and the pain will continue until the burn heals.

Postnasal drip is another source of a sore throat. When fluid drips from the nose down the back of the throat, it tickles and often generates a cough. The drip itself can be irritating, and the cough also can cause soreness.

Sore throats often result from dryness. In a particularly dry climate — including a household where there is dry heat running —

it is not uncommon to feel pain at the back of the throat. Drinking liquids or running a humidifier usually helps. This type of sore throat also tends to get better with time: as the day goes on, the dryness typically resolves.

What can I do?

It is important to ease the pain of a sore throat, especially if your child is refusing to eat or drink. When the cause is a viral or bacterial infection, there are a number of things you can do to help make your child more comfortable.

First, encourage liquids and don't worry about solids. If your child doesn't want to eat for a day or two, that's okay. But if he doesn't want to drink, he runs the risk of becoming dehydrated. Cool drinks tend to go down better than warm ones. Popsicles can be a good way to get some fluids into your child.

Occasionally, an anti-inflammatory such as ibuprofen (Advil or Motrin) will help minimize the inflammation and pain. If your child has a fever at the same time, the ibuprofen will treat that as well.

For a severe sore throat, "magic mouthwash" can help tremendously. This mixture of Children's Benadryl Allergy Liquid and Maalox coats the back of the throat and reduces inflammation (see page 11).

If a foreign body is the source of the throat pain and you think your child has swallowed something small and relatively blunt, you can try getting him to eat some bread to push it down into the stomach. This will relieve the sensation of having something caught in the throat. However, if your child is complaining of a foreign body sensation and you are not sure what he swallowed, it is best to call your doctor before proceeding.

If dryness is causing the sore throat, try running a humidifier or vaporizer. This will moisturize the air and soothe the throat.

When does my doctor need to be involved?

Call your doctor anytime your child is complaining of a severe sore throat. If he is refusing to drink or eat anything, you should contact your doctor.

If the sore throat continues for several days or is accompanied by other symptoms, such as vomiting, high fever, swollen glands in the neck, or rash, you should see your doctor.

What tests need to be done, and what do the results mean?

If strep throat is suspected, a strep test can be done. A sterile Q-Tip is rubbed against the back of the throat in the area around the tonsils. With a ***rapid strep test,*** the specimen is mixed with a chemical, and within five minutes the test will tell whether there is strep in the sample. With a ***culture,*** the Q-Tip is rubbed along a special gel-coated plate, and the plate is kept in an incubator for 24 to 48 hours. If strep is present, the bacteria will grow on the plate.

A rapid strep test is convenient, but it doesn't pick up all cases of strep throat. In fact, it is only about 80 to 85 percent sensitive. This means that 15 to 20 percent of strep cases register negative on the rapid test.

The culture is more sensitive. If the culture is negative after 48 hours, you can feel confident that your child does not have strep throat. Likewise, if it is positive, the infection is clearly present.

Most pediatricians perform cultures specifically looking for GABHS. However, sometimes a laboratory looks for other bacteria that may grow from the swab. It is important to realize that many bacteria live in the throat normally. These bacteria are called ***oral flora.*** When they are present in small numbers, they keep the teeth and mouth healthy. These bacteria may grow on a culture plate, but they almost never need to be treated.

What are the treatments?

Since only 20 percent of sore throats are caused by strep, most result from a virus. And with viral infections, getting better is only a matter of time. Of course, you can — and should — try to maximize your child's comfort. But antibiotics are recommended only when a specific bacteria, especially strep, is the proven cause.

Remember, bacteria other than GABHS live in the mouth normally. If a throat culture grows normal oral flora, an antibiotic should *not* be used. Just because there are bacteria present in the mouth and throat does not mean that they are causing a problem.

Overusing antibiotics is a serious problem. The risk of an adverse reaction — rash, diarrhea, or a full-blown allergy — to an antibiotic is 2 to 5 percent. By using these drugs inappropriately, there is a real chance that a child will have an unnecessary reaction. Also, many antibiotics are expensive. Therefore, their overuse drives up health care costs. But the most important issue related to antibiotic overuse is that the more often antibiotics are used, the more likely antibiotic resistance will evolve. Antibiotic resistance is a major public health concern. One child can actually pass on antibiotic resistance to another child by passing strains of bacteria that carry resistance. If antibiotics are used appropriately, they can save lives, prevent hospitalizations, and shorten the course of an illness. When used inappropriately, they put our entire community at risk.

If a sore throat is caused by a foreign body lodged somewhere in the back of the mouth or down the esophagus, the object needs to be removed. If drinking and eating do not push the object down into the stomach, or if the object is too large or sharp and there is concern about its moving through the gastrointestinal tract, it may need to be removed. A doctor who specializes in the intestinal tract, called a gastroenterologist, will perform this procedure using a narrow camera (called an **endoscope**) attached to a tool that can grab the object. Most toddlers need to be sedated for this procedure.

What are the possible complications?

The most serious complication of strep throat is **acute rheumatic fever (ARF).** Here the body's immunological response to strep cross-reacts with other parts of the body, first involving the large joints (knees, ankles, shoulders, and elbows) and later involving the skin, heart, and even nervous system.

When the heart becomes involved, ARF can cause permanent damage to the heart valves and in rare cases can be lethal. ARF is entirely avoidable with antibiotic treatment of strep throat. ARF was common before the discovery of penicillin, and many older adults who have had heart valve replacements had ARF as children. Nowadays ARF is rare in the United States, but it still exists in parts of the world where access to health care and antibiotics is poor and where overcrowding allows for the rapid spread of strep.

Another complication of the body's immune response to strep is **glomerulonephritis.** This problem results from the deposition of anti-strep antibodies in the kidneys. The antibodies clog the small filters that make up the kidneys. In order to continue to allow for drainage of waste products in the urine, the kidneys respond by becoming leaky. With glomerulonephritis, the urine often has blood and other debris in it. Most of the time, the situation is short-term, but glomerulonephritis can cause permanent kidney damage and even kidney failure.

Occasionally, glomerulonephritis is accompanied by abdominal pain, joint swelling, and a splotchy rash on the legs and buttocks. This constellation of symptoms is called **Henoch-Schoenlein purpura.** It, too, results from the deposition of the antibodies in various parts of the body.

Additional Resources:
http://www.nlm.nih.gov/medlineplus/encyclopedia.html (Click on "Si-Sp," then scroll down to "sore throat.")
http://www.chop.edu/ (Click on "your child's health" along left-hand margin, then go to "search" in upper right-hand corner and type in "pharyngitis.")
http://www.emedicine.com/med/topic2922.htm

SWOLLEN GLANDS IN THE NECK

What is happening inside my child's body?
The "glands" in the neck are **lymph nodes.** These nodes are part of the larger **lymph system,** a network of filters responsible for removing waste from the body. The lymph nodes serve as important components of the body's immune system because they produce immune cells that fight infection, and they aid in the disposal of bacteria and viruses.

The lymph system is made up of dozens of lymph nodes connected by lymphatic vessels. The most easily palpable nodes are in the neck, groin, armpits, and back of the head. When your child gets sick and the lymph system is working hard to clear the infection, lumps and bumps in these areas are not uncommon. Enlargement of the lymph nodes is called **lymphadenopathy.**

Any number of things can cause lymph nodes to enlarge. Conditions associated with inflammation (such as lupus) and cancer (such as lymphoma) can cause node swelling. Because the nodes are filters of infection, they themselves can become infected (called **lymphadenitis**). But by far the most common cause of lymph node enlargement is infection somewhere in the body, causing the nodes in that region to react and swell.

The glands in the neck generally swell in response to a few specific infections. **Strep throat** is the most common bacterial infection to cause neck node enlargement. This infection is caused by **Group A beta-hemolytic streptococcus (GABHS).** It is seen frequently in children because it is spread so easily by activities that children engage in regularly: sharing food and drink, exchanging toys that are wet with saliva, and so on. The bacteria grow and multiply at the back of the throat, where the tonsils and adenoids reside. These glands swell with infection, until eventually you can easily see and feel the lumps in the neck. Children with strep throat typically have at least one of the following symptoms: sore throat, headache, stomachache, nausea, vomiting, fever, or rash.

Viruses can also cause remarkable gland swelling in the neck. A wide variety of viruses will do this, including the seasonal viruses that cause **upper respiratory infections (URIs),** better known as "common colds."

There are other, less common viruses that cause lymphadenopathy in the neck. **Mononucleosis** (also known as **mono** or "the kissing disease" in teens and adults) is probably the most well known. This infection is caused by **Epstein-Barr virus (EBV).** It is estimated that about 95 percent of all adults have been exposed to this virus, because about 95 percent have developed antibodies against it. But only a small number of people actually get sick when exposed to the virus. Mono causes sore throat and extreme exhaustion. Children with mono can be so tired that they fall asleep during their favorite activities. Mono can also be associated with headache, stomachache, fever, and even concurrent strep throat.

Another virus associated with notable lymph node swelling in the neck is **cytomegalovirus (CMV).** CMV is similar to EBV in that most adults have been exposed (because most have antibodies against it) but the vast majority don't know it. Also like EBV, relatively few people get very ill when exposed to CMV. The symptoms of CMV can be nearly identical to those of EBV, which is not surprising given that both CMV and EBV belong to the family of viruses called the **herpesvirus group.**

It is important to recognize that lymphadenopathy is one of the most common symptoms seen in pediatric practices. It may be difficult for parents to tell the difference between worrisome and nonworrisome lymph node enlargement. The following general guidelines may help reassure you.

Benign lymphadenopathy that is associated with a common viral illness will generally be symmetric on both sides of the neck. The nodes can be large, but not golf ball size. They should not be warm or tender to the touch. And they are almost always associated with symptoms of a URI — cough, congestion, and runny nose — or a sore throat.

Malignant lymphadenopathy, which may signal cancer or other serious medical problems, tends to be associated with fevers, night sweats, weight loss, decreased appetite, or easy bruising and bleeding. Remember that this condition is drastically less common than benign lymphadenopathy caused by infection.

Lymphadenopathy is not limited to the neck. The nodes behind the ears or at the back of the scalp can become enlarged, as can the nodes in the groin or armpits. Again, when the swelling is symmetric and not tender to the touch, there is usually less cause for concern. Although the neck nodes can become very large, the nodes elsewhere in the body tend to grow only to the size of a pea or peanut at most.

When a lymph node is infected, it is called **lymphadenitis.** The node is usually enlarged and warm to the touch. There can be a red line visible on the skin starting at the node and moving up the extremity. It is rare for lymphadenitis to occur in more than one lymph node at a time.

What can I do?

There is not much that you can do about enlarged lymph nodes. If your child is having other symptoms, such as a sore throat, you can address those. But the nodes themselves should shrink over time.

Occasionally, an anti-inflammatory such as ibuprofen (Advil or Motrin) will help minimize node swelling. Ibuprofen is especially helpful if the swelling is associated with inflammation in the throat and painful swallowing.

Your child may not want to eat much, and that's okay. But drinking is very important because it will keep him well hydrated. Cool drinks tend to go down better than warm ones, especially with an associated sore throat. Popsicles can be a good way to get some fluids into your child.

When does my doctor need to be involved?

Call your doctor if the lymph nodes are remarkably enlarged or if there are associated symptoms such as high fever, painful swallowing, or vomiting.

Your doctor definitely needs to see your child if the swollen lymph nodes are unilateral (only on one side of the neck) or warm and tender to the touch. You should also call your doctor if the nodes do not disappear over time.

What tests need to be done, and what do the results mean?

Since the most common cause of lymphadenopathy is a viral infection, often no tests are done.

If your doctor suspects strep throat, a strep test can be performed. This is a simple swab of the throat that looks for bacteria. There is a 5-minute test (rapid strep test) and a 48-hour test (culture). The culture is sent only if the rapid test is negative or unavailable.

If the doctor suspects that the cause of the lymph node enlargement is mono or CMV, lab tests will be done. These include a complete blood count, specific EBV and CMV tests, and often a chemistry panel to look at liver function. The last test is important because both EBV and CMV can cause liver inflammation (hepatitis).

If there is concern that there may be other causes of the lymphadenopathy — such as a bacterial infection of the blood, an inflammatory illness, or cancer — a similar set of lab tests will be done. More specific lab tests can be added based on the level of suspicion.

Very occasionally, it is necessary to biopsy the lymph node in order to diagnose the problem. A biopsy is performed by an otolaryngologist (ear, nose, and throat doctor), a general surgeon, or a pathologist.

What are the treatments?

Because viruses are the most common cause of lymphadenopathy, and because viruses must run their course without specific treatment, usually no medicine is given. However, rest and fluids are an important part of healing. Especially with mono, which can cause enlargement of the spleen, avoiding contact sports is essential. The activities of a toddler or young child with an enlarged spleen should be restricted to avoid abdominal trauma: no wrestling with siblings, jumping off playground equipment, and so on until the spleen has shrunk.

If the lymph node swelling is due to a bacterial infection, antibiotics are necessary. The specific antibiotic will depend on the type of infection.

Other causes of lymphadenopathy require more specific treatments. Because they are fairly rare in the United States, their treatment is not covered here. See the resources at the end of this section.

What are the possible complications?

Lymphadenopathy has very few potential complications. **Lymphadenitis,** or infection of the node that is enlarged, is possible but not common.

Most of the complications associated with enlarged lymph nodes have to do with the underlying problem. In general, however, parents don't have to worry about enlarged lymph nodes. They usually indicate that the immune system is doing its job.

Additional Resources:
http://www.nlm.nih.gov/medlineplus/encyclopedia.html (Click on "Sq-Sz," and then click on "swollen glands" or go to "Lo-Lz," and then click on "lymph system.")
http://www.emedicine.com/PED/topic1333.htm

CROUP AND STRIDOR

What is happening inside my child's body?
Once you hear a *croup* cough, you will never forget it. The cough is harsh and dry, sudden and dramatic — often described as sounding like a barking seal. However, some children with croup have congestion, a runny nose, or even a wet cough. The hallmark of croup is that, wet or dry, the cough is harsh.

Inexplicably, croup almost always begins as the sun goes down and gets worse through the night. By the time the sun comes up the next morning, it is usually getting better. Its duration varies, sometimes lasting one night, sometimes five. It tends to be at its worst on the second night. Occasionally, the cough continues through the daytime, predicting a rough night to come.

The sound of a croupy cough tends to alarm the child who is producing it. In fact, the cough can be so loud and barky that it may cause your child to cry, which then exacerbates the cough.

It is important to remember that croup is always caused by a viral infection, and therefore it does not improve with antibiotics (antibiotics treat only bacteria). There are at least five or six different viruses that may lead to this classic cough. Therefore, to call a cough "croup" does not diagnose the cause of the cough. Instead, "croup" is a description, not unlike calling the sky "blue."

Stridor is a low-pitched or squeaky sound produced when your child inhales. Stridor results when the part of the airway right around the vocal cords narrows. This narrowing can be caused by infection, allergy, inflammation, a congenital problem, or even a foreign body (such as food or a small piece of a toy) lodged in that area. Unlike the croup sound, which is audible only with coughing, stridor is heard with each breath.

When infection causes stridor, it can be difficult to say whether the infection is viral or bacterial. The most dangerous type of infection associated with stridor is **epiglottitis.** This is a bacterial infection that causes swelling of the epiglottis, the piece of cartilage located at the base of the tongue. Epiglottitis causes sudden-onset respiratory distress that can escalate quickly. There can be so much swelling that air cannot get in or out of the lungs, resulting in complete obstruction of the airway, a medical emergency. A child with epiglottitis will look very sick and may be seated in a tripod position (sitting on his bottom, leaning forward onto his hands) to make himself comfortable. The most common cause of epiglottitis is a bacterium called *Haemophilus influenzae* type B (HiB). Fortunately, this bacterium is now very rare because children are vaccinated against it (see chapter 20). It is important to recognize that an undervaccinated or unvaccinated child is still at grave risk for epiglottitis from HiB.

Allergy can cause stridor if the tissue in the airway swells in response to an allergen. Severe allergy in the airway is called **anaphylaxis.** It is accompanied by swelling of the lips or tongue and hives on the skin. In the case of an allergic reaction, swelling on the outside of the body (skin, lips) may signal swelling on the inside (airway, lungs).

What can I do?

As long as your child is breathing comfortably, there are a few things you can try at home.

Sometimes sitting your child upright makes breathing easier by taking pressure off the airway.

Cool mist or cold air often helps reduce airway swelling, easing breathing. For croup, alternate between cool air (outside) and steam (from the shower), spending about 10 minutes in each. The combination soothes the throat and reduces swelling. This usually resolves croup completely. When you take your child from a warm, steamy bathroom out into the cool night air, don't forget to put a jacket or blanket around him.

One of the most important things you can do is keep your child calm. This reduces crying and diminishes stridor. A few minutes in front of the TV may quickly ease an exacerbation.

If your child has a fever, which is not uncommon with croup, give him a fever reducer such as acetaminophen (Tylenol) or ibuprofen (Advil or Motrin). This will make him more comfortable and slow down his breathing. (When a child has a fever, he will pant to "blow off" the fever.) Remember that a child should never be given aspirin.

When does my doctor need to be involved?

If your child is struggling to breathe, call 911.

If you think your child has respiratory distress, or if he has stridor, call your doctor. It can be difficult to tell whether your child's noisy breathing is worrisome, especially because croup can sound so dramatic. Your child will use certain techniques to get extra oxygen into his lungs, however. Call your doctor if your child displays two or more of these symptoms or if you have any doubt.

Flaring the nostrils with each breath. This allows more air to flow into the airway and lungs.

Visible flexing or contracting of the long muscles at the neck, between the jaw and shoulders. This pulls on the tops of the lungs, increasing the size of the lungs and their air capacity. The notch between the collarbones, called the sternal notch, may also be pulling in with each breath.

Visible flexing or contracting of the muscles between the ribs. This pulls on the lungs to open them horizontally. It also increases lung size and capacity. To see these muscles pulling, draw an imaginary line from your child's armpit to his hip. Halfway along that line, look for the ribs moving with each breath. They will look like a row of bucket handles moving up and down.

Moving the belly up and down in an exaggerated way with each breath. This forces the diaphragm down, increasing the depth of the lungs and their air capacity.

Breathing fast. This increases the flow of air into the lungs simply by speeding it up. Remember that a child who has a fever will breathe fast to "blow off" the fever. This is a very good way to help cool down the body; it is *not* a sign that he is having difficulty breathing. In the absence of a fever, the normal rate of breathing is age dependent: young toddlers may breathe 25 to 35 times a minute, while children over two years old breathe 20 to 30 times a minute. (Adults typically breathe 12 to 14 times per minute.) If your child has a fever, give him a fever-reducing medicine. When his temperature has returned to normal, recheck his respiratory rate.

These symptoms are helpful in assessing a (relatively) calm child. However, in a crying child, they are not necessarily accurate indicators of difficulty breathing. This is because a crying child will flare his nostrils, open his mouth, and breathe fast as part of crying. Breathing is covered in more detail in chapter 8.

When in doubt, call your doctor or 911 immediately. When your child is having difficulty breathing, you should *never* put anything into his mouth, including food or drink.

What tests need to be done, and what do the results mean?

If your child has classic croup, there are a number of ways to approach the problem. Most often, tests are not performed. Instead, a medicine is used to help open up the airway and ease the breathing. This is covered in more detail in the treatments section.

If your child has stridor and is having difficulty breathing that does not seem to be croup, an X ray of the neck and lungs may be done. This picture looks at how the structures are formed and shows how much swelling there is around the vocal cords. A neck X ray also can rule out other causes of noisy, distressed breathing. It can detect swelling in other parts of the neck, as well as some types of foreign bodies lodged in the airway.

Sometimes a liquid called **barium** is used during the X ray. The child drinks this liquid, which helps distinguish the airway from its neighboring esophagus.

In persistent or extreme cases of stridor, more extensive tests, such as a CT scan or MRI, may be done. In some cases, a tiny camera is inserted through the mouth and into the airway to take pictures. This procedure is called **endoscopy.**

Sometimes blood tests are necessary. Certain tests — complete blood count, sedimentation rate, and blood culture — can determine whether there is an infection. Others can measure the blood oxygen level. In classic croup, lab tests are almost never warranted. But with significant stridor, they become more important. All of these tests and studies are reviewed in chapter 19.

What are the treatments?

In most cases of croup, the home-based approach of steam alternating with cool air is enough to make your child comfortable and get him through the night. However, if your child is having difficulty breathing, medical intervention may be necessary. This is especially important when the breathing difficulty is caused by acute swelling in the airway.

Steroids are one of the most effective medicines used to treat severe croup and stridor. These potent anti-inflammatories rapidly reduce swelling inside the airway. Steroids have a bad reputation because after prolonged use, they can be associated with complications such as high blood pressure, weight gain, and skin changes. However, when used for a short duration (less than two weeks) and in relatively low doses, steroids are safe medicines with few side effects. In most cases of croup or stridor associated with respiratory distress, steroids are typically given for one to three days. Sometimes they are used only once. They can be given by injection, by mouth, or in a mist that is blown into the child's mouth and down into his lungs. The use of a mist is called a **nebulized treatment.**

Sometimes a muscle relaxant called **albuterol** is used to help ease respiratory distress. This medicine relaxes the muscles that line the airway and lungs, so that the tubes (bronchi) carrying air can open to their maximum size. For this reason, albuterol is called a bronchodilator. Albuterol is effective only when the muscles are clenched tight or in spasm. Therefore, if the cause of croup or stridor is obstruction in the uppermost part of the airway and is not associated with airway muscle spasm, albuterol is ineffective. Albuterol can be given in a liquid or nebulized form.

If the stridor results from severe allergy and anaphylaxis, a shot of **epinephrine** may be used on its own or in addition to steroids. Epinephrine also can be inhaled in a nebulized form. It works by a different mechanism than steroids. Like albuterol, it is a muscle relaxant, which means that it opens up the airways in the lungs. But it is much more potent than albuterol. Epinephrine occurs naturally in the body, but it can be supplemented with the manufactured form. It is administered in life-threatening situations ranging from respiratory distress to cardiac arrest.

When epinephrine is used in the emergency setting, it often quickly improves a child's breathing, causing stridor to subside. When the medicine wears off, however, the labored breathing and stridor may return. This is why a child who receives epinephrine will need to be observed for three to four hours before being discharged home.

When stridor is caused by a bacterial infection, antibiotics must be used. In severe cases, antibiotics are given intravenously (directly into the bloodstream) because a child with a swollen airway will have trouble swallowing medications. IV forms are also faster acting and often more potent.

A child with a bacterial infection of the airway — such as epiglottitis — has an airway emergency. He may need to have his airway examined by someone skilled in airway management, either in the emergency department or in the operating room.

What are the possible complications?
Croup and stridor can result in difficulty getting air into and out of the lungs. If air cannot get in or out, the body's oxygen level will drop. In the most extreme cases, if the airway becomes completely swollen or obstructed, your child could stop breathing.

A child's health is in jeopardy when he works hard to breathe for several hours or days. Eventually, the increased energy expenditure used for breathing will exhaust the child, and he will literally not have enough energy to breathe.

Another complication is spreading infection. Both viral and bacterial infections can spread from the airway to other parts of the body. The most common sites of spread are the lungs (***pneumonia***) and the bloodstream (***bacteremia*** or ***viremia***).

Additional Resources:
http://www.chop.edu/ (Click on "your child's health" along left-hand margin, then go to "search" in upper right-hand corner and type in "croup.")
http://www.lpch.org/DiseaseHealthInfo/HealthLibrary/respire/stridor.html
http://www.mayoclinic.com (Go to "search" in upper right-hand corner and type in "croup.")

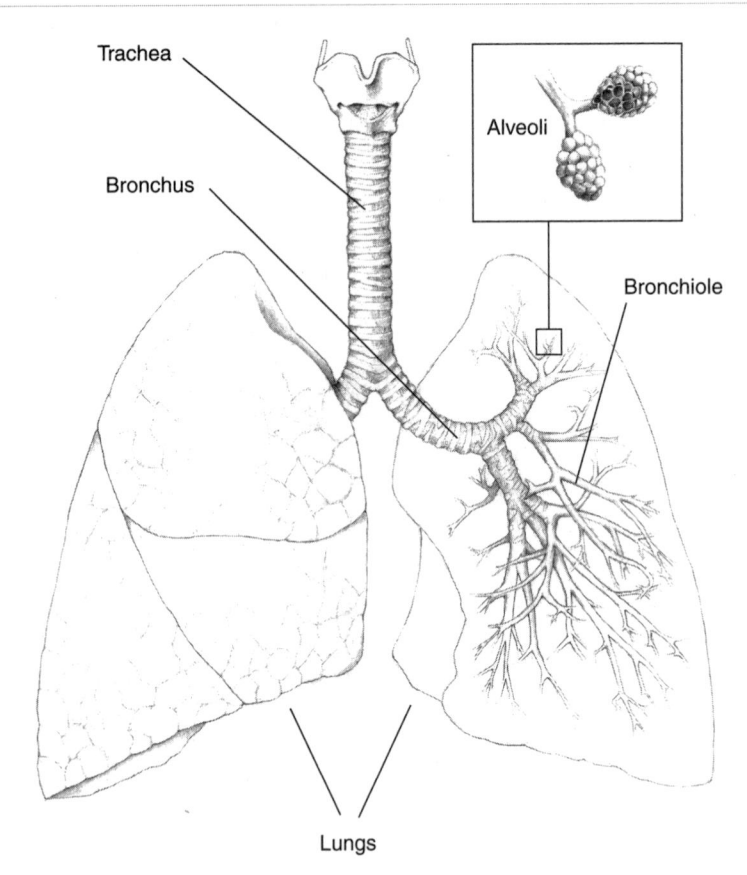

In the lungs, airways branch into smaller and smaller tubes. At the tip of each tiny airway, there is a cluster of cells (alveoli) responsible for the actual transfer of oxygen into the bloodstream.

8

Chest and Lungs

DIFFICULTY BREATHING, WHEEZING, AND ASTHMA

What is happening inside my child's body?
"Normal" breathing means different things for different children. One child breathes quietly, while another makes noise with each breath. A child at rest takes slow, deep breaths, while a running child breathes quickly. Given the range of normal, it can be difficult to tell when breathing is abnormal.

You will hear several terms used to describe "abnormal breathing." ***Labored breathing*** refers to rapid, often shallow breathing associated with increased effort to take each breath. ***Respiratory distress*** is an exaggerated form of labored breathing that is associated with not getting enough oxygen into the body.

Wheezing is a sound heard on exhalation, a high-pitched whistle. It may be associated with labored breathing or respiratory distress, or it may not. Wheezing is discussed in more detail later in this section.

The easiest way to understand why breathing may be labored is to understand the path that air follows from the nose and mouth down to the lungs. Air enters the airway through the nose or mouth and heads down the trachea, passing the vocal cords. It goes through the main stem bronchus into the right and left bronchi. It passes along an ever-narrowing channel of tubes, divided among the various bronchioles, eventually reaching the end of the lungs at grapelike sacks called alveoli.

There are some important general rules to know about the flow of air. First, air follows the path of least resistance. Therefore, if something is blocking one particular route, air will be less likely to flow in that direction and more likely to find an unobstructed path. Second, air is only 21 percent oxygen. When doctors talk about "air exchange" and the importance of air, they are usually referring to oxygen. If you recognize that oxygen is a relatively small component of air, you will understand why giving extra oxygen — increasing the relative percent of oxygen being inhaled in air — can often help a child with labored breathing or respiratory distress. The whole goal of breathing is to get oxygen into the body. The more difficult this goal is to accomplish, the harder a child will work to get it done.

The most common general cause of difficulty breathing is obstruction of the airway. What blocks the airway? Physical objects, such as accidentally swallowed toys, can do it. Mucus can block the airway, too. The mucus that complicates breathing is generally a byproduct of an infection. Other infections can physically block breathing by causing swelling within the airway. This swelling reduces the diameter of the airway, a form of obstruction. And any process that causes inflammation of the airway, such as allergy or asthma, causes obstruction and difficulty breathing for the same reason.

Asthma is the most common cause of breathing difficulty among children in the United States. It is estimated that 9 million American children are asthmatic. This represents 12 percent of all children in this country, a sharp increase from the 8 percent in 1995. Asthma is responsible for 4.6 million outpatient visits, more than 700,000 emergency room visits, and more than 200,000 hospitalizations among children each year.

Although asthma is typically equated with wheezing, this is not the right way to think about it. Asthma has three components: muscle hyperreactivity, mucus secretion, and inflammation. To have asthma, a child must have all three of these things going on in the lungs. In medicine, there is a saying: All that wheezes is not asthma.

Basically, when a child has asthma, this is what happens: The child is exposed to something that triggers her asthma — cigarette smoke, pollen, cat dander, even a virus. The irritant causes the muscles lining the medium-size airways to spasm, and the spasm causes the airway diameter to shrink. Normally open airways become small — acting as if they are obstructed — and smaller airways present increased resistance to airflow. When this happens, breathing is difficult, but it is generally easier for the air to get into the lungs than it is for the air to leave. This phenomenon causes a classic wheeze on the exhale but not on the inhale.

Meanwhile, the irritant also stimulates cells lining the airway to produce mucus. This is part of the normal immune system response, but with the narrowed diameter of the airways, the mucus can cause more harm than good. Thick mucus congests the airways, narrowing their diameter even more and adding to their obstruction.

Finally, inflammation occurs in the alveoli, the smallest, most distant part of the lungs. The alveoli are the sites of air exchange. When these sacks are coated with inflammatory cells, it becomes more difficult for oxygen to pass through them and into the bloodstream. Therefore, air exchange is reduced, and the efficiency of breathing is further reduced.

Because all three of these components contribute to the labored breathing of asthma, all three must be treated to resolve the problem. It is important to remember that just because a child wheezes, it does not necessarily mean that she has asthma. The converse is also true: not all children with asthma wheeze. In fact, there is a well-known variety of asthma called ***cough-variant asthma*** in which there is coughing rather than wheezing.

A child should not be called "asthmatic" after the first episode of wheezing, unless the episode was so severe that the child required hospitalization. Rather, the first episode of wheezing is usually called ***reactive airways disease (RAD).*** Typically, after three episodes of RAD, a child will earn the diagnosis of asthma.

What can I do?

If you think your child is in respiratory distress, is not breathing, or is struggling to breathe, call 911 and start CPR immediately.

Sometimes moisturized air can make breathing more comfortable. You can try using steam (such as a steamy bathroom) or cool mist (such as a vaporizer). Try this only when the breathing difficulty is mild, in conjunction with other treatments, and on the advice of your doctor.

If an irritant has triggered the breathing difficulty, remove the irritant. If you are indoors, go outside. A cigarette smoker can trigger an asthma attack in a bystander just by wearing a sweater or shirt saturated with smoke. Cats shed large amounts of dander, so even if a cat is removed from the room, the dander lingering on the carpet can cause the irritation to continue.

If your child is known to have RAD or asthma, your doctor may have already advised you about a medication regimen. These regimens are reviewed in the treatments section.

When does my doctor need to be involved?

If your child is struggling to breathe or appears not to be breathing at all, call 911 and start CPR immediately.

Anytime you suspect difficulty breathing, call your doctor. It can be difficult for you to tell whether a child's breathing is worrisome. Your child will use certain techniques to get extra oxygen into her lungs, however. Call your doctor if your child displays two or more of these symptoms or if you have any doubt.

Flaring the nostrils with each breath. This allows more air to flow into the airway and lungs.

Visible flexing or contracting of the long muscles at the neck, between the jaw and shoulders. This pulls on the tops of the lungs, increasing the size of the lungs and their air capacity. The notch between the collarbones, called the sternal notch, may also be pulling in with each breath.

Visible flexing or contracting of the muscles between the ribs. This pulls on the lungs to open them horizontally. It also increases lung size and capacity. To see these muscles pulling, draw an imaginary line from your child's armpit to her hip. Halfway along that line, look for the ribs moving with each breath. They will look like a row of bucket handles moving up and down.

Moving the belly up and down in an exaggerated way with each breath. This forces the diaphragm down, increasing the depth of the lungs and their air capacity.

Breathing fast. This increases the flow of air into the lungs simply by speeding it up. Remember that a child who has a fever will breathe fast to "blow off" the fever. This is a very good way to help cool down the body; it is *not* a sign that she is having difficulty breathing. In the absence of a fever, the normal rate of breathing is age dependent: young toddlers may breathe 25 to 35 times a minute, while children over two years old breathe 20 to 30 times a minute. (Adults typically breathe 12 to 14 times per minute.) If your child has a fever, give her a fever-reducing medicine. When her temperature has returned to normal, recheck her respiratory rate.

These symptoms are helpful in assessing a (relatively) calm child. However, in a crying child, they are not necessarily accurate indicators of difficulty breathing. This is because a crying child will flare her nostrils, open her mouth, and breathe fast as part of crying.

When in doubt, call your doctor or 911 immediately. When your child is having difficulty breathing, you should *never* put anything into her mouth, including food or drink.

What tests need to be done, and what do the results mean?

Respiratory distress is a sign that the lungs are working too hard to get oxygen into the body. Usually a child in severe distress is unable to get the oxygen she needs and will likely have a low oxygen level. The lower the oxygen level goes, the harder she will breathe in an attempt to get more oxygen in — a vicious cycle. Therefore, oxygen levels will be measured in your doctor's office or the emergency room. This is done in one of two ways. A ***pulse oximeter*** may be attached to a finger or toe, noninvasively estimating the oxygen saturation of the blood. Alternatively, blood may be drawn and analyzed to determine the **blood oxygen level,** a more accurate measure. Both of these methods are described in further detail in chapter 19.

An X ray will help to reveal improperly formed lungs, fluid (seen in many infections and in trauma), a foreign body, a collapsed lung, and even inflammation. First-time wheezing, especially in the absence of cold symptoms, usually requires an X ray to make sure nothing other than RAD is causing the problem.

Specific blood tests can be done to determine whether the underlying cause of the breathing difficulty is an infection. These tests include a complete blood count and a blood culture. A positive blood culture can identify the bacteria causing an infection and will help determine what antibiotic your doctor will prescribe.

What are the treatments?

If your child is having difficulty breathing, the treatment will depend on the cause. In the case of asthma, because there are three components contributing to the wheezing and difficulty breathing, all three need to be dealt with.

To treat the smooth muscle spasm along the airways, an inhaled muscle relaxant is used. The most common muscle relaxant is **albuterol.** This medicine relaxes the muscles that line the airway and lungs, so that the tubes carrying air can open to their maximum size. Because albuterol targets the muscles along the bronchi, it is called a **bronchodilator.** Albuterol can be given in a liquid or aerosolized (also called **nebulized**) form.

To help break up the mucus, an inhaled medicine called a **mucolytic** can be given in combination with albuterol in the same nebulizer machine. The most common mucolytic is **ipratropium bromide.**

To treat the inflammation in the alveoli, potent anti-inflammatory medications called **steroids** are used. In mild or moderate cases of wheezing, steroids can be given in the nebulizer along with the other medications. In more severe cases, they may be given in an oral form or even as a shot. Steroids rapidly reduce swelling inside the airway.

Steroids have a bad reputation because after prolonged use, they can be associated with complications such as high blood pressure, weight gain, and skin changes. However, when used for a short duration (less than two weeks) and in relatively low doses, steroids are safe medicines with few side effects.

If the cause of difficulty breathing is obstruction by a foreign body or a mass somewhere along the airway, the obstruction will need to be removed. Foreign bodies stuck in the lung almost always need to be taken out. This is covered in greater detail later in this chapter. Mucus can cause enough of an obstruction that it behaves like a foreign body, but it usually goes away on its own. In significant cases, interventions (such as deep suctioning) or medications can be used to help remove mucus.

If a bacterial infection is causing the respiratory distress, your doctor will prescribe antibiotics. However, if a viral infection is the cause, the infection will need to run its course because antibiotics don't work against viruses. The supportive treatments described earlier will help minimize symptoms while the body's own defense system does its work.

In all of these scenarios, supplemental oxygen may be needed. Supplemental oxygen helps to raise the level of oxygen in the bloodstream and to reduce the work of breathing. It can be beneficial even when the blood oxygen level is okay to begin with. Oxygen can be given mixed with aerosolized medicines through a nebulizer machine. It can also be administered on its own by a mask strapped over the nose and mouth or by a tube inserted directly into the lungs.

What are the possible complications?
The most serious complication of respiratory distress is ***respiratory arrest,*** with cessation of breathing. This can happen when the lungs are overwhelmed with infection or inflammation, when they are completely obstructed, or when the muscles of the lungs grow too tired to breathe after several hours or days of hard work.

Infection in the lungs can spread elsewhere in the body, causing infection in the blood (***bacteremia*** or ***viremia***). Less likely but still potential sites of spread include bones (***osteomyelitis***), urine (***urinary tract infection***), and even brain (***meningitis*** or ***encephalitis***).

An infected lung can form an ***abscess,*** a walled-off collection of fluid, or an ***empyema,*** a collection of pus adjacent to the lung. These collections of fluid or pus compound breathing troubles and provide reservoirs for infection.

The question of who has asthma and who doesn't is more complex than you might think. In general, one episode of wheezing with RAD is almost never called asthma unless it required hospitalization. By the third or fourth episode of RAD, however, a child is often labeled "asthmatic." Essentially, the more often a child has wheezing from RAD, the more likely it is that the child will wheeze again. In many cases, though, toddlers who wheeze "outgrow" their wheezing, and it doesn't return until their late teens or early adult years. This "honeymoon" period can be deceiving because even though no wheezing is heard, slow, chronic lung damage may be occurring. Therefore, toddlers who experience multiple episodes of wheezing are now treated aggressively with anti-inflammatory medicines daily. These medicines include steroids and the relatively new class of nonsteroidal medicines called ***leukotriene inhibitors.*** By giving your child a daily medicine, you can minimize recurrent episodes of wheezing and, more important, prevent chronic lung damage leading to severe adult asthma.

Additional Resources:

http://www.nlm.nih.gov/medlineplus/encyclopedia.html (Click on "Bl-Bz," then scroll down to "breathing difficulty." Or click on "Cp-Cz," then scroll down to "CPR.")

http://www.packardchildrenshospital.org (Go to "health library," then go to "search" in upper right-hand corner and type in "breathing difficulty.")

http://www.chop.edu/ (Click on "your child's health" along left-hand margin, then go to "search" in upper right-hand corner and type in "wheezing.")

BRONCHITIS

What is happening inside my child's body?

Bronchitis means inflammation of the ***bronchi.*** The bronchi are the large airways at the very top of the lungs. Air comes in through the mouth or nose, then travels down the trachea and into the bronchi. From there, it travels down increasingly smaller airways (called **bronchioles**) all the way out to the edges of the lungs, where oxygen is exchanged for carbon dioxide.

In medicine, "-itis" means acute inflammation. Therefore, bronchitis is inflammation of the bronchi, just as appendicitis is inflammation of the appendix. The term "bronchitis" is not used very often to describe illnesses among young toddlers; its use becomes more common as children get older. For infants and young toddlers, the term **bronchiolitis** is typically used. The difference between these two conditions is the area of lung involved. The bronchioles are farther down the respiratory tree than the bronchi. Your doctor can determine whether your child has bronchitis or bronchiolitis by listening to the lungs with a stethoscope.

The most common cause of bronchitis is a viral or bacterial infection. However, anything that causes swelling and inflammation can cause bronchitis, so allergies and intense irritation from something inhaled are certainly possibilities.

By far, the most common scenario is this: A child gets an **upper respiratory infection (URI).** In the course of this illness, a virus infects the upper airway, including the nose, sinuses, and throat. The virus itself can move farther down toward the lungs, infecting the bronchi. If it moves all the way down into the lungs, it causes **pneumonia.**

Sometimes bronchitis results from inflammation without actual infection. As the virus causes postnasal drip and a cough, the large airways can become irritated and swollen. The result may be symptoms of bronchitis even though the virus isn't physically in the bronchi.

Bacteria can cause bronchitis, too. A child with bacterial bronchitis will tend to be sicker than one with viral bronchitis — the fever is generally higher, and the symptoms come on faster. Otherwise, the viral and bacterial forms can look quite similar.

The hallmarks of bronchitis are a thick, wet cough with any of the following: fever, decreased energy, thick nasal congestion, sore throat, shortness of breath, wheezing, or chest pain. Many of these symptoms are nonspecific. Therefore, just because your child complains of a sore throat and has a thick, wet cough he doesn't necessarily have bronchitis. The most accurate way to diagnose bronchitis is for a doctor to listen to his chest.

What can I do?

Make your child comfortable. If he is running a fever, use a fever reducer such as acetaminophen (Tylenol) or ibuprofen (Advil or Motrin).

Many people believe that milk, cheese, yogurt, and other dairy products tend to increase congestion, thus increasing the thickness of the cough. Therefore, you may want to have your child stay away from dairy products as much as possible. In lieu of dairy products, encourage the consumption of clear liquids. If your child insists on drinking milk, use soy or rice milk, or dilute cow's milk with water.

Encourage your child to blow his nose often. This will minimize the risk of a secondary sinus or ear infection.

Over-the-counter cough suppressants may or may not help. At night, they can give your child a break from coughing, drastically improving sleep. During the day, however, it may be better to let your child cough. Coughing helps keep fluid and mucus from settling in the lower parts of the chest, thus reducing the likelihood of pneumonia. If the coughing is severely inhibiting your child's ability to maintain normal activities during the day, or if the coughing is so strong that it causes vomiting, a cough suppressant is appropriate. Specific cough suppressants are discussed in the treatments section.

When does my doctor need to be involved?

Take your child to see your doctor if the cough is getting steadily worse or if your child is having difficulty breathing. Coughing that is so severe that it causes vomiting usually warrants a visit to the doctor. If the cough is accompanied by a high fever, or if your child's energy is much lower than usual, contact your doctor.

What tests need to be done, and what do the results mean?

Tests are generally not done with bronchitis. The diagnosis can usually be made based on a history of recent events and a physical exam.

It can be difficult to determine the exact cause of bronchitis, and methods used in adults (such as stimulating a deep productive cough to get a sputum sample) are generally unsuccessful in children.

If your doctor is concerned about concurrent pneumonia, a chest X ray may be done. With bronchitis, the lungs may look normal on X ray. With pneumonia, collections of fluid will be visible.

If your child is having difficulty breathing, the doctor may check his oxygen level. This is most easily done using a pulse oximeter attached to a finger or toe.

What are the treatments?

If the cause of the bronchitis is a bacterial infection, antibiotics will be necessary. However, most cases are caused by viruses, and there are no specific medicines available to fight viruses. Sometimes with viral bronchitis, your doctor will suggest an antibiotic to prevent a secondary bacterial infection. However, this approach is not standard.

One exception to the rule that viruses aren't treated with specific medicines is **influenza.** Influenza, or true "flu," can cause sudden and severe illness, including bronchitis. There are several antiviral medications available to treat influenza. These medicines are expensive, and many of them are not yet approved for toddlers. However, if your child is diagnosed with influenza, your doctor may prescribe an antiviral medication such as Tamiflu to shorten the course of the illness and reduce its severity.

Fever reducers such as acetaminophen (Tylenol) and ibuprofen (Motrin or Advil) are commonly used with bronchitis. Ibuprofen also works as an anti-inflammatory medication, helping to minimize the swelling in the large airways.

Cough medicines may or may not be helpful with bronchitis. The most potent cough suppressant available is codeine. This medicine works by decreasing the gag reflex at the back of the throat. This reflex can account for coughing spells with URIs and bronchitis. Codeine also works by increasing sleepiness and minimizing activity. A child who runs around less and sleeps more is less likely to cough from activity and more likely to get the sleep he needs to get healthy again faster.

However, codeine does not always increase sleepiness. In fact, it can have the opposite effect — called a **paradoxical reaction** — in some children. Because codeine is such a potent medication, it is available only by prescription. Parents are advised to use it sparingly, as it will cause constipation if used too often, and it is not recommended for children under two years of age. It is also important to follow your doctor's dosing instructions, because an overdose of codeine can cause respiratory suppression. Overuse of codeine also can cause addiction.

A more commonly used cough medication is dextromethorphan. Several over-the-counter preparations combine this drug with guaifenesin, an expectorant that thins mucus in the respiratory tract.

For children who have wheezing associated with bronchitis, the smaller airways also need to be opened up. This is accomplished using a **bronchodilator** such as albuterol. Albuterol is covered in detail in the previous section on asthma.

What are the possible complications?

The most worrisome complication of bronchitis is **respiratory distress.** This does not happen very often because the large airways are large enough that they can generally tolerate some swelling and inflammation. However, in a small child, the airways are commensurately small. In such cases, bronchitis may cause significant difficulty breathing because the relative obstruction is greater.

Another complication of bronchitis is **pneumonia.** When the inflammation results in increased mucus and fluid production, the fluid can track down into the deep parts of the lung. This happens more frequently in young children who cannot (or do not know how to) cough the mucus up and out. Using too many cough suppressants also can lead to pneumonia.

Additional Resources:
http://www.emedicine.com/emerg/topic69.htm
http://www.chop.edu/ (Click on "your child's health" along left-hand margin, then go to "search" in upper right-hand corner and type in "bronchitis.")

◆ ◆ ◆

FOREIGN BODY IN THE LUNGS

What is happening inside my child's body?
A ***foreign body*** is any object that is not human. It can be a piece of food, a toy, a coin, or the top to a medicine container. It is possible for a foreign body to get stuck in a child's airway or lung. Although this is really not very common, it can be serious or even fatal.

The mechanism for how this happens is called ***aspiration.*** When a child aspirates, something that was in his mouth gets swept down into the airway or lung with a deep breath. Often aspiration is accompanied by coughing or gagging, but sometimes not. Small objects, such as a button or popcorn kernel, make it down to the deep part of the lung; bigger objects, such as a wheel from a toy car or a piece of a hot dog, get stuck higher up in the airway. Given the way the right and left bronchi are shaped, it is more common for objects to wind up on the right side of the lung than the left.

The degree of seriousness depends on how much the object is obstructing the passage of air. A big foreign body, such as a grape, can become lodged in the trachea or main stem bronchus. Such a blockage can almost completely restrict the passage of air down to the lungs, causing shortness of breath and even respiratory distress. Big pieces lodged up high can also cause irritation, so coughing, gagging, or choking frequently accompanies this scenario.

A small foreign body, such as a bead, can travel much farther into the lungs. In this case, there is usually very little difficulty breathing (especially right after the incident) because only a small section of the lung is affected. But eventually, inflammation will develop in the area where the object has settled. Both the foreign object and the inflammation may lead to infection.

What can I do?
If your child is not breathing, start CPR and have someone call 911 immediately.

If your child is choking, you can give back blows or use the Heimlich maneuver. Following the maneuver, sweep the mouth with your fingers to find and remove the object. Specific details about how to deal with choking are covered in basic first aid courses, and the importance of taking one of these courses cannot be overstated. It is worth noting that if your child is able to speak, it is *not* recommended to attempt the Heimlich maneuver or back blows. Likewise, if your child is awake, it is *not* recommended to check the mouth with your fingers.

If you aren't sure whether your child has aspirated something but he is breathing comfortably, there is not much you can (or need to) do at home. You need to see a doctor.

To avoid aspiration in the first place, make sure to keep all small toys out of the reach of a child. This is especially important around infants and young toddlers, who often put things into their mouths. Sort through an older child's toys and remove any pieces that might present a choking hazard to your infant or young toddler. Anything the size or shape of a grape can pose a hazard. Instruct your older child never to feed your infant or young toddler solid food. It is probably best to avoid having foods the size and shape of a grape in the house.

When does my doctor need to be involved?
Anytime you think your child has aspirated, you need to see a doctor.

What tests need to be done, and what do the results mean?
The first and most important step is for a doctor to listen to your child's breathing. Sometimes it is possible to diagnose aspiration when air movement through the chest is audible in some parts of the lung but not others.

Usually, if aspiration is suspected, a chest X ray is done. Unless it is made of metal or another material that shows up on an X ray, the object that was aspirated will not be visible. But a collapsed lung behind the object or fluid pooling around the object will be visible to someone who knows how to interpret X rays. If the X ray is inconclusive, other tests such as a CT scan may be done to help make the diagnosis.

What are the treatments?

The foreign body must be removed. How this is done will depend on how far down the object has traveled. An object up relatively high in the airway can often be retrieved using a special instrument called a **bronchoscope.** This is a tube that is inserted into the airway. It has a camera and a tool attachment for retrieving objects. Doctors qualified to perform this procedure include otolaryngologists (also called ENTs, or ear, nose, and throat doctors), general surgeons, and pulmonologists (lung specialists).

An object lower down in the lung may require surgery for removal. Sometimes the object is so low down that the only means of getting it out is to cut through lung tissue. Other times the object is not quite so deep but is lodged in such a way that it is difficult to remove using a bronchoscope.

Both bronchoscopy and surgery require anesthesia. Although some adults can cooperate with a doctor using a bronchoscope, most toddlers cannot. The degree of anesthesia necessary — whether your child needs to be put to sleep completely or a local anesthetic can be used along with a relaxant — depends on the approach used to remove the foreign body.

What are the possible complications?

The most serious complication is obstruction of the airway and inability to breathe. In the most extreme circumstances, this can lead to respiratory distress, oxygen deprivation, and even death.

Once an object has made its way down into the lungs, the main complication is infection. **Pneumonia** is infection of the lung tissue. An **abscess** is a walled-off infection. It is similar to pneumonia, but the infection is sealed off by a thick capsule of tissue. An abscess is much more difficult to treat than pneumonia because the capsule prevents penetration by antibiotics. Therefore, an abscess generally needs to be drained.

Additional Resources:
http://www.emedicine.com/ped/topic286.htm
http://www.healthcentral.com/mhc/top/000036.cfm

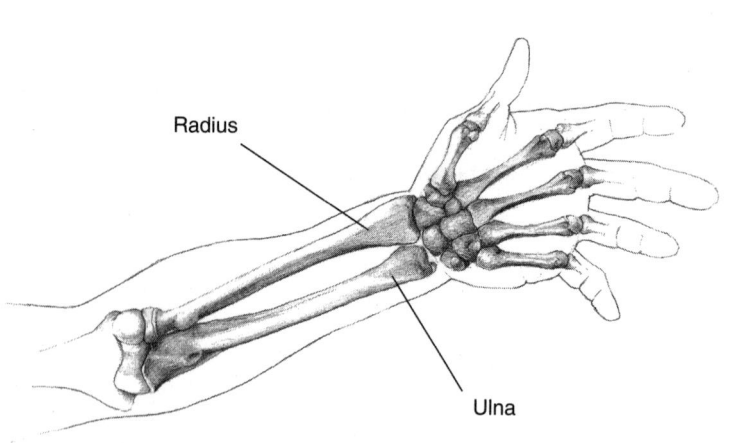

The lower arm has just two long bones while the wrist
and hand are made up of many small bones that fit together
like pieces of a puzzle.

9

Arms and Hands

NURSEMAID'S ELBOW

What is happening inside my child's body?
With ***nursemaid's elbow,*** the end of one of the bones in the forearm (the radius) moves out of its usual position in the elbow. The head of the radius is normally held in place by a piece of tissue called the ***annular ligament.*** When a toddler is pulled by the wrists and hands, the trajectory of the force pulls the annular ligament over the head of the radius and into the joint space, causing nursemaid's elbow. This can happen when you are trying to help your child stand, when you grab her hand to cross the street, when you try to prevent a fall, or when you play games involving lifting and swinging.

If your child has nursemaid's elbow, she will hold her arm in a very specific position: slightly bent at the elbow, hanging by her side, palm facing her belly. She will refuse to use that arm, even to reach out for her favorite food or toy. If she tries to use it, she will probably cry or wince in pain.

The elbow itself always looks perfect with nursemaid's elbow: no swelling, no redness, no bruises. This helps distinguish it from a broken bone or a bad sprain.

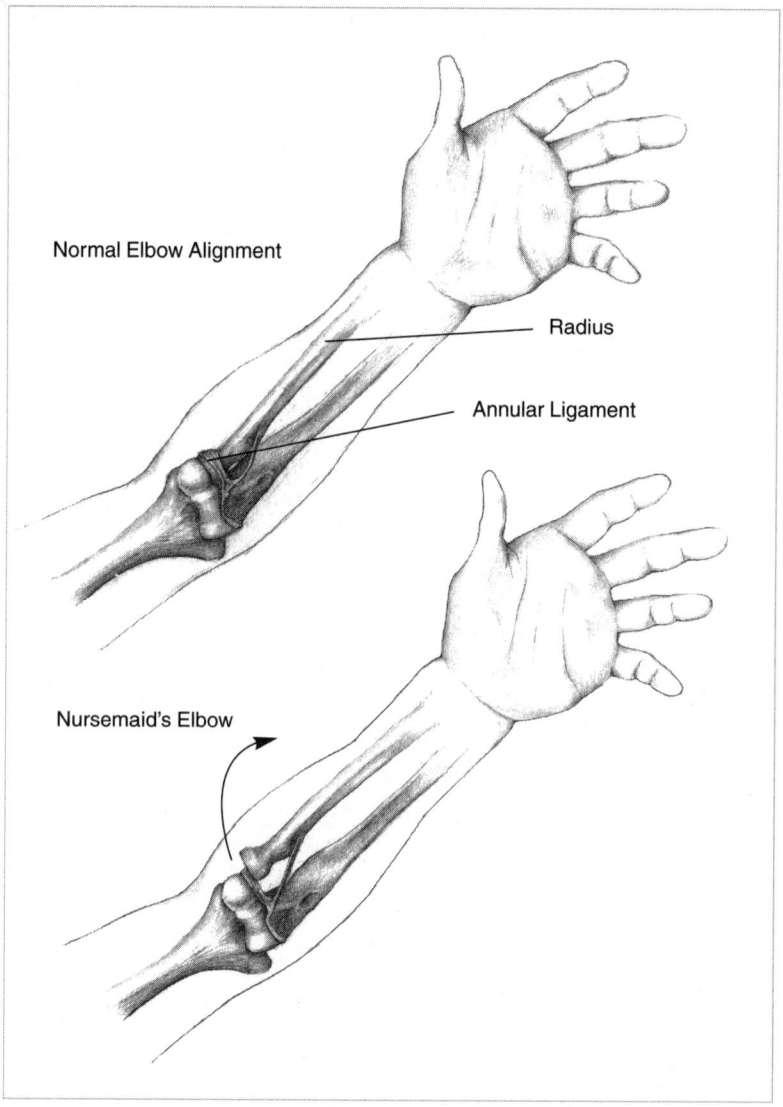

"Nursemaid's elbow" results from the head of the radius shifting off its normal resting spot. The head of the radius is usually held in place by the annular ligament.

Once your child has had nursemaid's elbow, there is a slightly greater chance that she'll have it again in the future. After age four, nursemaid's elbow is uncommon regardless of your child's history.

What can I do?

If you know how to fix nursemaid's elbow, then you can do it yourself. The steps are reviewed in the sidebar on page 162. If you don't know how, or if you are uneasy about doing it, leave the elbow alone. If you are unsure whether it is nursemaid's elbow, it is best not to manipulate the arm.

If the incident that caused the injury was not witnessed, or if it was witnessed but does not fit the classic story of nursemaid's elbow (if there was no pulling on the wrist or arm), the injury is likely to be something else, such as a broken collarbone or arm. It is very painful to manipulate the arm when there is a fracture, so this is not recommended. Again, if you are not sure whether it is nursemaid's elbow, leave it alone and let a doctor take a look.

When does my doctor need to be involved?

Call your doctor if you are unsure whether your child's injury is nursemaid's elbow. It can be difficult to distinguish a break or sprain from nursemaid's elbow, especially if you have never seen these before. Be sure to call or visit your doctor if your child is having significant pain or absolutely refuses to move the arm.

What tests need to be done, and what do the results mean?

Tests are generally not done for nursemaid's elbow. Your doctor can make the diagnosis by looking at the way your child is holding her arm, examining her elbow (and finding that it is normal), and obtaining the history of how it happened. When there is doubt, an X ray may be done to make sure there is no fracture.

What are the treatments?

Nursemaid's elbow is treated by putting the ligament back in its original position, a technique called **reduction.** This technique is very simple and is outlined in the sidebar on page 162. Within

HOW TO FIX NURSEMAID'S ELBOW

1. *Face your child. Hold the elbow of the affected arm in one of your hands.*
2. *With your other hand, take hold of the hand and wrist of the affected side.*
3. *In one careful but swift motion, turn the palm of your child's hand so that it faces the ceiling. Lift the hand up to the shoulder on the affected side by bending the elbow completely. Straighten the elbow by bringing the hand back down to your child's side.*
4. *You may feel a pop in the elbow either when you bend the arm or when you straighten it. Or you may feel nothing.*
5. *Leave your child's arm and hand alone for a few minutes. Although she may cry when you are doing the maneuver, as soon as you are done, she should calm down quickly. Within five minutes, she will be able to use the arm again.*

five minutes of a successful reduction, your child will be happy and using her injured arm once again.

What are the possible complications?

Nursemaid's elbow has no long-term complications. Once it is reduced, the pain is gone, and your child can resume normal activity. However, once your child has had nursemaid's elbow, there is a slightly increased risk that it will happen again.

Additional Resources:
http://www.nlm.nih.gov/medlineplus/ency/article/000983.htm
http://www.med.umich.edu/1libr/pa/pa_nursmaid_hhg.htm
http://www.fpnotebook.com/ElbowNursemaidsReduction.jpg

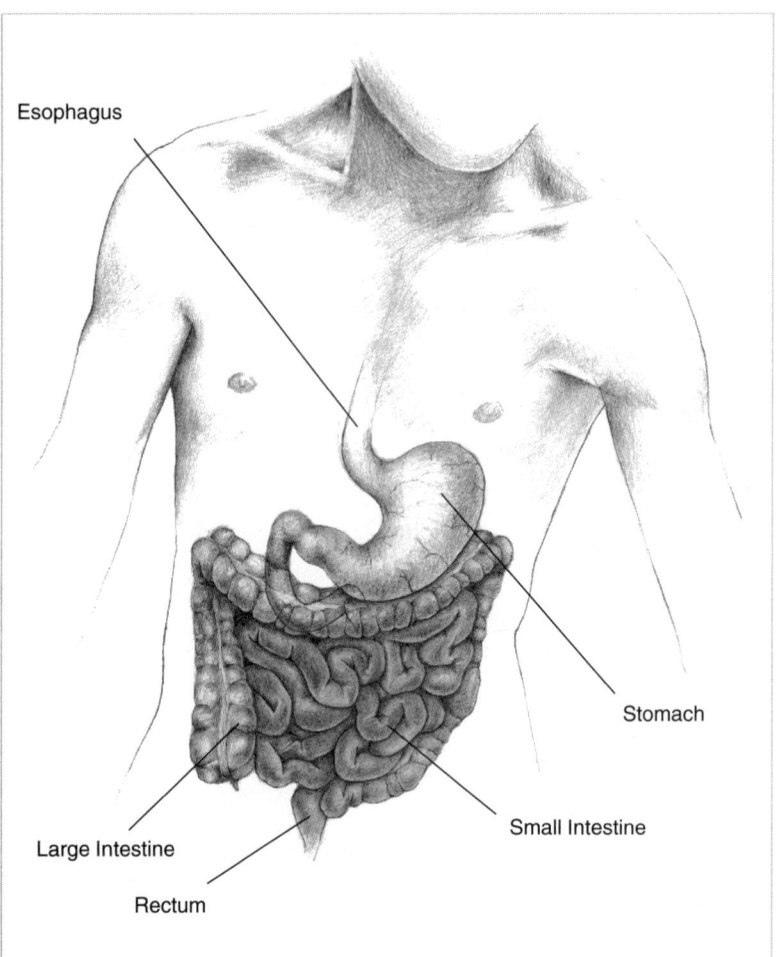

Esophagus

Stomach

Large Intestine

Small Intestine

Rectum

The gastrointestinal tract is like a long, convoluted hose.
Food enters via the esophagus and stomach,
and waste leaves via the rectum.

10

Stomach and Intestine

CONSTIPATION

What is happening inside my child's body?
Some toddlers poop three times a day, and others go once every three days. Both are normal. Just because one child poops less frequently than another does not mean that the child is constipated.

The definition of constipation has two parts. First, a constipated child goes less frequently than what is usual for him. Second, the stool is firm and difficult to pass. If the stool comes out soft, no matter how long it has been since your child's last bowel movement, he's not constipated.

Why do many parents automatically think that when their child poops infrequently, he is constipated? It is because the longer stool stays in the colon and rectum, the more firm it becomes. One of the jobs of the colon is to remove water from stool. So it stands to reason that when the stool sits for a prolonged period of time, more water is removed from it, and the stool becomes hard and dry. (The opposite also is true: in the case of diarrhea, when stool passes through the intestine rapidly, there is not much time for the colon to remove excess water, and so it comes out wet and runny.)

A constipated child will eventually become uncomfortable. Older kids complain of lower abdominal pain, while younger toddlers often simply whine or cry while squatting. The pain generally comes from a spasm of the muscle in the anus (called the **anal sphincter**). These spasms can further slow down pooping, worsening constipation and creating a vicious cycle (it hurts, so he won't go; he won't go, so it hurts).

A child's appetite can diminish with constipation, partly because of the associated abdominal pain and partly because the retained stool makes a child feel "full."

When constipated stool finally comes out, it may well hurt. Constipated stool that is large and dry can tear the skin around the anus when it is passed, resulting in drops of bright red blood. Such a tear is called an **anal fissure.** Fissures sting when urine or stool come into contact with the torn skin. If you look closely at your child's bottom, you can usually see an anal fissure right at the anus. Again, this creates a vicious cycle: for the broken skin to heal, the stools must be soft, but for the stools to be soft, your child must be willing to poop frequently.

There are many causes of constipation, but the most common is diet. Certain foods firm up stool, causing constipation; others help soften it, so their absence leads to hard stool. Fluids are also important. For stool to remain soft, your child must drink a minimal amount of liquid. The combination of not enough liquid and a constipating diet can quickly lead to painful bowel movements.

Another cause of constipation is constipation itself. If your child has ever passed a painful stool, you know that he does not want to repeat this uncomfortable experience. Constipation begets constipation because a child will hold his stool in an effort not to feel the discomfort of having another painful bowel movement. This response is not entirely unreasonable. The pattern is especially difficult to curb in toddlers, because they are too young to reason with but too old to forget the prior pain. But once your child returns to normal, soft, painless stools, he is likely to resume regular pooping.

What can I do?
There are two steps you can take to help your constipated child: (1) solve the immediate problem and (2) help prevent it from recurring.

For the urgent situation, you can try giving your child prune or pear juice. Sometimes these work instantly, but more often they take a few days.

Put some petroleum jelly (Vaseline) or another lubricant around your child's anus to help ease the passage of the stool. The lubrication will minimize the risk of tearing the skin when the stool comes out. It also will help the stool to slide out more easily, and its application can encourage a bowel movement by stimulating the anus to contract.

If your child is extremely uncomfortable, you may want to be more aggressive. One approach is to use a rectal thermometer coated with petroleum jelly. Inserting a rectal thermometer stimulates the anal sphincter and often causes a child to poop shortly thereafter. Suppositories can be used in a similar manner. These are discussed in the treatments section. If you help move your child's bowels with a thermometer or a suppository, do it only once or twice before speaking with your doctor. Parents who rely too heavily on this technique find that the child becomes dependent on it and cannot have a bowel movement without help.

To prevent future constipation, try to remove constipating foods — such as rice, starches, and bananas — from your child's diet. Just as important, add foods that help keep the stool soft and moving, such as sweet fruits (apricots, prunes, peaches, pears, and plums) and fibrous vegetables (peas and spinach). These dietary changes should be continued until the stool is consistently soft. Then you can resume a more normal diet, reintroducing the foods that are considered constipating and watching to see what happens.

When does my doctor need to be involved?
Call your doctor if your child is in pain, if the constipation continues for several days, or if it is getting worse. You should certainly call if your child is having vomiting due to the constipation or a fever along with the constipation.

The first time your child has blood in his stool, it can be difficult to tell whether the blood is from an anal fissure or from bleeding within the intestine. Either way, call your doctor. Blood in the stool is covered in more detail later in this chapter.

What tests need to be done, and what do the results mean?
If your child has mild constipation that is readily resolved with
dietary changes, prune juice, a rectal thermometer, or over-the-
counter treatments, no tests need to be done.

However, if the constipation is not easily treatable, or if it wors-
ens despite attempts to treat it, tests should be done. An X ray can
show how much stool remains in the intestine. It can also identify
structural abnormalities of the intestinal tract.

More invasive tests, such as colonoscopy or biopsy, can be
done as well. These are not common but are sometimes helpful
in chronic cases. Gastroenterologists are doctors who specialize
in the intestinal tract and are trained to perform these tests. Again,
it is unusual for constipated toddlers to require such invasive
tests.

Very occasionally, blood tests are done to determine whether
there might be an underlying cause of the constipation. These
include tests to assess thyroid function, calcium level, lead level,
and celiac disease antibodies. Abnormalities in any of these areas
can point toward the source of chronic constipation.

In extreme cases, an MRI may be considered. This test can look
at the structures and nerves around the intestine. Ongoing or particularly severe constipation can be caused by a mass pushing
against the intestine and blocking normal flow. It also may be a
result of inadequate nervous system input to the intestine.

Hirschsprung's disease is the absence of nerves at the end
of the colon. These nerves are necessary to help keep the bowels
moving, so without them, severe constipation will result. This
uncommon problem can be diagnosed only by biopsy, and treatment requires surgery.

A **tethered cord** is an anomaly along the spinal cord that
sometimes causes constipation. The nerves traveling from the
spinal cord to the bowel become entrapped or inflamed, interfering with their ability to function properly. Tethered cord is discussed at length in chapter 14.

What are the treatments?
There are two routes to treat constipation: from the top (through
the mouth) and from the bottom (up the rectum).

Stool softeners are taken by mouth. They pass through the stomach into the intestine, helping to soften the forming stool by increasing its water content. Prune and pear juice work as stool softeners, as do corn syrup and mineral oil. Prescription stool softeners are available as well. Lactulose is a nonabsorbable sugar that draws water into the colon quickly. Other stool softeners include milk of magnesia and docusate (Colace).

To treat your child from the bottom end, you can use a *suppository* or *enema.* These treatments provide anal lubrication and stimulate the rectum to contract at the same time. The stimulation helps move the bowels. Glycerin suppositories (sized for children) are semisolid, so they dissolve quickly once in the anus. Enemas are liquids that are squirted into the anus.

Do not use anal stimulation regularly without speaking with your doctor. You do not want your child to become dependent on this as a means of moving her bowels. Furthermore, as almost any toddler will tell you, this is *not* the preferred method of treatment.

What are the possible complications?

Regular constipation can cause slow weight gain or even weight loss. This happens because ongoing constipation will interfere with your child's appetite.

Severely impacted stool that cannot come out despite all efforts can lead to a *toxic megacolon.* The colon becomes extremely distended and can even rupture. This very rare but worrisome consequence of constipation can be life threatening and requires immediate medical attention.

Additional Resources:

http://www.mayoclinic.com/ (Go to "search" in upper right-hand corner and type in "constipation children.")

http://www.drhull.com/EncyMaster/C/constipation_infant.html

http://www.nlm.nih.gov/medlineplus/encyclopedia.html (Click on "C-Co," then scroll down to "constipation" or click on "Ah-Ap," then scroll down to "anal fissure.")

◆   ◆   ◆

GASTROENTERITIS (STOMACH FLU), VOMITING, AND DIARRHEA

What is happening inside my child's body?
Stomach flu is a general phrase describing vomiting and/or diarrhea. It is a catchy term that has stuck over the years. The more correct medical name is **gastroenteritis.** The phrase "stomach flu" is a misnomer because this illness is not caused by or in any way related to the infection influenza.

Most types of stomach flu are extremely contagious, so siblings and parents are likely to get sick as well. The typical incubation period is 48 to 72 hours. Infants tend to have more diarrhea and less vomiting; adults sometimes report only nausea, but it is so intense that they can lose their appetite for days.

The stomach flu usually begins with vomiting that lasts anywhere from 12 to 24 hours. This can vary widely, ranging from sporadic vomiting every couple of hours to intense repeated vomiting. Eventually, the contents of the stomach may be emptied, and your child will begin dry heaving, with nothing coming up.

Diarrhea typically follows vomiting by about a day or so, but the two can occur simultaneously, and in some cases the diarrhea even precedes the vomiting. Diarrhea means watery and frequent stools. The stools are not just soft; they are liquid. The diarrhea seen with most forms of stomach flu is voluminous, watery, foul-smelling, and associated with crampy abdominal pain. It will generally last anywhere from three to seven days, but it can persist for up to two weeks before the stools normalize completely.

Generally speaking, diarrhea is caused by intestinal-wall swelling. This interferes with normal absorption, leaving in the intestine water and nutrients that usually move out of the gut and into the bloodstream. This extra water gives the diarrhea its characteristic liquid consistency. Significant diarrhea also changes the normal balance of bacteria in the gut. It is important to remember that bacteria are normal inhabitants of the intestine. Bacteria help break down food and produce byproducts (such as vitamin K) that are used by the rest of the body. When the number and types of bacteria change dramatically, the consistency of the stool will change, too.

Anything that inflames the intestine can cause diarrhea. Possible sources of inflammation include food allergy, diseases of the immune system, or infection. The most common virus to cause diarrhea among young children is rotavirus. Other viruses that can be to blame for stomach flu include astrovirus, adenovirus, and Norwalk virus. Bacteria such as salmonella, shigella, campylobacter, and E. coli also can cause gastroenteritis. Worldwide, the most infamous bacterial cause of stomach flu — and one of the leading causes of death in developing countries — is cholera.

Ironically, the medicines that treat bacteria — antibiotics — can cause diarrhea, too. Antibiotics can change the balance of bacteria that normally reside in the intestine or can cause an allergic reaction. Each may result in profuse diarrhea.

Regardless of the underlying cause, once diarrhea starts, it can be difficult to stop. This is because the intestine becomes very irritated. The more irritated it is, the more blunted the normally absorptive surfaces become. It takes time for these surfaces to return to their baseline. Especially in the case of an intestinal infection, it is often best to let diarrhea run its course rather than try to stop it with medicine. The sooner the infection has left the gut, the sooner the gut can begin to heal.

What can I do?

What to do depends on where you are at in the course of the illness. The main thing you want to do is prevent your child from becoming dehydrated.

For vomiting: If your child has just begun with vomiting, the best first step is to stop giving him all solids and most liquids. Your child will probably refuse to eat anyhow, so the solids part is easy. But after a few bouts of vomiting, he is likely to become fairly thirsty. Try to wait 45 minutes to an hour after the last episode of vomiting to give him something to drink.

Then start with clear liquids and small sips. If you offer your child eight ounces in a cup, he may drink it all (or a significant portion of it), and almost certainly it will come right back up. So start by offering little bits — on a spoon, in a medicine dropper, in the form of a soaked washcloth or a Popsicle. The goal is to get a teaspoon or so of liquid into your child every few minutes.

Once your child is able to tolerate small sips, you can slowly increase the amount. Offer a half ounce or an ounce at a time every several minutes. Gradually, you will get up to several ounces at a time, but this takes a few hours. Remember to stick with clear liquids such as water, watered-down juice, or rice water. Don't give into your child's pleas for large amounts of liquid or for milk. These are the two surefire ways to prolong the vomiting. If he refuses everything but milk, try soy milk or rice milk, but even so, dilute it with water. If all he will take (or all you have) is cow's milk, water it down significantly.

For diarrhea: When your child has stopped vomiting (or if your child never vomited in the first place) and he is coping with only diarrhea, you want to rehydrate him as aggressively as possible. Excessive diarrhea can lead to dehydration when a child poops out more liquid than he takes in.

Clear liquids are the best for rehydration. You can give water, rice water, or any other clear liquid. Most juices exacerbate diarrhea, except for white grape juice, which can alleviate it. Rehydration drinks contain electrolytes to replace those that are lost during ongoing diarrhea. Unfortunately, these drinks are not safe if they are the only thing consumed for more than 24 hours. Also, some of these drinks are so unpalatable that they make kids

---

RICE WATER RECIPE

To make rice water, boil one liter of water. Add about one cup of rice and cook for 5 to 10 minutes until the water is starchy. Then pour the liquid into a container. Some people like to add one teaspoon of sugar and a pinch of salt to the liquid. Once it has cooled to room temperature, you can give your child the rice water. You can do whatever you like with the leftover rice.

throw up. If nothing else, you want to do your best to keep up with the fluid losses and not give something that is going to cause your child to lose more liquids.

When your child feels ready to start eating solids, give them to him. To help firm up the stool, give your child bland, constipating foods such as rice, pasta, crackers, or bananas. The old recommendation was to follow the BRAT diet: bananas, rice, applesauce, and toast. But it turns out that any bland food is fine. If your child wants chicken, go for it. In fact, proteins are helpful in healing the intestine. Just stay away from spicy foods, sugary foods, and dairy products. Spicy foods will upset a relatively empty stomach. Sugar draws more water into the intestines, which can worsen diarrhea. And dairy products seem to exacerbate diarrhea almost immediately. If your child insists on milk, try soy or rice milk instead of cow's milk, and dilute them if you can.

Some children with stomach flu will refuse to drink anything except water or watered-down juice, both of which offer almost no calories. If your child falls into this category, you may think he is becoming dehydrated because he will almost certainly have a diminished energy level. However, if he is urinating and the inside of his mouth is moist, he is not dehydrated. This confusing picture results from good liquid intake without nearly enough calories. To help boost your child's energy, try to get some calories in him by giving juice or rice water with sugar added.

It is not uncommon for the diarrhea to last three to seven days (and sometimes longer) with gastroenteritis.

When does my doctor need to be involved?
Call your doctor if (1) your child won't drink anything at all, (2) he takes little sips but vomits immediately thereafter, or (3) the vomiting goes on for hours and you seem unable to find a window of 45 minutes since the last episode. Children who have persistent vomiting or are unwilling to drink may become dehydrated.

In some cases, the nausea is so debilitating that a child will refuse liquids entirely. In other cases, the diarrhea is so voluminous that despite drinking fairly well, the child is losing more fluids than he is taking in. Dehydration also can occur gradually if diarrhea persists over an extended period of time and is not getting better. Call your doctor if your child has any of these.

Remember, too, that a child who is drinking but is not getting many (or any) calories can become lethargic. If your child's energy level is significantly depressed, you will need to contact your doctor. When in doubt, pick up the phone.

If you think that the cause of the diarrhea is a medication (such as an antibiotic), you should call your doctor. The medicine may need to be changed or stopped.

What tests need to be done, and what do the results mean?

In general, children with vomiting or diarrhea rarely need lab tests. However, if the diarrhea goes on and on (certainly if it has lasted longer than two weeks), or if it has become bloody, the stool should be checked for specific infections. In many cases, even if an infection is identified, medication is not given. Ironically, this is because the medication can make things worse.

Infections that begin in the intestine can spread to the bloodstream and then to other parts of the body. In an ill-appearing child, blood tests such as a complete blood count and a blood culture may be done to determine whether an infection has spread.

If your child is so dehydrated that he requires IV fluids, he will likely have his labs checked as well. A complete blood count, blood culture, and electrolyte panel are standard.

In rare cases, if your child has recurrent vomiting and an obstruction in the bowel is suspected, an X ray of the abdomen will be done.

What are the treatments?

There are two goals in treating gastroenteritis: stop the vomiting and diarrhea in order to prevent dehydration, and then rehydrate.

There are medicines available to help stop vomiting. These are usually given as a rectal suppository because a vomiting child will not be able to keep down an oral medicine. In the hospital, these medicines are also available as shots or can be given through an IV. The most common of these medicines is promethazine (Phenergan), which slows the motion of the intestine, preventing vomiting and therefore helping with oral rehydration. Promethazine can cause sleepiness, however. This effect sometimes outweighs the benefit because it may be difficult for a tired child to increase his fluid intake.

There are also medicines available to help stop diarrhea, but these are generally not recommended for toddlers. Antidiarrhea medicines such as loperamide (Imodium) will significantly slow diarrhea, but they also will slow the passage of whatever infection is causing the problem. If the infection lingers, so will most of the symptoms. Until the underlying infection is passed, a child cannot recover completely. This is why, when diarrhea is the result of an infection, the infection is typically left untreated. It will almost always resolve spontaneously.

If your child has a parasitic infection such as giardia causing his symptoms, he will need a specific antibiotic. Parasites do not get better on their own. Another infection that requires medication is a bacterial infection that has moved from the gut into other parts of the body.

Rehydration is the main treatment for gastroenteritis. Many strategies can be tried at home, as described previously. If your child is unable to drink or if he is significantly dehydrated, he may need an IV. When an IV is used, a solution containing sugar and salt is run directly into a vein. This increases the blood volume and eventually maintains the fluid level in the body despite ongoing losses in the stools. When a child is dehydrated, his heart has to work harder to pump blood around his body, and there is less blood available to the various organs. When the blood volume increases with IV fluids, the heart doesn't have to work as hard, and the organs get more of the nutrients they need. This is described in more detail in the section on dehydration in chapter 18.

If your child's diarrhea is the result of an antibiotic, your doctor may reduce the dose or stop it altogether.

What are the possible complications?
Massive or ongoing diarrhea can cause ***dehydration.*** It is important to be able to recognize the signs of dehydration, which are covered in chapter 18. You may groan at the notion of having to

go to the doctor's office or the emergency room for an IV, but remember that IV fluids can be lifesaving. IV rehydration is not available in many parts of the world, and this is why dehydration is a leading cause of death worldwide.

Frequent vomiting can eventually lead to a tear in the esophagus called a ***Mallory-Weiss tear***. The result is bright red blood visible in the vomit.

Other common complications are far less worrisome. Many of the infections that cause gastroenteritis may also cause body rashes. These rashes range from pink to red, flat to raised, splotchy to confluent. They most often appear on the chest and back but can show up just about anywhere.

Diaper rashes result from frequent diarrhea. The watery stools contain bile, and this bile irritates and eventually breaks down the skin of the buttocks. The more frequently your child poops and the more watery the stools become, the more likely it is that your child will wind up with a rash. This is obviously worse for a child in diapers. To add insult to injury, when you wipe your child's bottom, you will likely further irritate the skin and exacerbate the rash. Sometimes sitting your child in lukewarm water for a few minutes is the least irritating way to clean his bottom.

There are ways to minimize diaper rash in this situation. For toddlers still in diapers, change the diaper as soon as possible, avoiding prolonged contact between the stool and the skin. For potty-trained toddlers, recognize that accidents are common when your child is having a bout of diarrhea, so look out for soiled underpants and don't be surprised if he reverts to diapers for a short time. Keep your child's bottom as clean and dry as possible, washing with plain water instead of perfumed soaps or wipes. Often a thin layer of diaper cream, especially one with zinc, will help heal the skin and prevent more irritation.

Constant diarrhea inflames the lining of the intestine, decreasing the absorption of nutrients and minerals. Typically, when a child who has just gotten over the stomach flu drinks milk or eats dairy products, his diarrhea returns. Some children are unable to tolerate diary products for several days (or even weeks) after having the stomach flu.

To complicate matters, during an episode of gastroenteritis, the intestine loses many of the normal bacteria that live on its walls. These bacteria are critical to digesting food and forming stool. The absence of these bacteria can continue to cause problems long after the stomach flu has run its course. **Probiotics** such as **lactobacillus acidophilus** can help to repopulate the intestine with normal bacteria.

Additional Resources:
http://www.chop.edu/ (Click on "your child's health" along left-hand margin, then go to "search" in upper right-hand corner and type in "diarrhea.")
http://www.niddk.nih.gov/health/digest/pubs/diarrhea/diarrhea.htm
http://www.cincinnatichildrens.org (Click on "search" in upper right-hand corner and type in "gastroenteritis.")

◆　　◆　　◆

BLOOD IN THE STOOL

What is happening inside my child's body?

Although it is not normal to have blood in the stool, it is not uncommon either. How and where the blood appears is significant, providing clues about where in the intestinal tract the bleeding is coming from.

The redder the blood, the fresher it is. Most of the time, bright red blood in the stool comes from the very end of the intestine or from a tear in the skin on the anus. If the blood is mixed into the stool, the bleeding is likely from the intestine. Bright red blood separate from the stool (in the diaper or on toilet paper) represents tearing of the anal skin, called an **anal fissure.**

Old blood looks brown (like coffee grounds) or black. This blood has been in the stomach and intestine for a while by the time it is passed out through the stool. Exposure to the acids along the digestive tract makes the blood darker.

In rare circumstances, bloody stools look uniformly maroon, like currant jelly, or grossly bloody, like catsup. This isn't subtle — you won't miss it. This type of bleeding typically occurs when there is a large bleed somewhere high up in the intestine, either in the stomach or in the small bowel. Blood is a cathartic: it makes the bowels move faster. With lots of blood present, the bowels move significantly faster than usual. And when the bowels move faster, the contents pass through more quickly, preventing the blood from turning brown or black. (It doesn't have a lot of time in the intestine to be exposed to digestive enzymes.) Therefore, the classic major intestinal bleed is watery and bright red. Currant jelly stools are associated with **intussusception** — an uncommon condition in which one piece of bowel telescopes into another, cutting off its own blood supply and causing significant pain.

Blood can appear in the stool for a number of reasons. Ulcers, infections, and tears in the tissue lining the stomach or intestine can all cause bloody stools. In fact, anything that inflames or tears the lining of the gastrointestinal tract can cause bleeding. Sometimes blood in the stool will be the first sign of a disease affecting the whole body. One example is a food allergy. Another is **inflammatory bowel disease** (and within this category, **Crohn's disease** and **ulcerative colitis**).

Anal fissures are most commonly the result of a large, hard stool passing out the bottom, stretching the skin and causing it to break. This is why anal fissures are often associated with constipation.

Red stools don't necessarily have blood. Certain foods and medicines can stain the stool, creating the appearance of blood. Beets are the most common culprits. (They can also turn the urine red.) An antibiotic called rifampin can do the same thing. Ingested red crayons or red Play-Doh will pass into the stool and make it look red as well.

What can I do?

The first time you see blood in the stool, you should call your doctor. If your child is still in diapers, save the diaper with the bloody stool so that the doctor can see the color of the blood and where it is relative to the stool.

If your child has recurrent bloody stools, what you do will depend on the cause of the problem. Constipation, causing an anal fissure, is treated with stool softeners and lubrication. A food allergy is treated by avoiding the offending food. You and your doctor will come up with a plan depending on your child's underlying issue.

When does my doctor need to be involved?
Call your doctor anytime you see blood in the stool for the first time. Even if you have seen blood in the stool before, you should contact your doctor if you see copious amounts of blood or if your child is pale, lethargic, or significantly irritable.

What tests need to be done, and what do the results mean?
The decision of whether to do lab tests will depend on what the stool looks like (Is there a little blood or a lot? Is it bright red or brown? Is it occasional or persistent?) and on how your child appears.

In general, if there is blood only around the edges of the stool and an anal fissure is suspected, tests are not done.

If there is only a small amount of blood mixed into the stool (sometimes along with mucus) and your child looks otherwise well, tests are generally not done.

If the blood in the stool is persistent, increasing, bright red, or associated with fever, or if your child appears ill, tests will be done. These may include stool tests, blood tests, and imaging (X ray or ultrasound).

Different stool tests yield different kinds of information. The presence of blood can be documented (called **heme positive** stools). Signs of irritation in the bowel include the presence of **white blood cells** (a sign of inflammation) or **eosinophils** (markers of allergy). Stool cultures will identify specific infections. Some of these tests require separate stool samples collected in specific containers. Naturally, if your child is still in diapers, the samples are easier to collect. In general, stool samples need to be fresh. This is why even when you bring a diaper to the doctor's office, you may need to collect the stool another time.

If blood tests are done — and this is an infrequent occurrence — they generally include a complete blood count and a blood culture. Sometimes an electrolyte panel and liver function tests are run to assess whether other organs are affected. Specific problems such as celiac disease, food allergy, or inflammatory bowel disease may be identified with blood tests.

An X ray or ultrasound (or both) may be done to take a picture of the intestine. Neither of these studies is perfect, but both can show contrast between solid, liquid, and gas, creating an image of what is going on inside. An X ray is especially helpful if the doctor suspects an obstruction somewhere along the intestinal tract.

In some cases, intestinal bleeding may need to be evaluated with pictures of the inside of the intestinal walls. A gastroenterologist (a doctor specializing in the intestinal tract) will take these pictures using a tiny camera. When a camera is inserted into the stomach via the mouth, the procedure is called **endoscopy;** when it is inserted into the large intestine via the anus, it is called **colonoscopy.** This technique allows for clear pictures of the bowel, but it is quite invasive and therefore is used only when necessary.

What are the treatments?
The treatment always depends on the source of the bleeding. Infections associated with bloody stools are rarely treated unless they also cause significant illness, either by spreading to other parts of the body or by leading to dehydration. But certain infections — such as a parasite or the bacteria *C. difficile* — do need to be treated with specific medicines.

Inflammation along the bowel wall may need to be treated if it is severe or if it is associated with a systemic illness. **Steroids** are strong anti-inflammatory medicines that can help to heal the bowel lining. Although steroids are exceptionally helpful in treating inflammatory disorders, they are necessary only in a small subset of children.

If an obstruction or intussusception is the cause of blood in the stool, the bowel must be released. This requires either an enema using a liquid visible on X ray (called a **barium enema**) or surgery.

Anal fissures can be treated with a lubricant, such as petroleum jelly (Vaseline), applied to the anus. This will help a subsequent stool slide out without reinjuring the torn skin. Stool softeners and a diet oriented toward softening the stool will help address constipation, thereby reducing the bulk of the stools passing through the anus. Anal fissures (and constipation in general) can be very hard to treat in toddlers. It can be difficult to convince a strong-willed child that pooping will actually make things better when the child is well aware that it was pooping that caused the pain in the first place. Such circumstances can lead to a cycle of constipation and reinjury to the anal skin. This topic is covered in greater detail earlier in this chapter in the section on constipation.

What are the possible complications?

The most worrisome complication of bloody stools is loss of blood, with subsequent **anemia.** An anemic child feels tired and doesn't gain weight or grow as well as she could. Severe anemia can cause problems with other organs in the body.

Blood in the stool can cause **rashes** on the bottom, because bloody stools are more irritating to the skin than normal stools. Steps to minimize this are the same for bloody stools and for diarrhea. If your toddler is still in diapers, change the diaper as soon as possible, avoiding prolonged contact between the stool and the skin. If your toddler is potty trained, recognize that accidents are common when your child is having a bout of bloody stools, so look out for soiled underpants and don't be surprised if she reverts to diapers for a short time. Keep your child's bottom as clean and dry as possible, washing with plain water instead of perfumed soaps or wipes. Often using a cream to create a thin barrier, especially one with zinc, will help heal the skin and prevent more irritation.

Abdominal pain is often associated with blood in the stool. Remember that blood is a cathartic: it makes the stool move more quickly through the intestine. This may cause cramping. Also, the underlying issue causing the bleeding — whether it is an infection or inflammation — may cause cramping or abdominal pain on its own.

Additional Resources:
http://www.mayoclinic.com (Click on "search" in upper right-hand corner and type in "bloody stool.")
http://www.cincinnatichildrens.org (Click on "search" in upper right-hand corner and type in "intussusception.")
http://www.tch.harvard.edu (Go to "My child has:" in upper right-hand corner and type in "bloody stool.")

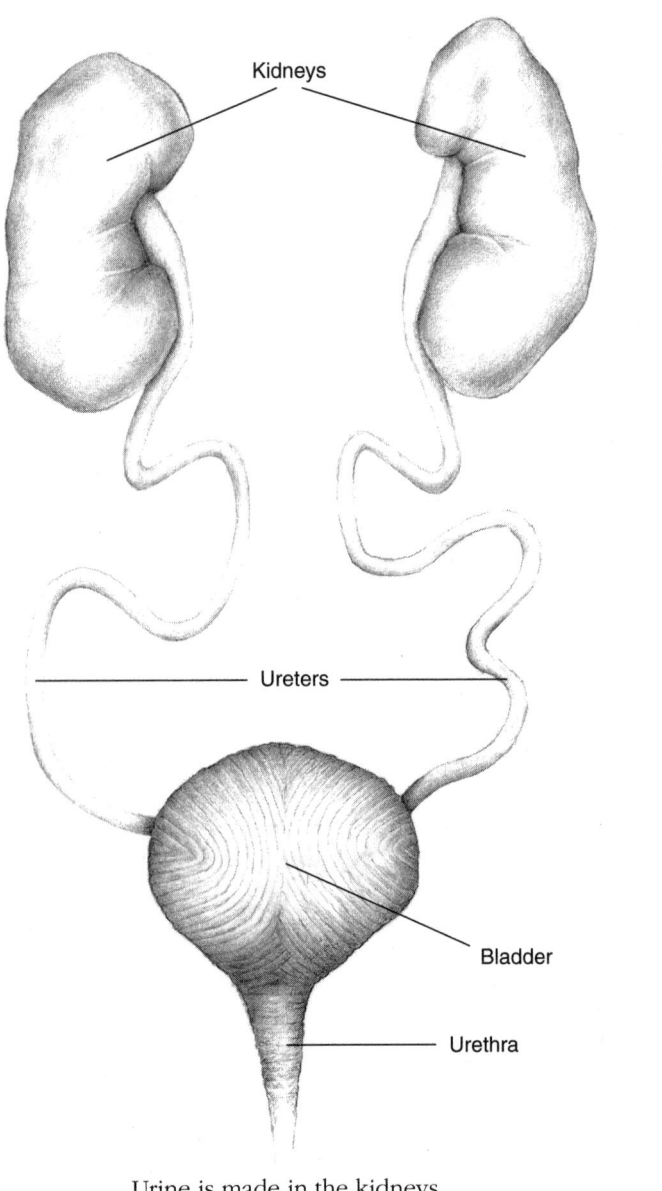

Kidneys

Ureters

Bladder

Urethra

Urine is made in the kidneys.
It flows down the ureters and is stored in the bladder
until it exits the body via the urethra.

11

Bladder and Urinary Tract

◆

PAINFUL URINATION AND URINARY TRACT INFECTION

What is happening inside my child's body?
Urine is produced in the kidneys. It flows from the kidneys down tubes called ureters into the bladder, where it remains until your child is ready to urinate. The urine leaves the bladder and exits the body through the urethra.

Even though urine is a collection of waste materials, it is relatively colorless and odorless, and it should always be painless to urinate. Sometimes, though, the urine will look dark yellow — for instance, when your child has not had enough to drink. And occasionally it will have a strong smell because some waste products (as with that of asparagus) carry an odor. A single episode of smelly or dark urine is rarely a cause for concern.

When these features persist or when your child begins to complain of pain, your child's urine may be infected. If it is, the problem can reside anywhere along the tract, from the kidneys down to the urethra. This is why it is called a ***urinary tract infection (UTI).***

In toddlers, the most common cause of a UTI is bad luck. For a child in diapers who sits in poop, the bacteria that normally live in the intestine and are shed in the stool can easily attach themselves to the urethra. Under the right circumstances, the bacteria move up the urethra toward the bladder, where they multiply and cause symptoms. For a child out of diapers who wipes her bottom on her own, stool can easily be smeared onto the skin around the vagina and urethra. Again, if the circumstances are right, the bacteria may ascend up to the urinary tract.

UTIs are more common in girls than boys. This is because the distance from the tip of the urethra to the bladder is shorter in girls than in boys. In boys, the length of the penis adds a significant — often insurmountable — distance for the bacteria to ascend. This added distance provides an extra level of protection for boys.

There are other causes of a UTI aside from bad luck. Unusual anatomy of the urinary tract will result in an abnormal flow of urine. This creates areas where urine can pool, and these areas are prone to infection. Another cause of a UTI is holding the urine for extensive periods of time. Urine that stagnates in the bladder is more likely to become infected than urine that moves out of the body on a regular basis. Again, this has to do with pooling: when urine pools, it is no different from any still body of water (such as a pond at the park), and bacteria tend to grow there.

We think of urine as always flowing down the urinary tract, but it can actually flow backward, from the bladder up the ureters and toward the kidneys. This is called **vesicoureteral reflux,** or **reflux** for short. Reflux can occur as a result of a UTI and will generally go away when the infection is treated. Reflux can also be the cause of a UTI. For example, an anatomical abnormality in the urinary tract can cause reflux, which in turn can cause pooling of urine and ultimately a UTI. Whether the reflux or the UTI comes first is important because recurrent reflux can be a source of recurrent UTIs.

The two most common symptoms of a UTI are urinary frequency (a feeling that you have to urinate much more often than usual) and painful urination. Some children complain of intense abdominal pain either at or below the belly button. Others don't complain of pain but instead dance around, wiggling from the low-grade discomfort. Fever can be associated with a UTI, especially when the infection has moved all the way up to the kidneys. Vomiting also can be associated with a UTI, because the stomach sits just above the bladder.

In medical jargon, the suffix "-itis" means inflammation. Therefore, **urethritis** means inflammation of the urethra. Unlike a UTI, urethritis is not caused by an infection. But the symptoms of a UTI and urethritis can be very similar, so the two are often confused. Here are a few ways to tell them apart. With both a UTI and urethritis, there is often itching or burning. But with urethritis, the burning tends to happen only at the beginning of urination, while with a UTI, it continues through the entire stream. This information can be difficult to elicit from a toddler. Other distinguishing features include the following: There is often abdominal or pelvic pain between episodes of urination with a UTI, but not with urethritis. The urine can look cloudy or dark with a UTI, but it is usually a normal clear yellow with urethritis. There is typically a sense of urgency and needing to go to the bathroom often with a UTI, but not with urethritis. And while UTIs are more common among girls than boys, urethritis occurs in both genders.

Urethritis is caused by irritation at the tip of the urethra. It can come from mechanical irritation, such as tight pants rubbing in the area or self-stimulation (masturbation). It can also come from chemical irritation, the most common culprit being the bubble bath. Even if your child has always loved the bath and has never had a problem before, sitting in soapy water for a long period of time can lead to urethritis.

Whether your child has a UTI or urethritis, you generally won't see any irritation or redness when you look at the vagina or penis. Likewise, there usually isn't any rash or discharge associated with either problem.

What can I do?
Because most toddlers get UTIs as a result of poor hygiene, stagnant urine, or bad luck, the best way to try to avoid a UTI is to teach good hygiene and to urge bladder emptying.

If your child is still wearing diapers, try to change diapers with poop relatively quickly and clean the area well so that the stool does not linger around the urethra.

For a potty-trained child, teach her to wipe from front to back and to wipe well, to help avoid getting poop in the urethra. Also encourage your child to listen to her body, urinating when she feels the urge and not waiting indefinitely. And teach her to take time when she does go to the bathroom, so that she empties all of the urine from her bladder. A child in a rush may have urine left in the bladder, a risk for infection and for accidents.

Even if it is uncomfortable for your child to urinate, encourage her to do so. This will minimize the risk of developing a UTI if she doesn't have one yet.

Make sure your child bathes without bubble bath until the pain has completely resolved. Instead of soap, put some baking soda in the bathwater and let her soak for a short time. The baking soda will soothe an inflamed urethra. During a UTI or urethritis, do not wash the genitals with soap, because this can sting and prolong the inflammation. Once the pain has resolved, I recommend avoiding bubble baths altogether. If your child insists, put only a small amount of bubble bath in the water and do not allow her to soak for indefinite periods of time.

Minimize rubbing and further irritation by helping your child choose loose-fitting pants or skirts. Potty-trained children should wear loose-fitting, white cotton underwear. The dye used to color underpants can sometimes irritate an already inflamed area. It also helps to discourage bike riding and horseback riding. These activities result in rubbing that can exacerbate urethritis.

When does my doctor need to be involved?

Call your doctor if your child's urine is persistently dark or foul-smelling, especially frequent, or painful. Even if your child does not have a fever with any of these symptoms, your doctor is likely to check for a UTI.

Anytime you can't tell whether it's a UTI or urethritis that is causing your child's discomfort, you should see your doctor. A simple urine test can distinguish between the two. If your child has had urethritis before and you are confident that there is no UTI, you do not need to see the doctor right away.

Anytime your child has significant lower abdominal or pelvic pain — with or without urination — you should contact your doctor.

What tests need to be done, and what do the results mean?

The tests used to check for a UTI are urinalysis and urine culture. A **urinalysis** is a preliminary test that indicates whether there is any likelihood of a UTI. It can be done in a laboratory or using a simple dipstick method in a doctor's office. It takes only a few minutes and can suggest the presence of an infection. A piece of paper (or dipstick) is dipped into the urine and then removed. After two to three minutes, the paper changes color to signify what components have been found in the urine. A positive urinalysis, suggesting that there is an infection in the urine, shows that there are **leukocytes** or **nitrites** in the sample.

If the test is positive (or if it is negative but your child's symptoms really seem to indicate a UTI), a **urine culture** will be done. A small amount of urine is transferred onto a special plate and left in an incubator for 24 to 48 hours. If bacteria grow on the plate, your doctor will identify the bacteria and prescribe an antibiotic that is effective.

Most potty-trained toddlers can produce a urine sample when asked, but toddlers in diapers generally need help with urine collection. Each of these tests is discussed in detail in chapter 19.

A urinalysis and a urine culture can be collected at the same time, as long as a sterile cup is used during the collection. A non-sterile cup can contaminate the urine culture, leading to false-positive results.

After the first (or certainly the second) UTI, it is standard to take a picture of the urinary tract to make sure there is no anatomical reason for the infection. Three tests can be used. An **ultrasound** illustrates the size and structure of the bladder, ureters, and kidneys. Ultrasound is entirely noninvasive but is not as definitive as the other two tests. A **voiding cystourethrogram (VCUG)** uses a special dye to light up the bladder, the ureters, and sometimes the kidneys. The dye is injected directly into the bladder using a tube inserted into the urethra. An X-ray device (called a *fluoroscope*) takes pictures to see whether the dye stays in the bladder or refluxes back up into the ureters and even the kidneys. An alternative detailed imaging study is a ***Tc-dimercaptosuccinic acid scan (DMSA scan).*** For this scan, a chemical is injected into a vein and is filtered out of the bloodstream through the kidneys. As the material flows through the urinary system, it outlines the urinary tract, identifying any abnormalities.

An ultrasound can be done during a UTI, but a VCUG or DMSA scan should be done only after the UTI is resolved. This is because a lingering infection can cause reflux of the urine, resulting in false-positive results. These results suggest abnormal anatomy of the urinary tract when in fact the urinary tract is structurally normal. Once a UTI is completely gone, a VCUG or DMSA scan will accurately represent the structure of the kidneys, ureters, bladder, and urethra.

What are the treatments?

A UTI is treated with an antibiotic. The precise antibiotic depends on the bacteria causing the infection. A urine culture will determine both the bacteria and the specific antibiotics to which the bacteria are sensitive.

If your child has an anatomical problem causing a predisposition to UTIs, surgery may be needed. This decision will depend on the type of anatomical abnormality and the severity of the UTIs. Some children outgrow the problem without needing surgery. Others get recurrent infections until the problem is corrected.

It is not uncommon for a child with recurrent UTIs to be placed on prophylactic antibiotics. This means that a daily low dose of an antibiotic is administered to keep the urine from getting infected. The rationale for prophylactic antibiotics is that a child with a mild problem may avoid recurrent UTIs and should eventually outgrow the anatomical issue. Sometimes this approach helps obviate the need for surgery.

Adults with UTIs often use a pain reliever called phenazopyridine (Pyridium). This medication quickly relieves the pain associated with a urinary infection. However, it is not approved for use in children. The best approach to manage acute pain associated with a UTI is to use acetaminophen (Tylenol) or ibuprofen (Motrin or Advil).

Urethritis has no specific medical treatment. Aside from the techniques to minimize local irritation suggested earlier in this chapter, only time will help resolve the inflammation. Unfortunately, there are no specific medications that relieve pain associated with urethritis. An anti-inflammatory, such as ibuprofen, may be worth a try.

What are the possible complications?

When bacteria multiply in the urine and travel up the urinary tract, the kidneys themselves can become infected. This condition is called **pyelonephritis.** An infected kidney can scar, and the kidney tissue can become permanently damaged. Ultimately, but very rarely, this can lead to kidney failure.

The bacteria causing a UTI can also move to other parts of the body. The most common secondary site of infection is the bloodstream (**urosepsis**).

A UTI can be associated with blood in the urine. The medical term for this is **hematuria.** Occasionally, the blood is visible, making the urine look red, but more often the blood is invisible and detected only on urinalysis. This is called **microscopic hematuria.** The blood typically comes from inflammation of the bladder walls. But sometimes, when the infection travels all the way up to the kidneys, the bacteria deposit there, clogging the kidney infrastructure and interrupting the kidneys' ability to work properly as filters. Excess waste, including blood, spills into the urine. The medical term for this sequence of events is **glomerulonephritis.** Mild glomerulonephritis may resolve on its own, but occasionally it leads to significant kidney malfunction and may need to be treated with a variety of medications, from **steroids** (to help reduce inflammation) to **diuretics** (to help facilitate urination).

Urethritis has no major long-term complications. In the short run, it can lead to a UTI because the pain associated with urination can cause a child not to want to urinate. Holding the urine for extended periods of time is a clear risk factor for UTI.

Additional Resources:

www.packardchildrenshospital.org/ (Go to "health library," then go to "search" in the upper right-hand corner and type in "urinary tract infection.")

http://www.duj.com/peduti.html

http://www.tch.harvard.edu (Go to "My child has:" in upper right-hand corner and type in "urinary tract infection.")

http://www.nlm.nih.gov/medlineplus/encyclopedia.html (Click on "U," then scroll down to "urine — bloody.")

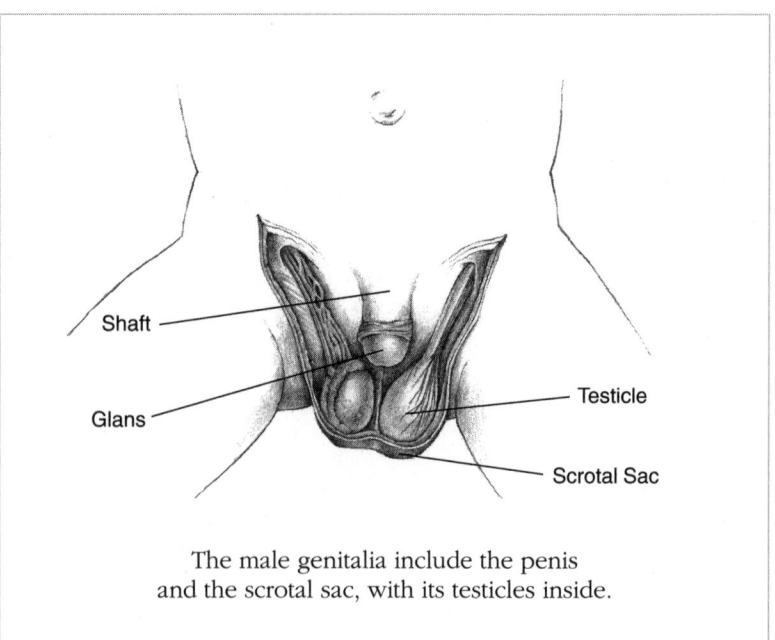

The male genitalia include the penis
and the scrotal sac, with its testicles inside.

12

Penis and Scrotum

UNCIRCUMCISED PENIS: PARAPHIMOSIS AND PHIMOSIS

What is happening inside my child's body?
If your child is not circumcised, the area under his foreskin *never* needs to be vigorously cleaned. It may collect some normal debris, but this white or cheesy material causes no harm. Eventually, the foreskin will retract on its own, but more often than not, this doesn't happen until well into the toddler years — around age three or older.

In fact, forcibly pulling the foreskin back, called **retraction,** can cause irritation and swelling. In extreme cases, the foreskin can become so tight that it limits the penis blood flow, causing the head to swell, a phenomenon called **paraphimosis.** As the head engorges, the foreskin acts like a noose, further restricting the blood flow to the head of the penis. Reduced blood flow results in less oxygen to the penis. Eventually, the foreskin cannot be returned back over the head of the penis. This requires emergency intervention by a doctor.

Sometimes the foreskin is not at all retractable because its opening is too narrow. This is called **phimosis.** Phimosis is normal among uncircumcised boys and typically resolves by school age. If you try to retract the foreskin and your son has a little bit

of phimosis, the tip of the foreskin can tear and scar, and phimosis can become permanent.

What can I do?

You should never do anything special with an uncircumcised
penis. Instead, employ a "hands-off" policy. If your child is still in
diapers, wipe him with each diaper change, but never forcibly
pull back the foreskin to clean underneath it. Once your child is
potty trained, show him how to dry off his penis when necessary.
Of course, most boys discover their penis in the infant or young
toddler years, so the "hands-off" policy applies only to parents
and caretakers.

When does my doctor need to be involved?

Your doctor needs to be called immediately if the foreskin is
pulled back over the head of the penis and it cannot be returned
to its usual position (paraphimosis).

Also call your doctor if there is bulging of the foreskin with urination. This is a sign of phimosis — the opening of the foreskin
is too tight, and urine becomes trapped behind the foreskin.
Trapped urine is a breeding ground for bacteria and can eventually lead to a skin infection or a **urinary tract infection (UTI).**

What tests need to be done, and what do the results mean?

The only time a test is necessary is in the case of phimosis with a
suspected UTI. When this happens, a urinalysis and urine culture
should be done to determine the appropriate treatment. These
tests are reviewed in chapter 19.

What are the treatments?

In some cases of paraphimosis, when the foreskin is stuck below
the head of the penis, a lubricant can be put on the penis, allowing the foreskin to slide back into its original position. However,
if the swelling is extreme, the doctor may need to cut a small hole
in the foreskin so that the tension can be released and the foreskin can return to its usual position. If that does not work, an
emergency circumcision may need to be done.

For phimosis, a steroid cream can be applied to the tip of the foreskin to reduce inflammation, relaxing the tight opening. If this treatment is used, the steroid cream needs to be applied several times daily for a few weeks. If phimosis causes a UTI, your child will need to be given antibiotics. The treatment of UTIs is covered in detail in chapter 11.

What are the possible complications?

The most worrisome complication of paraphimosis is tissue death (also called **necrosis**). The foreskin entraps the head of the penis, starving it of its essential nutrient, oxygen. This is why paraphimosis is a medical emergency and requires immediate treatment.

Phimosis can cause a UTI. UTIs are relatively uncommon in boys (compared with girls). According to some studies, the risk of a UTI in uncircumcised boys is as much as 10 times the risk in circumcised boys. These infections are generally easily treated with antibiotics.

Phimosis can also be associated with a skin infection along the foreskin, shaft, or glans. Such an infection, called **cellulitis,** can be extremely painful. It requires oral antibiotics and sometimes surgical cleaning.

Additional Resources:

http://www.packardchildrenshospital.org (Go to "health library," then go to "search" in upper right-hand corner and type in "phimosis.")

http://www.chop.edu/ (Go to "your child's health" along left-hand margin, then go to "search" in upper right-hand corner and type in "phymosis" or "paraphymosis.")

http://www.urologychannel.com/emergencies/ (Go to "paraphimosis" on left-hand margin.)

◆   ◆   ◆

TESTICULAR TORSION

What is happening inside my child's body?
Testicular torsion literally means "twisted testicle." Inside the scrotum, each testicle is wrapped in a sack called the **tunica vaginalis** and hangs from a stringlike structure called the **spermatic cord.** The spermatic cord is a conduit that contains the nerves and blood vessels supplying the testicles. Each testicle is affixed to its tunica vaginalis, anchoring it within the scrotal sac. If the point of attachment is in the wrong place, the testicle can rotate, twisting the spermatic cord and its contents. When this happens, blood can no longer move easily up and down the spermatic cord. Poor blood flow leads to redness, swelling, and loss of oxygen at the testicle, all of which can be extremely painful. With enough loss of blood flow, the starved testicle can become permanently nonfunctional.

Testicular torsion is very rare. Most cases are seen in adolescents and adults. However, it can occur in young boys. Symptoms of torsion include pain, swelling or redness of the scrotum, and vomiting. Regardless of age, it causes excruciating pain.

What can I do?
Anytime testicular torsion is suspected, you should call or visit your doctor immediately. There is nothing for you to try at home.

When does my doctor need to be involved?
Testicular torsion is a surgical emergency. If it isn't fixed right away, the consequences can be permanent. The maximum time from onset of torsion to surgery is four to six hours; beyond that, the testicle is not salvageable. Testicular torsion is one of those better-safe-than-sorry situations: don't hesitate to call the doctor even if you are not sure your son's condition warrants it.

What tests need to be done, and what do the results mean?
When the child's inner thigh is stroked, the testicle on that side leaves the scrotum and rises into the pelvis. This is known as the

cremasteric reflex. This reflex goes away when the testicle is twisted. Therefore, one of the easiest tests to determine whether there is testicular torsion is to try to elicit the cremasteric reflex.

A complete blood count is often checked to make sure an infection is not the cause of the symptoms. The blood count is often normal with torsion. Although an infection in the testicle can cause pain, the pain of torsion is usually more severe.

An ***ultrasound*** can be performed to look at the testicular structure. If the ultrasound has ***Doppler*** — a mode that detects blood flow — it can help determine whether the testicle has actually twisted and cut off its own blood supply.

If the diagnosis is still uncertain, a ***radionuclide scan*** of the testicle can be helpful. This test looks at the testicle and its blood flow. It is helpful in differentiating torsion from other conditions because it can demonstrate blood flow — or lack thereof — to the testicle. Radionuclide scanning has an accuracy rate of 90 to 100 percent. However, this test can take time to schedule and administer, and if torsion is suspected, sufficient time may not be available.

What are the treatments?

If the testicle is twisted, it is sometimes possible for it to be untwisted by hand. Physical rotation of the testicle in the scrotal sac is called ***manual detorsion.*** This can solve the problem immediately. Pain relievers are often given prior to the procedure because untwisting a testicle can be as painful as having it twisted in the first place. In fact, rotation of the testicle may need to be attempted two or three times before complete detorsion is accomplished. The benefit of this procedure is that it requires no surgery, but the success rate is only 30 to 70 percent.

The alternative to manual detorsion is surgery. The scrotum is opened, and the testicle is untwisted. Then an ***orchiopexy*** is performed. This procedure attaches the testicle to the scrotum so that it cannot twist again. Tunica attachment happens during fetal development, and abnormal attachment on one side predicts abnormal attachment on the other. Therefore, if one testicle experiences torsion, there is a good chance that the other testicle will experience torsion at some point in the future. For this reason, most surgeons will perform an orchiopexy on the nontorsed testicle as well.

What are the possible complications?

The most severe complication of testicular torsion is permanent testicular nonfunction, or "testicular death." This can happen when the blood supply to the testicle is cut off for more than six hours. When the testicle dies, it must be surgically removed, because it becomes a source of potential infection. This increases the chances of infertility, since the body's sperm production is reduced by half.

Additional Resources:

http://www.packardchildrenshospital.org (Go to "health library," then go to "search" in upper right-hand corner and type in "testicular torsion.")

http://www.nlm.nih.gov/medlineplus/encyclopedia.html (Click on "T-Tn," then scroll down to "testicular torsion.")

http://www.urologychannel.com/emergencies (Go to "testicular torsion" on left-hand margin.)

http://www.chop.edu/ (Go to "your child's health" along left-hand margin, then go to "search" in upper right-hand corner and type in "testicular torsion.")

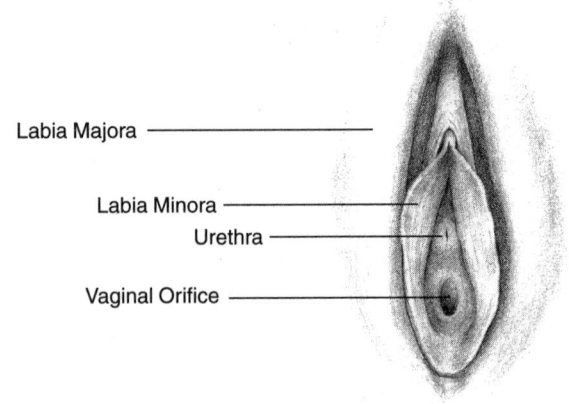

Labia Majora

Labia Minora

Urethra

Vaginal Orifice

The female genitalia includes two pairs of lips (labia)
and two openings: one to the vagina and one to the urethra.

13

Vagina

◆

LABIAL ADHESION

What is happening inside my child's body?
The vagina is surrounded by two pairs of skin folds that look like lips, hence the name ***labia*** (Latin for "lips"). The outer pair is called the ***labia majora*** and inner pair the ***labia minora.*** Sometimes the labia minora stick together, narrowing or closing entirely the vaginal opening. This is called a ***labial adhesion.*** Most labial adhesions are so small — extending only a millimeter or two — that they go unnoticed by both parents and doctors.

The adhesions occur as a result of inflammation along the labia. The surface becomes sticky, and a small scar forms. Labial adhesions can appear anytime throughout the infant or toddler years, and most disappear on their own over time. The adhesions are sensitive to hormones, and they actually resolve in the presence of estrogen. This is why most adhesions go away during puberty if they haven't disappeared before then.

What can I do?
If you notice an adhesion, bring it to the attention of your doctor. There is very little you need to do on your own at home.

When does my doctor need to be involved?

Most labial adhesions do not require medical treatment. However, if the adhesion is large, covering most of the vaginal opening, there is a slightly increased risk of bleeding or infection, especially **urinary tract infection (UTI).** You should call your doctor if you notice redness or bleeding in the area or if your daughter complains of pain with urination.

What tests need to be done, and what do the results mean?

No tests need to be done with labial adhesions. However, the presence of an adhesion can increase the risk of UTI. If a UTI is suspected — if your child is complaining of pain with urination or of the need to urinate frequently — her urine should be checked with a urinalysis and a urine culture. UTIs are covered in detail in chapter 11.

What are the treatments?

Labial adhesions can be treated using an estrogen cream applied directly to the area. Hormones (namely estrogen) help to dissolve the adhesions quickly and easily. However, this treatment provides only a short-term solution. Once the cream is no longer applied, the adhesion may return. If this happens, the cream can be repeated as needed. In general, estrogen creams are used only with an adhesion large enough to present a risk of infection.

What are the possible complications?

An adhesion can cause a UTI because it provides a place for urine to pool inside the vagina. Stagnant urine, like any other stagnant fluid, is more likely to breed infection than moving fluid. A UTI can cause fever, burning with urination, foul-smelling urine, and frequent urination. For more on UTIs, see chapter 11.

Labial adhesions are known to recur even after several rounds of treatment with an estrogen cream. Repeated use of the cream can result in a change in the pigmentation (color) of part of the labia. Given the location of the tissue, the loss of pigmentation is generally not considered a significant side effect. In rare cases, the estrogen cream will stimulate the growth of hair around the vagina. When use of the cream is discontinued, the hair will go away.

Additional Resources:
http://www.keepkidshealthy.com/toddler/toddler.html (Go to "search" in upper left-hand corner and type in "labial adhesion.")

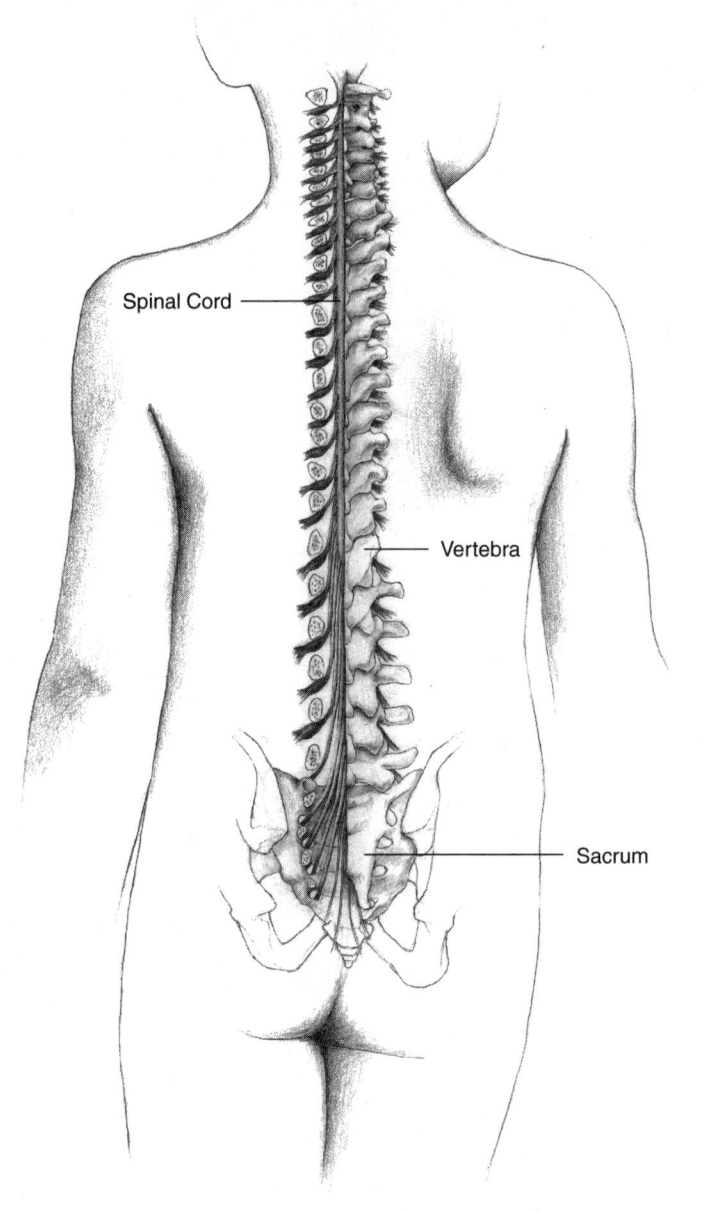

Spinal Cord

Vertebra

Sacrum

The spine starts all the way at the top of the neck and extends almost to the buttocks. The nerves of the spinal cord are protected by prominent bones called vertebrae.

14

Back

TETHERED CORD

What is happening inside my child's body?
The "cord" in tethered cord refers to the spinal cord. The "tether" refers to a sticking point. The spinal cord normally hangs down between the bones of the spine, called ***vertebrae.*** A sheath of tissue surrounds the cord, enclosing it along with fluid, called ***cerebrospinal fluid (CSF).*** As your child grows, so do the spinal cord and its surroundings.

Occasionally, the spinal cord is restricted and cannot grow. This can happen when the cord or its sheath becomes affixed to the surrounding bony structures. Initially, this causes no problems. But as a child grows, the stuck cord cannot stretch. Instead, the nerves of the cord are slowly pulled taut. Eventually, the nerves cannot perform their usual functions, such as transmitting impulses to muscles in various parts of the body.

The symptoms of a tethered cord really depend on where along the spine the cord is stuck. This location will determine which nerves are pulled. By far the most common place for a tether to occur is toward the bottom of the spine, at the L4–L5 level. The *L* is short for ***lumbar,*** the section of the spine that goes (approximately) from the bottom of the ribs to the hips. The numbers refer to vertebrae, which you can feel as you run your hand up and down your child's back. The vertebrae are counted from top to bottom, so L1 is at the top of the lumbar section of the spine, closer to the ribs, and L5 is at the bottom, near the hips.

A tether in the lower lumbar region is especially significant because the nerves that travel to the bowel and bladder exit the spinal cord at that level. Therefore, when the cord tethers there, the symptoms usually involve the bowel and bladder: constipation, urinary retention, or urinary tract infection (UTI). Nerves that exit the spinal cord below the level of the tether also become impaired. This means that nerves traveling to the legs and feet are usually involved when a cord becomes tethered. The result is a tingling sensation ("pins and needles") or weakness in the feet or legs, but no symptoms in the back, where the tether actually exists.

What causes a cord to tether? Usually there is an underlying anatomical irregularity. Sometimes the sheath that encases the spinal cord gets trapped between vertebrae during fetal development. When only the sheath is involved, the condition is called a **meningocele.** When both the sheath and the cord beneath it are involved, it is called a **meningomyelocele.** Cysts or other masses also may develop along the inside of the spinal column. These masses may create sticking points for the spinal cord. Or the spine may curve, as is the case with **scoliosis,** trapping the spinal cord.

In toddlers, it can be very difficult to diagnose a tethered cord. Whereas adults can describe tingling in their toes and numbness in their legs, toddlers usually cannot. Toddlers are also more likely just to keep on going despite new sensations or increased difficulty moving. Therefore, a tethered cord is suspected when a constellation of symptoms appears: changes in gait or foot coordination; complaints of feeling funny tingling or "sleepiness" in the toes, feet, or legs; changes in urinary patterns and bowel patterns; and recurrent UTIs.

What can I do?

If you suspect that your child has a tethered cord, you should contact your doctor. There is nothing you can do at home to address the symptoms.

When does my doctor need to be involved?

Whenever a tethered cord is suspected, your doctor should be involved. Likewise, contact your doctor if your child is having tingling or weakness in his legs and feet or if he is having new-onset constipation and urinary retention.

What tests need to be done, and what do the results mean?

To make the diagnosis, the doctor must visualize the tether. In some cases, an X ray of the spine is sufficient. However, the vast majority of cases require an MRI to show exactly where the tether is located. While an MRI is a very sensitive test, it does not pick up all tethers. Therefore, in cases where a child is experiencing increasing symptoms of a tethered cord despite a normal MRI, exploratory surgery may be performed.

Bowel and bladder function need to be monitored closely. If the nerves traveling to the bowel and bladder have been stretched and injured, they can become permanently damaged. Therefore, even if the tether is repaired with surgery, problems with constipation and recurrent UTIs may persist.

Bladder function is often evaluated by a urologist. Urine cultures may be done sporadically to make sure silent infections are not recurring.

Parents generally monitor bowel function at home. If constipation does not resolve and becomes increasingly problematic, a gastroenterologist can help with the situation.

What are the treatments?

If the cord is tethered, surgery is a must. Otherwise, the nerves will become increasingly damaged as the child grows. In the case of a tether at or below the lumbar spine, ongoing nerve injury will affect foot and leg function, as well as the bowel and bladder. The surgery is generally quite simple: a neurosurgeon uses an

MRI and the child's symptoms to locate the tether, then goes into the spinal canal at that point to release the cord.

The cure rate for a tethered cord is quite high, especially if it is diagnosed early, before too many symptoms of nerve damage appear. There are no medicines that can be used in lieu of surgery.

What are the possible complications?

The complications of a tethered cord are the same as the symptoms: nerve damage, depending on where the tether resides. Because lower lumbar tethers are the most common, damage to the nerves going to the feet, legs, bowel, and bladder tend to be the most common neurological complications from surgery.

Other surgical complications include bleeding, infection, and retethering. The cord can retether because the area that is released might have some inflammation, which provides a site for potential scarring.

The longer the tether remains and the more a child grows while the tether exists, the more chronic the nerve damage will be. The longer nerve damage occurs, the more likely it is to become permanent.

Additional Resources:

http://www.packardchildrenshospital.org (Go to "health library," then go to "search" in upper right-hand corner and type in "tethered cord.")

http://www.cpmc.columbia.edu/ (Go to "search" in upper right-hand corner and type in "tethered spinal cord.")

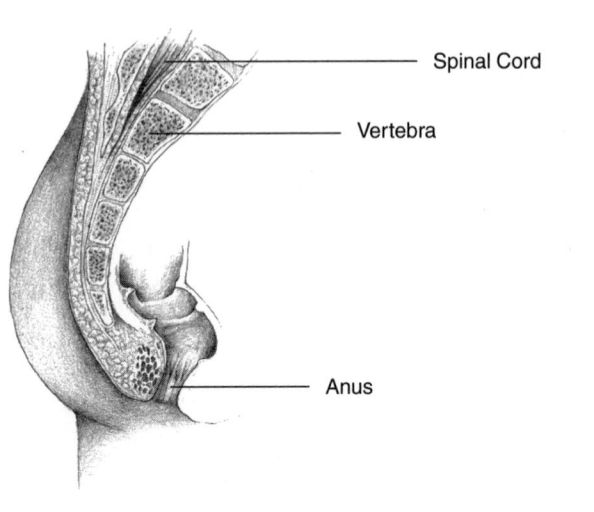

The bottom marks the end of both the gastrointestinal tract (anus) and the spine.

15

Anus

---◆---

ANAL FISSURE

What is happening inside my child's body?

An **anal fissure** is a tear in the tissue around the bottom, the puckered ring where stool leaves the rectum. This area tears easily when a child is constipated and has a large, hard stool. Small cuts in the skin around the anus result in bright red spots of blood. If your child is in diapers, you will see blood in the diaper next to the stool, or the blood will be visible when you use wipes. If your child is potty trained, the toilet water may look red, or there may be blood on the toilet paper. In either case, with anal fissure blood is never actually mixed into the stool.

Anal fissures hurt because (1) it hurts to tear the skin around the anus, (2) it stings when stool or urine come into contact with the tear or when the injured skin is wiped clean, and (3) the anus spasms as a result of the fissure, and these spasms are uncomfortable. Although the skin heals relatively quickly, every time another sizable stool comes along, it can reinjure the broken skin. For this reason, a toddler with an anal fissure may try to avoid pooping. This creates a vicious cycle because the child will hold in his stool and become increasingly constipated. When he finally does poop, he will be significantly more likely to retear his anus.

Stools must be soft in order not to tear the irritated skin, but for the stools to be soft, the child must be willing to pass them with relative frequency.

What can I do?

If you are not sure whether your child has an anal fissure, you can shine a flashlight onto his bottom and look for a small, slitlike tear just inside the ring of anal tissue. Sometimes the area will be slightly red, or there will be a spot of dried blood at the site.

To help relieve the stinging, put a small amount of a color-free, perfume-free lubricant, such as petroleum jelly (Vaseline), around the anus. This will lubricate the skin so that the next time your child poops, the stool can pass more easily through the anus. Apply the lubricant using your pinkie finger, not a Q-Tip or other narrow tool. You can repeat this every few hours or with each diaper change until a stool is passed without tearing the skin.

To minimize pain with wiping, avoid perfumed wipes, which will sting when they come into contact with the tear.

If your child is constipated, it is critical that you address that issue, because chronically hard stools will continuously retear the skin. Constipation is covered in detail in chapter 10.

When does my doctor need to be involved?

If you are not sure whether an anal fissure is the source of your child's bleeding, you should call your doctor. You should also call if the bleeding amounts to more than a few drops of blood, if it increases, if it persists, or if the blood is mixed into the stool. Anytime you are unsure, ask your doctor.

What tests need to be done, and what do the results mean?

Anal fissures do not require any tests. But if the blood is mixed into the stool rather than coating it or sitting beside it, the source of bleeding is likely somewhere inside the intestine rather than an anal fissure. If intestinal bleeding is suspected, a stool sample should be tested for infection, inflammation, and other causes of intestinal bleeding. This topic is covered in chapter 10.

What are the treatments?

The primary treatment for an anal fissure is lubrication of the anus to help the stool slide through more easily.

Sitz baths are also helpful. These warm-water baths contain various mild agents that help soothe the skin.

Remember, if your child's constipation is the underlying cause of the fissure, the constipation must be treated. Stool softeners are very effective. For information on treating constipation, see chapter 10.

What are the possible complications?

A **chronic fissure** is one that will not heal. Such a fissure can develop when the same tear is continually reopened before it has time to heal. Fissures can also bleed excessively or become infected. All of these complications are extraordinarily uncommon.

> *Additional Resources:*
> http://www.mayoclinic.com/ (Go to "search" in upper right-hand corner and type in "constipation children.")
> http://www.nlm.nih.gov/medlineplus/encyclopedia.html (Click on "A-Ag," then scroll down to "anal fissure" or click on "Ch-Co," then scroll down to "constipation.")

PINWORMS

What is happening inside my child's body?

A pinworm is a short, skinny parasite — 5 to 10 millimeters long — that lives in the human colon (large intestine). Its proper name is *Enterobius vermicularis*. The female pinworm crawls out of the anus and lays her eggs on the skin. When the temperature is right (98° to 99°F), the eggs mature into an infectious form.

The eggs are then passed from person to person by the fecal-oral route: wiping or itching, followed by poor (or no) hand washing, allows pinworm eggs to collect on a person's hands. The eggs are then transferred to sheets, clothes, carpets, toilets and bathroom fixtures, eating utensils and glassware, sandboxes, and so on, where they can be picked up by another person. They can also be passed directly from the hands of the host to the hands of another person. It is estimated that 40 million people in the United States have or have had pinworms.

Once a person ingests pinworm eggs, the eggs make their way to the small intestine, where they hatch. About a month later, they are ready to move toward the large intestine and repeat the cycle. The time from ingestion of the eggs to itching on the bottom is usually two to four weeks.

When the worms crawl out of the anus and deposit eggs on the skin, they cause itchiness. The classic indicator of pinworms is itching around the anus at night, right about bedtime. Girls can have vaginal itching as well because the worms can migrate forward into the vagina. Pinworms can also be associated with behavioral changes, such as restlessness and irritability, in toddlers.

What can I do?
The worms are easily visible. If your child is complaining of itching, have him lie facedown with his bottom in the air. When you shine a light at his anus, you will see threadlike worms or small yellow egg sacks. If you see pinworms on your child, you should treat them medically. They will not go away on their own.

You can do a lot to prevent pinworms, however. Thorough hand washing is the best prevention. Other basic hygiene measures, such as daily bathing and wearing clean underwear, will help minimize pinworm infections.

When does my doctor need to be involved?
Call your doctor if the itching intensifies despite treatment. If your child has scratched so much that you think the skin is broken, you should contact your doctor.

What tests need to be done, and what do the results mean?
The only test used to confirm the presence of pinworms is a very simple one called the "Scotch tape test." Both parents and doctors can perform this test. With your child on his hands and knees, press the sticky side of a piece of clear Scotch tape against the

anus. Sometimes it helps to use a tongue depressor to gently press the tape to the skin. When the tape is removed seconds later, eggs and worms will stick to it. They should be easily visible.

What are the treatments?

Mebendazole (Vermox) is the most common treatment for pinworms. This antiparasitic is given one time, then typically repeated one to two weeks later. It is available as a single-dose chewable tablet, making it easy to give toddlers.

What are the possible complications?

Pinworm eggs may cohabitate with an intestinal infection called *Dientamoeba fragilis*. Infection with *D. fragilis* can cause chronic gastrointestinal upset and in some cases diarrhea.

Additional Resources:
http://www.biosci.ohio-state.edu/~parasite/enterobius.html

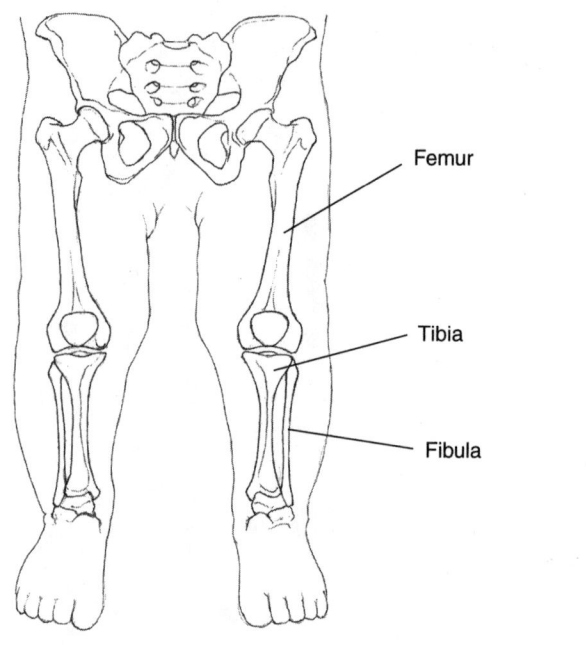

The bones of the legs include the femur, the tibia, and the fibula.
The head of the femur fits into the hip socket.

16

Legs and Feet

◇

BOWLEGS AND KNOCK-KNEES

What is happening inside my child's body?
As toddlers learn to walk and then run, the shape of their legs changes. Initially, a toddler walks with a wide-based gait, and her legs typically look bowed — as if she just got off a horse. By two or three years of age, the base narrows, and the legs straighten out. Often the feet begin to point inward, and the knees may even knock together. The technical term for bowlegs is ***varus deformity*** and for knock-knees ***valgus deformity***.

Most children develop straight legs with no more bowing or knocking by seven or eight years of age. But occasionally, the process is exaggerated, and the varus or valgus is extreme. This results in difficulty walking and running, causing the child to trip and fall more than other children.

Bowlegs are normal — to an extent. The legs can become too curved when one side of each leg grows more quickly than the other. When you look at your child straight on, you can draw an imaginary line down the middle of her body, starting at her head and traveling down to the space between her feet. The side of the knee closest to the line is called the ***medial*** side; the side farthest

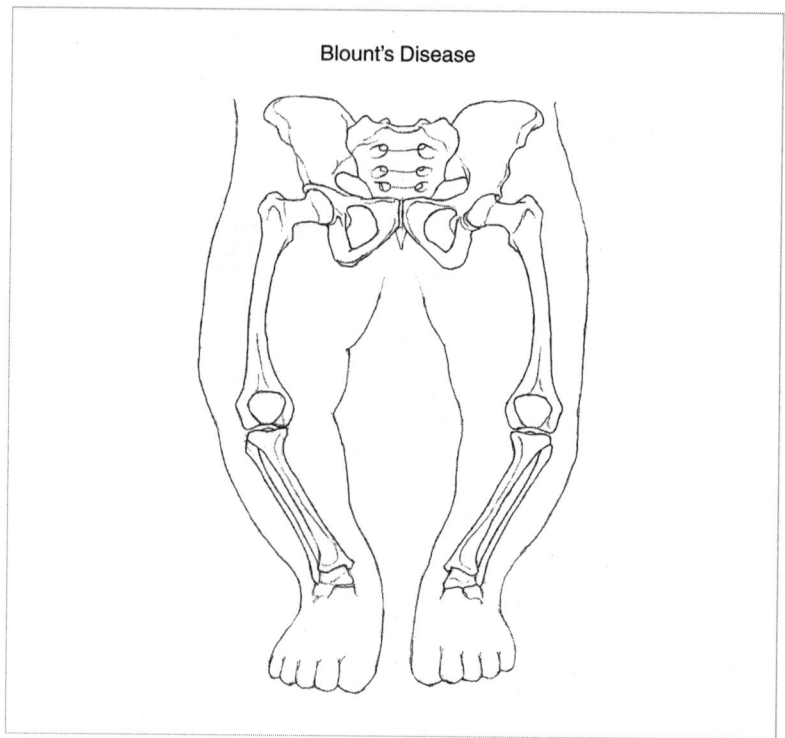

Blount's Disease

Toddlers' legs are not always perfectly straight.
In Blount's disease, they are bowed to an extreme.

from the line is called the *lateral* side. With severe bowing of the legs, the lateral sides of the growth plates near the knees grow faster than the medial sides, causing the bones to curve in a C shape. This condition is called ***Blount's disease.***

Knock-knees evolve very differently. As the legs straighten by age two or three, increasing pressure is put on the medial sides of the feet. If a child has flat arches or has trouble distributing the weight of her body across each of her feet, the medial side will bear more of the weight, and the feet will roll in toward the midline of the body. In turn, the ankles will roll inward, and the knees will follow, "knocking" together. Often the thighs will rub together in the midline as well. Most of the time, when a knock-kneed child moves her weight onto the lateral sides of her feet

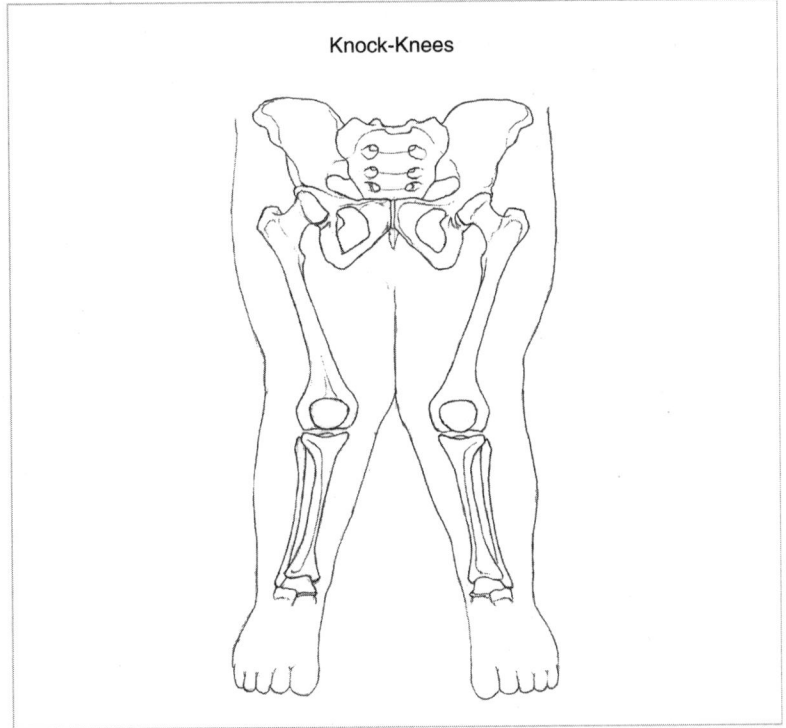

Knock-Knees

Even when knock-knees seem extreme, they can straighten
on their own with time. Often knees knock as a result
of ankle weakness or flat feet.

(for instance, when she wears shoes with arch support), her
thighs and knees will come apart, and her ankles will straighten.

What can I do?
Nothing needs to be done for normal bowlegs. For knock-knees,
try putting your toddler in shoes with arch support.

When does my doctor need to be involved?
Bowing and knocking are normal — to a degree. If your child is
having difficulty walking or running because of the shape or
position of her legs, you'll want your doctor to observe her in
motion. Also, if the legs look different, with one significantly
more bowed or knocked than the other, let your doctor know.

Remember that most bowing corrects itself by age three. If this hasn't occurred, you may want to speak with your doctor. Severe bowing can be associated with other bony problems elsewhere in the body, such as vitamin D deficiency (also called **rickets**).

What tests need to be done, and what do the results mean?

Tests do not need to be done when bowlegs or knock-knees are part of the normal continuum of development. If, however, the shape is extreme or is interfering with your child's movement, X rays may be done.

What are the treatments?

In the past, many children with bowlegs or knock-knees were put in braces or casts. Today children are treated much less aggressively because it is recognized that these treatments didn't do much good.

For severe or persistent bowing or knocking, your doctor may recommend that your child see an orthopedist about every six months. Bracing, casting, or surgery are needed only in the most extreme cases.

What are the possible complications?

There are no complications of normal bowlegs or knock-knees. However, if the positioning does not resolve on its own, or if it becomes exaggerated, the other bones and muscles from the hips down to the feet can be affected.

Additional Resources:

http://www.orthoseek.com/ (Click on "orthopedic topics," then scroll down to "bowlegs" or "knock-knees.")

http://www.nlm.nih.gov/medlineplus/encyclopedia.html (Click on "Bl-Bz," then scroll down to "bowlegs" or "Blount's disease.")

◆   ◆   ◆

FLAT FEET

What is happening inside my child's body?
The sole of the foot is flat along the base of the toes, around the outer side, and all the way back to the heel. The inner side has a slight C-shaped curve, and it rises up above the rest of the sole to form an arch. This is called the ***medial arch.*** It is most noticeable when standing, because this is the part of the foot that doesn't touch the ground.

Absence of an arch causes the foot to roll in toward the midline of the body. In medical terms, this is called ***pes planus.*** More commonly, it is known as flat feet.

Various muscles and ligaments combine to make the arch, but the process takes time. This is why infants and even many toddlers have flat feet with no or minimal arches. With time, the muscles strengthen and the ligaments, especially at the ankle, tighten up and do a better job of holding the foot in place. The medial arch appears around two years of age, but it won't look like an adult arch until about kindergarten age.

The arch is easily obscured by excess fat. Fat pads are normal in infant and toddler feet. Sometimes the fat collects underneath the arch, making the arch appear smaller. Flat-footedness is exaggerated when a child stands, because the fat obscures the usual space between the floor and the bottom of the arch. However, when a child dangles her feet while sitting in a chair, the arch is more noticeable.

So feet can appear flat because of minimal arches or because of weak ankles that allow the foot to roll inward. Either problem usually resolves on its own with time. And it is uncommon for flat feet, whether temporary or permanent, to cause significant difficulties with walking.

What can I do?
You really don't need to do a thing if your toddler has flat feet, unless she is complaining of pain. You can let her run around

barefoot at home, and you need only insist that she wear shoes when she is outside, in order to protect the feet from potential injury by contact with glass shards or nails, for example. Shoes do not "treat" flat feet. But to make your child more comfortable, choose shoes with good arch support.

When does my doctor need to be involved?

Let your doctor know if your child complains of pain. Most often pain associated with flat feet is in the feet, ankles, or knees. Also tell your doctor if your child is having difficulty running or walking because of the positioning of her feet.

What tests need to be done, and what do the results mean?

Flat feet do not require any specific tests. Simply by watching your child walk, your doctor can usually determine the extent of the problem.

What are the treatments?

Toddlers rarely need to be treated for flat feet. However, when the problem is severe enough that it causes pain or difficulty walking, **orthotics** may be necessary. Orthotics are special soles that can be put inside regular shoes. They provide extra support for the arches, helping to position the feet during walking and running. Although orthotics can be very helpful, they can also be quite costly because children outgrow them rapidly.

Years ago, children were routinely fitted with special shoes and sometimes even braces for foot problems. Parents who used these devices in childhood often worry that their children will need them, too. It is important to remember that the approach to foot problems in young children has changed dramatically over the past few decades. Braces and special shoes generally are not prescribed these days because flat-footedness is often considered short-term and benign.

What are the possible complications?

The main complication of flat feet is pain. The pain comes from a shift in the distribution of body weight. The foot is designed to support the weight of the body in very specific ways. When the positioning of the foot changes, so does the weight-bearing responsibility in the foot and subsequently in the ankle and knee. When parts of the body that are not designed to bear certain types of weight suddenly have that responsibility, significant pain can result.

In some cases of flat feet, the toes or heels may rub against your child's shoes, causing blisters or calluses.

Additional Resources:
http://www.orthoseek.com/ (Click on "orthopedic topics," then scroll down to "flat feet.")

◆ ◆ ◆

INGROWN TOENAILS

What is happening inside my child's body?
An **ingrown toenail** is a toenail that grows into the surrounding skin, causing swelling and often pain. It is seen most commonly in the big toe, sometimes on only one side of the nail but often on both.

When the nail drives into the skin, it is perceived as a foreign body. A foreign body is any nonorganic source of irritation, or something that doesn't belong in the part of the body where it is currently located. The area becomes inflamed, with associated swelling and redness. Sometimes pus forms under the surface of the skin. The area grows increasingly tender as the nail digs deeper into the skin.

In toddlers, the most common cause of an ingrown toenail is simply the way the nail grows naturally. The big toenail especially tends to fan out toward the tip of the toe. Trimming the nails of a toddler can be very difficult. If the task is left undone, or if the nail is trimmed so that the edges are either higher than or lower than the middle section of the top of the nail, the skin will wrap around the toenail, creating an ingrown nail.

Toe positioning can also cause the problem. When toes overlap or press into each other, the skin surrounding a nail can be redirected. When this skin is pushed over the edge of the nail, the nail will grow into the skin.

Sometimes the growth happens so insidiously that it will not cause any pain. Rather, you may simply notice a calloused area at the edge of a toenail with no redness or swelling.

What can I do?

When you trim your child's toenails, try to trim evenly across the top. Rounding the corners of the nails is a risk factor for developing ingrown nails.

If your child has an ingrown nail, try massaging the area to relieve pressure. Do not do this if the area is extremely tender, red, or warm. Rub gently on the nail and its surrounding skin, starting on the nail and moving horizontally onto the skin. You can do this with clean, dry hands or using a lubricant such as petroleum jelly (Vaseline). This sort of massage often helps most just after a bath, when the skin is soft and supple.

You may want to apply an antibacterial solution to help disinfect the irritated skin. For example, you can use hydrogen peroxide to clean the skin or a topical cream or ointment such as Neosporin to moisturize and sterilize it.

Do *not* try to clip the offending part of the nail by cutting vertically next to the inflamed skin. If this needs to be done, a professional using sterile instruments should perform the procedure.

When does my doctor need to be involved?

If the skin is tender, red, or warm, or if there is pus in the area, it may be infected. For any of these symptoms, call your doctor.

What tests need to be done, and what do the results mean?

Tests are unnecessary with ingrown toenails.

What are the treatments?

Ingrown toenails causing inflammation and infection of the skin may need to be removed. A podiatrist typically does this. It is a simple, in-office procedure, though keeping your toddler still may not be so simple. The skin is numbed, then the nail is trimmed so that it no longer protrudes into the skin. When possible, the nail is cut in such a way that it will regrow properly, rather than back into the surrounding tissue.

When the ingrown nail has resulted in infection, the infection needs to be treated. If this cannot be done with topical creams, ointments, or antibacterial washes, oral antibiotics may be necessary. Oral medication is required only when the ingrown nail has become remarkably infected and the infection is getting worse or not getting better.

What are the possible complications?

The main complication of an ingrown toenail is pain. Occasionally, shoe-wearing habits need to be adjusted to give the toes additional room to spread out. Narrow, close-toed shoes can exacerbate the problem while flip-flops and open-toed shoes can aid healing.

Spreading infection is also a potential complication. Although this is unusual, the skin surrounding the ingrown nail can become infected, as can the soft tissue in the rest of the toe. Ingrown nails almost never cause infections that spread to other parts of the body.

Finally, it is not uncommon for ingrown nails to recur. Therefore, once the redness, swelling, and irritation associated with an ingrown toenail resolve, there is a reasonable chance that the problem will come back in the future.

Additional Resources:
http://www.nlm.nih.gov/medlineplus/encyclopedia.html (Click on "I-In," then scroll down to "ingrown toenail.")

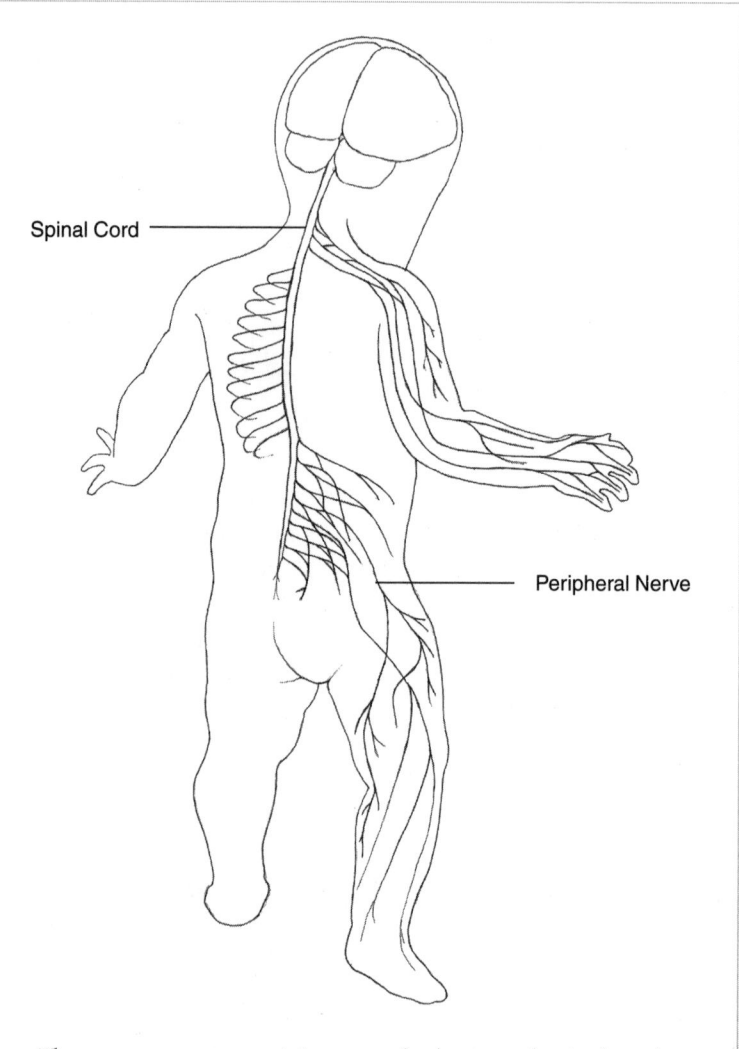

Spinal Cord

Peripheral Nerve

The nervous system originates at the brain and spinal cord.
An intricate network of peripheral nerves travels
to the muscles and organs.

17

Nervous System

◆

SEIZURES

What is happening inside my child's body?
Nerves are very similar to wires in that they carry signals from one place to another. Nerves are designed to tell a muscle, an organ, or another nerve what to do. To send the message quickly and efficiently, a nerve — like a wire — is insulated. This way, a message can travel along a nerve rapidly, without stimulating a neighboring nerve.

The brain is a massive and highly organized collection of nerves that controls all of the body's functions. When nerves in the brain fire inappropriately, the result can be a ***seizure.*** Seizures produce a sudden change in behavior, such as jerking, twitching, rhythmic shaking, or a combination of all three. A sudden increase in the electrical activity in the brain is the cause of a seizure.

How do you distinguish between benign jerking motions and a true seizure? Try to stop the jerking by putting pressure on the affected limb. If you cannot stop the jerking and you continue to feel the muscles rhythmically contracting and relaxing, your child is having a seizure. The jerking movements of a seizure usually last only a minute or two, rarely longer than five minutes. When these classic types of seizures involve the entire body, they are called **generalized** or **tonic-clonic seizures.** When only one part of the body is involved, such as the right arm, it is called a **focal seizure.** Breathing can stop during generalized seizures, although this is uncommon.

In some seizures, there will be no jerking at all. Instead, your child may stop moving and stare off into space. This is called an **absence seizure.** You can tell that this is a seizure because she cannot be engaged during the episode — she will not make eye contact and cannot respond to her name. After a minute or two, the seizure will resolve. Breathing is never compromised in a simple absence seizure.

Following any type of seizure, the child will be extremely tired, and often she will go to sleep. One exception to this rule is a very brief seizure lasting only a second or two. This type of seizure is less likely to be followed by a sleepy phase, and given its brevity, it may go unnoticed altogether.

The most common type of seizure in children ages six months to six years is called a **febrile seizure.** It is caused by a rapidly rising temperature. Approximately 2 to 5 percent of all children experience at least one febrile seizure by age six. With a febrile seizure, a child's arms and legs will jerk rhythmically and symmetrically. Most febrile seizures are not followed by a sleepy phase.

There are literally dozens of other causes of seizures, including an infection, a mass, and ingestion of a poisonous substance. Seizures can also be hereditary, meaning that they run in families. These various causes of seizures are not covered in detail here but are discussed in the resources listed at the end of this section.

If a child has recurrent seizures that are thought not to be febrile seizures, she is given the diagnosis of **epilepsy.** A diagnosis of epilepsy does *not* mean that a child has a severe neurological disorder. Although epilepsy can result from severe brain injury, it can also occur in healthy children with otherwise completely normal brains. In fact, many bright young children have epilepsy in early childhood and then grow out of it in a couple of years.

What can I do?

If you think your child is having a generalized seizure and this is the first time, call 911. Make sure your child is in a safe place (such as on the floor) and watch her carefully. If your child has had multiple seizures, you will quickly learn how to manage them and how to determine when to call a doctor or 911.

Do not attempt to put anything into the mouth of a child who is having a seizure. Although it may look as if your child could bite her tongue while seizing, putting an object in the mouth to prevent this can lead to other complications.

Vomiting can occur during a seizure. When this happens, there is a risk of choking on the vomit. If your child vomits during a seizure, turn her head gently to one side to help reduce the chances of her swallowing or inhaling the vomit. Remember, do not put anything in her mouth during the seizure.

A child who is holding a sharp or blunt object (such as scissors or a pen) can hurt herself involuntarily during a seizure. The best way to avoid this is to remove anything your child is holding in her hands when she begins to seize.

A child can fall during a seizure or can roll off a high surface such as a couch or bed. If you think your child is having a seizure, try to move her to a safe place such as the floor.

If the seizure is caused by a fever, give your child a fever-reducing medicine as soon as the seizure has stopped. Remember, don't put anything in a child's mouth during a seizure. If you are not sure whether your child has a fever, check her temperature. Using a rectal thermometer is best, although an older toddler can often cooperate with an oral thermometer. Acetaminophen (Tylenol) or ibuprofen (Motrin or Advil) can be used. Aspirin should never be given to infants or children without a doctor's involvement. Continue to monitor your child's temperature closely so that a febrile seizure does not occur again after the fever-reducing medicine has worn off.

If your child exhibits intermittent jerking or other behaviors that you think may represent a seizure, try to capture an episode on video so that you can show your doctor.

When does my doctor need to be involved?
The first time a child has a generalized seizure, call 911 for an ambulance. Your doctor will be involved, but this usually happens once you are already in the emergency room. You should

not call your child's doctor in lieu of 911 if your child appears to be having a seizure.

Whenever your child has a seizure, you will want to contact a doctor. The only exception to this is if your child has seizures routinely and you are comfortable managing them on your own.

What tests need to be done, and what do the results mean?

The first time a child has a seizure, it is imperative to determine the cause. For children with recurrent seizures, the cause is usually the same, so repeated lab tests are usually not necessary.

The most common causes of seizures can be identified with a few simple tests, including a complete blood count and a blood culture, an electrolyte panel, a glucose (blood sugar) test, a urinalysis and urine culture, and a lumbar puncture (also called a spinal tap). Each of these tests is discussed in detail in chapter 19. Many times, these tests will determine the root cause of the seizure. Note that the seizure itself will affect some of the test results. Therefore, your doctor will interpret the results in the context of the clinical situation.

In addition to lab tests, an imaging study of the brain can help to determine the cause of the seizure. A CT scan or MRI will show a mass, concussion or bleed, skull fracture, or even evidence of an infection around or within the brain. All of these conditions can be responsible for a seizure.

Sometimes it is helpful to look at brain wave activity using an **electroencephalogram (EEG).** This test is performed with wires attached via stickers to the scalp. The EEG can demonstrate ongoing subtle seizure activity, providing clues to the underlying cause.

What are the treatments?

The appropriate treatment for a seizure depends on its underlying cause. If your child has had a febrile seizure in the past, anytime she has a fever the priority will be to get the temperature down quickly. If your child has a bacterial infection, she will be treated with antibiotics.

If there is an abnormality on a CT scan, MRI, or EEG, treatment will depend on the specific problem identified. Such structural or functional problems are not common, and the list of potential causes is beyond the scope of this book. Information on possible causes is available in the resources listed at the end of this section.

If your child has recurrent seizures, she may be treated with a type of medication called an **anticonvulsant** to try to prevent future seizures.

What are the possible complications?

One serious complication of a seizure is the cessation of breathing. Because multiple nerves fire during a seizure, many muscle groups are stimulated at once, and many normal functions, such as breathing, can be compromised. In the most extreme case, a child may appear to turn blue during the seizure. In this case, CPR should be performed. Normal breathing will usually resume immediately after the seizure ends.

Vomiting can lead to aspiration of the vomit. Aspiration can in turn cause a lung infection (**pneumonia**), although this is quite uncommon.

Head trauma can occur when a child falls during a seizure. A seizing child can roll off a couch or bed or can even fall from the standing position. If this happens, you will want to make sure that she does not have a **concussion**. Because vomiting (sometimes) and sleepiness (often) go along with seizures, determining whether your child has a concussion after a fall during a seizure can be difficult. It is likely that she will need to see a doctor or have a CT scan to make sure. Concussions are discussed in chapter 2.

Additional Resources:
http://www.pediatricneurology.com/seizures.htm
http://www.ninds.gov/disorders/febrile_seizures/febrile_seizures.htm
http://www.nlm.nih.gov/medlineplus/encyclopedia.html (Click on "S-Sh," then scroll down to "seizures" or click on "F," then scroll down to "febrile seizure.")
http://www.cincinnatichildrens.org/ (Click on "health topics" and "your child's health," then go to "search" in the upper right-hand corner and type in "seizure.")

18

The Whole Body

FEVER

What is happening inside my child's body?
It is normal for body temperature to fluctuate throughout the day. It goes up when you sleep under a warm blanket or when you exercise. It goes down when you swim in cold water or spend significant amounts of time in the cold outdoors. Body temperature fluctuates in children just as it does in adults.

A *fever* is a rise in body temperature beyond normal daily variability. Average body temperature is 98.6°F (37°C). A fever is generally considered to be any temperature above 101°F (38°C).

When the body gets warm, there are built-in mechanisms designed to cool it down. The heart beats faster, and the blood vessels dilate, causing the skin to look flushed and feel warm. By moving closer to the skin's surface, the blood can be cooled, and the fever should go down.

Most of the time, a fever is not harmful. Rather, it is the body's natural response to infection or inflammation. And when the fever is not too high, the mechanisms for cooling usually work well. This is especially true when the fever is "low-grade," lingering between 99° and 100.5°F.

A fever between 101° and 104°F is significant but not worrisome. Generally speaking, when your child has a fever in this range, he will feel sluggish or uncomfortable. His appetite will likely be minimal, but he should be willing to drink. Fever-reducing techniques tend to be very helpful because they will make your child feel better, improve his appetite, and relieve most aches and pains.

A high fever is one above 104° or 105°F. A temperature this high is not uncommon in toddlers. In fact, it is the rare child who does not have a fever like this at one point or another. When the temperature goes this high, the body's mechanisms for cooling are generally insufficient. This is when the use of fever reducers and other techniques tends to be very important.

What can I do?

The most important thing to do when your child seems to have a fever is to take his temperature. You will want to know how high the fever is so that you can decide whether to give him medicine. If you speak with your doctor, it is likely the doctor will ask how high the fever is.

There are many ways to measure your child's temperature. Mercury thermometers — the old-style long, narrow, glass tube thermometers — used to be very common, but they have recently been taken off the market. Most thermometers are now made of plastic, are digital, and contain no heavy metal.

A **rectal temperature** is the most accurate measure; however, most toddlers will not comply with this technique. In general, a rectal temperature is taken with a digital thermometer inserted about half an inch into the rectum. You can use petroleum jelly (Vaseline) or any other lubricant around the anus and on the thermometer to make the insertion easier. The sensation is odd, but it should not hurt.

Many older toddlers can cooperate with taking an **oral temperature.** Insert a clean digital thermometer under your child's tongue and have him close his mouth. The digital reading is usually completed within seconds, rather than the two to three minutes it took with the old-style mercury thermometers.

The temperature also can be taken under the arm. This is called an **axillary temperature.** Just place the thermometer under your child's arm (in the armpit) and wait for the reading. Although this may seem simple, the arm must stay close to the side of the body throughout the process. Otherwise, you will be measuring the temperature of the air more than your child's body temperature.

Ear thermometers have recently become very popular. This device is placed in the ear canal, and with the press of a button, it bounces a light off the eardrum to measure the body temperature. An ear thermometer can be used only once the ear canal is large and straight enough to provide a direct line to the eardrum. Therefore, an ear thermometer works in older toddlers but not necessarily in younger ones. Also, if a child has accumulated a lot of wax in his ear canal, the reading from an ear thermometer will be inaccurate.

There is a lot of disagreement about the accuracy of nonrectal temperatures. Although oral or ear temperatures may represent the true body temperature, they may also be off by a degree or more. If your child cannot cooperate with the temperature taking, the measurement may be even less accurate. Alternative means of measuring temperature — for instance, the paper strip thermometers laid across the forehead — may seem easier, but these are highly unreliable.

If your child has a fever over 101°F, he will probably feel bad. This is the point at which you will want to take steps to reduce the fever and help alleviate the symptoms.

A lukewarm bath helps drive down body temperature. Make sure the bath water is not too cold. This is important because a cold bath will actually have the opposite effect: the body will try to conserve heat, and the temperature will go up. If your child won't get into the tub, a cool compress on the forehead and chest can be effective. And make sure to dress your child in loose, airy clothing or even no clothes at all.

Some parents use rubbing alcohol on the chest to help cool down their child. This is not dangerous, but it generally isn't recommended because the alcohol can dry and irritate the skin.

Over-the-counter fever reducers are very effective. These medicines are described in the treatments section.

When does my doctor need to be involved?
Call your doctor if your child is having other symptoms along with the fever, such as extreme sleepiness (lethargy), repeated vomiting, a spreading rash, or behavior changes. It is a good idea to call if the fever goes above 104°F or if the fever cannot be controlled despite using fever-reducing medicines and techniques.

What tests need to be done, and what do the results mean?
Whether tests need to be done depends on how your child looks. If your child is eating and sleeping well and has periods of playfulness, and if his fever is low or can be well controlled, it is likely that he has only a mild illness. If, however, the fever is high or your child is behaving as if he is sick — sleeping a lot more or less than usual; refusing to eat or drink; acting especially moody; complaining of a headache, ear pain, a sore throat, belly pain, or diarrhea — there is likely an infection somewhere in the body. An infection is also likely if the fever persists for more than five to seven days. Although none of these symptoms individually indicates that the fever is a sign of something serious, together the constellation of symptoms may suggest a type of infection that needs to be identified and treated.

The type of test done really depends on what your doctor sees when examining your child. If his throat looks red and infected, your pediatrician will often take a throat culture to check for **strep throat.** If your child is complaining of pain with urination, or if the urine has a foul smell, a urine culture may be done to look for a **urinary tract infection (UTI).** If it is flu season and your child has flulike symptoms (severe muscle aches and vomiting), a test can be performed using mucus from the nose or throat to check for the presence of **influenza.** A child with tremendous congestion, a harsh cough, and breathing difficulty may be tested for **respiratory syncytial virus (RSV)** using a nasal wash. Sometimes these tests are available in doctors' offices; other times they must be done at a laboratory or hospital.

If your child has a persistent fever (longer than five to seven days) and no source is apparent, or if your child appears to be very ill, blood tests will probably be done, including a complete blood count and a blood culture. Urine tests may be prescribed as well. For an extremely ill child, a spinal tap also will be performed, and the child will likely be hospitalized.

If coughing or vomiting is associated with the fever, an X ray may be done. The need for this depends on the history of the illness and what your doctor finds when she examines your child.

What are the treatments?

The two fever-reducing medicines available over the counter are acetaminophen (Tylenol) and ibuprofen (Motrin or Advil). These are available in infant drops, children's liquid, and children's chewable tablets. Acetaminophen is also available in a rectal suppository.

Acetaminophen can be given at any age. It is dosed by weight, 10 to 15 milligrams per kilogram of body weight. It is important to dose acetaminophen appropriately, as overdoses may be toxic. Make sure to read the labels of all over-the-counter cough and cold remedies, as many of these contain acetaminophen. Never give more than one acetaminophen-containing medicine at a time.

Ibuprofen can be given only after six months of age. It, too, is dosed by weight, 10 milligrams per kilogram of body weight.

The dosing of these medicines is usually listed on the back of the bottle. The recommendations can be confusing, so if you have any questions, call your doctor.

If your child has a high fever, or if the fever does not respond to one of these fever-reducing medicines, acetaminophen and ibuprofen can be used together or alternated. Call your doctor for information about how to combine them.

"Baby aspirin" is for teens and adults, not for infants or children. Aspirin should not be given to a toddler routinely because it has been associated with ***Reye's syndrome.*** Very occasionally, a toddler will have an illness that requires treatment with aspirin. In these cases, aspirin will be administered to a toddler only under the supervision of a doctor.

If an infection is identified as the source of the fever, your child may need an additional medicine to treat the infection. Bacterial infections are treated with specific antibiotics depending on the type of bacteria. Generally speaking, within 24 to 72 hours of starting an antibiotic, the fever should resolve. Viral infections usually cannot be treated with specific medicines, so they must run their course, often with the help of fever reducers and pain relievers. The main exceptions are influenza ("the flu") and herpes simplex virus (HSV), for which there are effective antiviral medications.

What are the possible complications?

The most common — and perhaps the most feared — complication of a fever is a ***febrile seizure.*** This is a convulsion that occurs when the temperature rises quickly. Febrile seizures are covered in chapter 17.

Infections can spread from one part of the body to another. One infection can also predispose a child to another. The classic example of this is a viral upper respiratory infection (URI) that causes fluid to accumulate in the middle ear, eventually leading to a bacterial ear infection. When your child's fever seems to be improving over a few days and then suddenly becomes worse again, you should suspect a secondary infection.

Additional Resources:

http://www.medem.com (Go to "search" in upper left-hand corner, type in "fever," and scroll down to "fever — understanding fever.")

http://www.packardchildrenshospital.org (Go to "health library," then go to "search" in upper right-hand corner and type in "fever.")

http://www.cincinnatichildrens.org (Click on "health topics" and "your child's health," then go to "search" in upper right-hand corner and type in "temperature taking.")

http://www.mayoclinic.com/ (Go to "search" in upper right-hand corner and type in "fever.")

http://www.ninds.nih.gov/health_and_medical/disorders/reyes_syndrome.htm

DEHYDRATION

What is happening inside my child's body?
Water is the single largest component of the human body, accounting for most of its weight. We lose water through sweat, tears, saliva, urine, stool, and even a little with breathing. We replenish it with food and drink.

A ***dehydrated*** child has too little fluid. She may be taking too little in (by refusing to drink or eat) or putting too much out (with vomiting or diarrhea) or both. How do you know when your child is getting dehydrated? The answer is that everything gets dry: your child will not make as much urine as usual, and when she does urinate, it will look darker than normal; she will have fewer tears; the inside of her mouth might be dry; and her tongue will be rough like sandpaper.

The most common cause of dehydration in toddlers is stomach flu. The medical term for this condition is ***gastroenteritis.*** A child with gastroenteritis loses fluid when she vomits and has diarrhea. There can be trouble replenishing this fluid because of her refusal to drink or inability to keep liquids down. It is relatively easy to get dehydrated this way. Gastroenteritis is discussed in detail in chapter 10.

Other causes of vomiting or diarrhea can also lead to dehydration. These include intestinal obstruction (from a hernia, for example), food allergy, infection, and bowel inflammation (for instance, celiac disease). With any of these, fluid loss can outpace replenishment, and your child can become dehydrated.

Sometimes dehydration results only from refusal to drink. Remember that the body loses water throughout the day, so without drinking, the body's water surplus is not maintained. Infection of the mouth or throat is the most common reason for a toddler to refuse to drink. Viruses (such as ***Coxsackie virus,*** which causes ***hand-foot-mouth disease***) and bacteria (such as ***Group A beta-hemolytic streptococcus,*** which causes ***strep throat***) can cause so much pain that toddlers will refuse liquids.

In the most severe cases, a child won't even swallow her own saliva.

Dehydration is classified as mild, moderate, or severe. Because water is such a large component of body weight, water loss causes weight loss. Therefore, weight loss can be used as an estimation of water loss and, by analogy, an estimation of the severity of dehydration:

Category of Dehydration	Body Weight Loss
Mild	3–5%
Moderate	6–10%
Severe	>10%

Oftentimes a precise pre-illness weight is not known, so this measure cannot be used. Instead, dehydration is classified based on symptoms. A child with **_mild dehydration_** may have dry lips, but the inside of her mouth will still be moist. She will urinate with relatively normal frequency and still cry tears. A child with **_moderate dehydration_** will have dry lips and less saliva than usual. She may urinate less frequently than normal, but still typically three or more times in a 24-hour period. She will make tears with crying. A **_severely dehydrated_** child will look quite ill. The lips and inside of the mouth will be dry. There will be no tears with crying. Urine output will be significantly decreased, sometimes only once in 24 hours (or none at all). Her eyes will often look sunken, and her energy level will be quite low. The skin may lose its normal elasticity, so that when it is pinched, it will hold the shape of a tent. This is called "tenting."

What can I do?
The most important thing is to recognize when your child is becoming dehydrated. If your child is mildly dehydrated, try your best to hydrate her. There are rehydration drinks, available in supermarkets and drugstores, that contain electrolytes meant to replace those lost during ongoing diarrhea. Unfortunately, these drinks are not safe if they are the only nutrition consumed for more than 24 hours. Also, most of them taste awful. Therefore, in

addition to these, give your toddler clear fluids, diluted juices, flat soda, or starchy water such as rice water.

Remember that if your child will drink but not eat, she is getting limited calories. Eventually, the lack of calories will cause her to feel weak or sleepy.

The key to replacing fluids is to do it slowly. If your child has been vomiting, she will eventually become thirsty. If she drinks a large amount, chances are that she will vomit up the fluids she has drunk. Small sips stay down longer. You may be surprised by how small the volume of liquid can be — sometimes only one teaspoon every 5 to 10 minutes — but this is enough to begin to turn things around. A toddler can get very upset when she is thirsty and you are slowing down her fluids. One easy way to minimize the struggle is to soak a washcloth in water and let her suck on it. Popsicles work well, too. The worst way to slowly rehydrate your child is to pour a big glass of something and say, "Now drink this just a little bit at a time."

If your child has only diarrhea, then she will be able to keep liquids and solids down, but they may go straight through her. To help firm up her stools, you can give her bland, constipating foods such as rice, pasta, crackers, or bananas. The old recommendation was to follow the BRAT diet — bananas, rice, applesauce, and toast — but it turns out that any bland food is fine. If your child wants chicken, go for it. Just stay away from spicy foods, sugary foods, and dairy products. Spicy foods will upset a relatively empty stomach. Sugar will draw more water into the intestine, which can worsen diarrhea. And dairy products seem to exacerbate diarrhea almost immediately. If your child insists on milk, try soy or rice milk instead of cow's milk, and dilute them if you can.

When your child's dehydration is the result of pain and subsequent refusal to drink, give her a pain reliever. You can use acetaminophen (Tylenol) or ibuprofen (Advil or Motrin). Both are effective pain relievers, but ibuprofen may cause stomach upset, especially in a child who is having stomach pain already. Another handy pain reliever is called "magic mouthwash." This combination of Maalox and Children's Benadryl Allergy Liquid coats the mouth and throat and reduces local pain caused by inflammation (see page 11).

When does my doctor need to be involved?

If your child has a significantly depressed energy level, call your doctor. If she is not arousable, call 911.

Anytime you suspect that your child is moderately or severely dehydrated, call your doctor immediately. Telltale signs of dehydration are a dry mouth with little or no saliva, no tears with crying, and poor urine output.

If diarrhea is ongoing for several days but your child is happy, eating and drinking well, and not dehydrated, you do not need to worry. However, if your child has had diarrhea for two weeks, notify your doctor. Also call your doctor if you notice blood in your child's stool.

What tests need to be done, and what do the results mean?

Standing your child on a scale and measuring her weight is an easy way to judge whether she is dehydrated. If your child has been weighed recently, the degree of weight loss can be measured. If not, at least checking the weight now will provide a baseline to determine how your child is doing over the next few days.

Depending on the suspected cause of dehydration, other tests may be done. A stool sample can be checked for infections such as viruses, bacteria, and parasites. A complete blood count and blood culture indicate whether the infection has spread to the bloodstream. Checking electrolytes may be necessary when vomiting or diarrhea is excessive, because these can alter the normal balance of electrolytes in the blood. Urine tests, such as urinalysis and urine culture, are also sometimes done, because vomiting can be a consequence of a urinary tract infection (UTI).

Imaging studies, such as X rays and CT scans, can look directly at the intestine and also at surrounding structures that may irritate the intestine. These studies will help rule out bowel obstruction, appendicitis, and other underlying causes. Remember that these tests are not commonly done in toddlers with garden-variety vomiting and diarrhea.

What are the treatments?

A dehydrated child needs to be rehydrated. The simplest way to do this is to have your child drink. In cases where a child cannot or will not drink, fluids must be given intravenously.

Oral hydration is preferred to IV hydration, but it works only if your child can drink fluids and keep them down. To help facilitate this, your doctor may prescribe an antiemetic medicine that minimizes vomiting. The most common medicine, promethazine (Phenergan), can be given by mouth or as a rectal suppository.

IV fluids are needed when your child is unable to tolerate oral hydration or when she is severely dehydrated and cannot replenish her fluids even with oral hydration. Typically, IV fluids make a child feel better with remarkable speed. Once an IV is started, most doctors are careful not to discontinue it until a child is able to hydrate by mouth. This is because no one wants to poke a child with a needle to place an IV more than once. The amount of IV fluids required to rehydrate a child depends on the degree of dehydration: a moderately dehydrated child may need IV fluids for only a few hours, while a severely dehydrated child may need them for days.

Ultimately, either the underlying cause of the dehydration will resolve on its own or it must be treated. Viruses and most bacteria run their course without requiring special medicines, but some intestinal infections, such as parasites, need to be treated. Also, there can be a mechanical reason why a child is vomiting, such as an intestinal obstruction. In such cases, an interventional or surgical procedure may be required.

What are the possible complications?

Untreated severe dehydration can have life-threatening complications. Because water is the primary component of the bloodstream, when a person is dehydrated, the bloodstream dries up. The body can go into **shock** as a result of too little blood volume. **Seizures** can result from too little blood flow to the brain or from electrolyte imbalances. In the most extreme cases, dehydration can lead to death.

HERNIAS

What is happening inside my child's body?

The word **hernia** means a bulge through an abnormal opening. Usually one organ, such as the intestine, bulges through a muscle. Hernias can occur just about anywhere in the body, but the two most common places in toddlers are the groin and the belly button.

In the groin, the intestine can push through a muscle in the floor of the pelvis, appearing anywhere along the groin all the way down to the scrotum. Such hernias are especially common in boys because during development in utero, the testicle descends into the scrotum through an open tubelike structure called the **processus vaginalis.** The processus vaginalis is actually an outpouching of the abdomen. It normally closes and shrinks before birth, but when it fails to close, it provides a conduit into the scrotum. The intestine can slip down this conduit, resulting in a hernia. This type of hernia, called an **inguinal hernia,** accounts for about 80 percent of all hernias in humans. Though more common in boys, inguinal hernias can occur in girls, too. In girls, the ovary and fallopian tubes are more likely than the intestine to protrude through an open processus.

Hernias exist elsewhere, too. In the abdomen, a pair of stomach muscles run vertically from the ribs to the pelvis. The muscles are parallel and are connected from top to bottom by a thick and durable sheet of tissue called a fascia. If the muscles aren't completely attached by this fascia, the intestine can protrude through

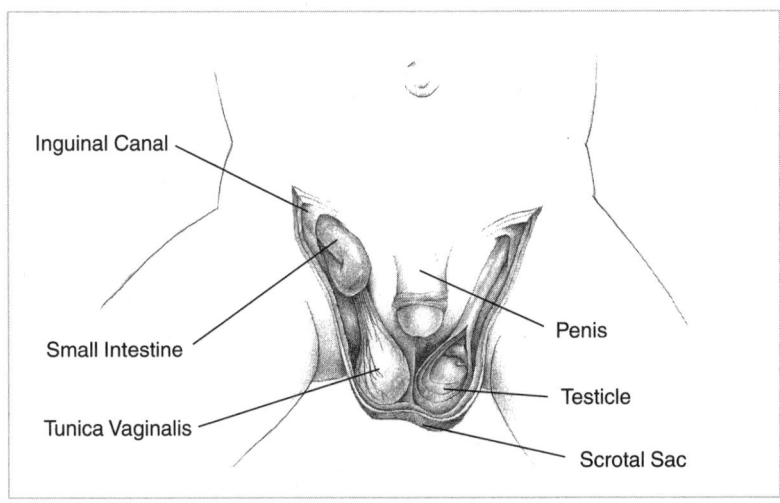

Inguinal Canal

Small Intestine

Tunica Vaginalis

Penis

Testicle

Scrotal Sac

An inguinal hernia occurs when the intestine pushes through a weakness in the inguinal canal. Oftentimes with straining (as with crying), a bulge forms along the groin.

the resulting hole. The most common point of weakness is right at or around the belly button, making the belly button look like an "outie." A hernia of this type is called an ***umbilical hernia.*** The actual hernia is made of a sac protruding through the opening between pieces of muscle and tissue in the abdominal wall. This opening is called the ***umbilical ring.***

Hernias can be small or large. They can be present all the time, or they can come and go. Visible hernias usually pop out when pressure is exerted — with crying, straining, or coughing, for example — causing the intestine to bulge through the hole in the muscle. Although they pop out, sometimes a remarkable amount, most hernias pop back in.

If a hernia remains pushed out, it is usually easy for you to apply gentle pressure and push it back in. When your child is straining or crying, it will be more difficult to do this; but when he is calm, it should be quite easy to apply gentle pressure and watch the hernia (temporarily) go away. This is called ***reduction.***

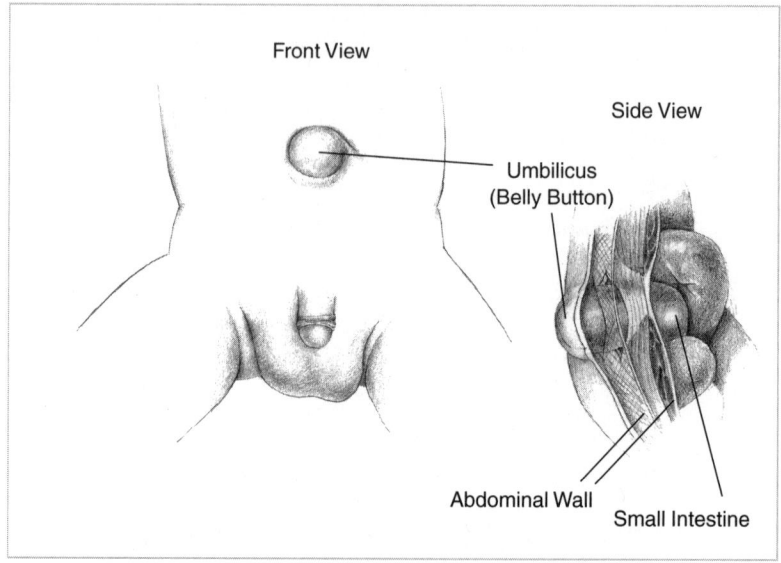

An umbilical hernia results from a weakness in the muscular wall.
The intestine beneath bulges through anytime there is straining
(as with crying).

What can I do?

If you notice a hernia, you can gently apply pressure to push the bulge back in or just leave it alone.

You need not — and really cannot — do anything to help a hernia go away permanently. It is an age-old myth that you can tie a coin to a string and wrap the contraption around a child's waist to push the belly button back in when he has an umbilical hernia. Given the reason the hernia exists in the first place, it is easy to see why this does not work.

When does my doctor need to be involved?

Your child needs to be seen by a doctor if his hernia is not reducible or if the area around the hernia looks red, hot, or swollen. If your child has a hernia and he is vomiting, is complaining of pain, is inconsolable, or has a fever, call your doctor immediately. Remember, with pressure from crying or straining, the hernia will pop out and will be difficult to reduce.

If you are noticing the hernia for the first time and it is reducible, let your pediatrician know. In this case, there is no urgency to call your doctor, but she should eventually evaluate any suspected hernia.

Vomiting and acute pain are worrisome because a hernia can become *incarcerated.* This occurs when the intestine gets stuck in the muscle, swells, and cannot be pushed back in. To further complicate matters, incarcerated hernias can become *strangulated.* In this scenario, the blood supply to the part of the intestine that is stuck becomes compromised, starving that part of the intestine of important nutrients, including oxygen.

Both incarcerated and strangulated hernias are medical emergencies. Strangulated hernias must be treated immediately with surgery, because the part of the intestine deprived of oxygen can die, becoming nonfunctional and a potential site of infection. Incarcerated hernias may not require urgent surgery, but they need to be examined by a doctor (often a surgeon) quickly to prevent strangulation. It is impossible to tell the difference between an incarcerated and a strangulated hernia just by looking at your child. To make the diagnosis, a doctor must examine your child or an ultrasound needs to be done to check for bowel swelling and blood flow in the area of the hernia.

What tests need to be done, and what do the results mean?

The most straightforward test is to apply gentle pressure to the hernia to see if it can be reduced. You or your doctor can perform this test. If a hernia cannot be easily reduced, it may be incarcerated or strangulated.

In the case of a strangulated or incarcerated hernia, an ultrasound will help the doctor tell whether there is still blood flowing to the part of the bowel stuck in the hernia. This in turn will determine whether emergency surgery is needed.

What are the treatments?

The treatment for a normal, reducible hernia depends on where it is located. Umbilical hernias are watched over time. Once a child reaches two years of age, 95 percent of all umbilical hernias close on their own. If a hernia has not closed by kindergarten, you may choose to have it closed surgically for cosmetic reasons.

Inguinal hernias rarely close on their own and almost always need to be repaired surgically. Although reducible hernias do not require immediate surgical repair, most surgeons agree that it is better to operate on an inguinal hernia soon after it is diagnosed rather than to wait for it to become incarcerated or strangulated.

Because inguinal hernias tend to appear on only one side, there exists a controversy over what to do about the other side. Some surgeons believe that if one side is repaired, the other side should be checked for a hernia as well. By sewing the processus vaginalis closed on the opposite side, a future hernia and its complications can be avoided. Other surgeons disagree, opting to operate on both sides only if the child is at known increased risk for having two hernias.

All strangulated hernias and some incarcerated hernias must be treated with immediate surgery. The only difference is that an incarcerated hernia may be operated on within hours, while a strangulated hernia should be operated on within minutes, if possible. The piece of intestine stuck in the gap between the muscles is pushed back in, and the gap is sewn closed. Sometimes the bowel is swollen or has had minimal blood flow while entrapped. In very extreme cases, when a segment of bowel has been so severely deprived of oxygen that it is no longer functional, it needs to be removed.

What are the possible complications?
The most severe complication of a hernia is incarceration or strangulation, but these are quite rare. Remember, when a child is crying, a hernia will always be difficult to push back in.

When a hernia is strangulated or incarcerated, the bowel will become obstructed, and the child will vomit. This can eventually lead to dehydration. A child with a strangulated hernia will almost certainly have pain as well.

Additional Resources:

http://www.packardchildrenshospital.org (Go to "health library," then go
    to "search" in upper right-hand corner and type in "hernia.")

http://www.caps.ca/guests/statements/hernia.htm

http://www.cincinnatichildrens.org/ (Click on "health topics" and "your
    child's health," then go to "search" in upper right-hand corner and type
    in "hernia.")

http://www.nlm.nih.gov/medlineplus/encyclopedia.html (Click on "H-Hf,"
    then scroll down to "hernia" or click on "U," then scroll down to
    "umbilical hernia.")

◆   ◆   ◆

BREATH-HOLDING SPELLS

What is happening inside my child's body?

A breath-holding spell is precisely what it sounds like: a child holds her breath until she turns blue or even passes out. The spell is triggered by a stimulus that causes the child to be angry, frustrated, surprised, frightened, or uncomfortable. She will begin to cry, but shortly thereafter she will become quiet, exhale, and stop breathing. That's when she'll become either pale or bluish, and she may lose consciousness. Usually within seconds, she will wake up and return to her normal activity level. The whole episode can last anywhere from a couple of seconds to half a minute.

Breath-holding spells are involuntary and are not associated with any other behavioral or physical problems. With some children, the spells occur infrequently (perhaps every few months), but with other children, they occur several times a day. The first spell usually occurs between 6 and 18 months of age. Half of the children who experience breath-holding spells will stop having them by five years of age. The spells will stop for almost all children by age seven.

No one really understands why certain children have breath-holding spells and others do not. Furthermore, what is going on in the body is not entirely understood. One theory is that hyperventilation followed by a deep exhale reduces the flow of blood back to the heart, which, seconds later, means there is decreased blood flow to the brain. This causes a child to become pale or blue and pass out. Another theory is that children with breath-holding spells have more dramatic drops in their blood pressure than children who don't experience the spells. Again, following a stimulus, a drop in blood pressure results in decreased blood flow back to the heart, which in turn causes reduced blood flow to the brain.

At first it can be difficult to tell the difference between a breath-holding spell and a **seizure.** However, whereas breath-holding spells tend to be brought on by a precipitating event and almost always involve crying during the spell, seizures are not brought on by any particular stimulus and almost never involve crying. Also, during a breath-holding spell, you may notice that your child's heart rate slows down considerably. By contrast, during a seizure, the heart rate speeds up rather than slowing down. Finally, most children are extremely sleepy after a seizure. After a breath-holding spell, however, there is only a brief period of fatigue lasting seconds or minutes, and more often there is no fatigue at all.

What can I do?

If there is any doubt as to whether your child is having a breath-holding spell and you do not know why your child has turned blue and stopped breathing, you should begin CPR. Usually, by the time you make this snap decision, the breath-holding spell will be over, and your child will be coming to.

No matter how dramatic a breath-holding spell appears, you do not need to do anything. Your child will begin to breathe and wake up on her own. You may wish to place your child somewhere safe (for example, lay her on her back on the floor) and remove any objects from her hands.

Again, the best way to treat a breath-holding spell is to help prevent it. If you know that a certain reaction or behavior by you will trigger a spell, avoid that reaction or behavior. Continue to set limits for your child. Don't let breath-holding spells scare you away from good parenting, but do it in a way that causes the least amount of reaction and frustration.

When does my doctor need to be involved?

Let your doctor know if your child has breath-holding spells. If you are not sure that what your child is experiencing is in fact a breath-holding spell, call your doctor.

What tests need to be done, and what do the results mean?

If your doctor cannot be sure that your child had a breath-holding spell and not a seizure, your child will likely have an evaluation to rule out a seizure. The tests might include an ***electroencephalogram (EEG)*** and sometimes an imaging study such as a CT scan or MRI. Seizure evaluation and management are discussed in detail in chapter 17.

Sometimes there may be concern that breath-holding spells are related to heart function. This is especially common when the spells involve a blue color change. If cardiac problems are suspected, tests may include an ***electrocardiogram (EKG)*** and an ***echocardiogram (ECHO),*** and a simple chest X ray.

In some cases, blood work is done to evaluate a child with breath-holding spells. Although this is largely considered unnecessary, checking hemoglobin and serum ferritin may be worthwhile. These tests look for ***anemia*** (low iron level), which may play a part in breath-holding spells.

What are the treatments?

There are no specific treatments for breath-holding spells. Many children outgrow them by the end of the toddler years, and all children outgrow them by age seven. However, minimizing the triggers that lead to the spells can help reduce their frequency, especially if your child is having many per day.

There is a theory that iron supplementation reduces the frequency of breath-holding spells. Initially, toddlers with these spells were thought to be anemic, and when they were treated appropriately, their breath-holding spells decreased. However, even children who are not anemic may have fewer breath-holding spells when treated with iron. Therefore, some doctors recommend a daily iron supplement for all children with breath-holding spells.

What are the possible complications?

Children do not die from breath-holding spells. Although the spells look dramatic and many children will turn blue and lose consciousness, breath-holding spells are benign.

Probably the most common complication of a breath-holding spell is injury from passing out. Falling can result in head trauma or a broken limb. A child who is holding something sharp, such as scissors, while having a breath-holding spell can cut herself.

Rarely, a child's EKG will show **long QT syndrome.** This heart rhythm abnormality can be associated with a risk of sudden death in both children and adults. Among children with breath-holding spells, long QT syndrome is generally seen when the spells are provoked by excitement, not anger or fright. The best way to rule out long QT syndrome is with an EKG. If it is determined that your child has long QT syndrome, you will likely be referred to a pediatric cardiologist for evaluation. It is important to realize that children with breath-holding spells often have normal EKGs and children without breath-holding spells can have long QT syndrome.

Additional Resources:
www.chop.edu (Click on "your child's health" along left-hand margin, then go to "search" in upper right-hand corner and type in "breath holding.")
http://www.med.umich.edu/ (Go to "search" in upper right-hand corner and type in "breath holding spells.")

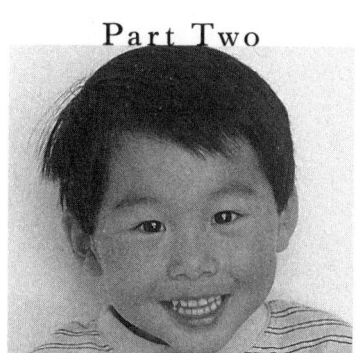

Part Two

Tests and Vaccines

19

Lab Tests and Radiology Studies

BLOOD CULTURE

A blood culture looks for infection in the blood.

Unlike most other blood tests, a blood culture requires that the skin be specially cleaned before the needle is inserted. This helps avoid contamination by the bacteria that normally live on the skin. A tourniquet is placed just above the area where the blood is to be drawn. This pressure restricts blood flow through the vein, causing the vein to engorge with blood. After the needle is inserted into the vein, blood is collected in a syringe or vial. Once the blood has been collected, the tourniquet and needle are removed, and the puncture site is covered with a piece of gauze or a bandage.

Then the blood samples are placed in different environments — some with oxygen, some without, and each with a specific set of nutrients. The samples are placed in a warm incubator for 48 to 72 hours, sometimes longer. Bacteria, viruses, or yeast can be cultured, and organisms are identified by their growth patterns and appearance. Antibiotics are added to growing colonies. When colonies stop growing in the presence of certain antibiotics, the bacteria in those colonies are deemed sensitive to those antibiotics. This helps to identify bacteria that are resistant to various antibiotic drugs.

Often more than one blood culture will be performed. This is because there is a higher likelihood that the infection will be found if more than one test is done. These tests must be done at different times, and therefore the blood must be redrawn with a new needle stick.

Although the blood-drawing procedure for a blood culture is very specific in order to maintain the sterility of the sample, blood for other tests — ones that don't require such stringent sterility — can be drawn at the same time. For instance, if a patient needs both a culture and a complete blood count, blood for both tests can be drawn with a single needle stick. However, the reverse is not true. If a nonsterile sample is being collected and at the last minute a blood culture is desired, unless the skin is prepared using the appropriate measures, another needle stick will be required for the culture.

Additional Resources:
http://www.labtestsonline.org/ (Go to "search" in upper right-hand corner and type in "blood culture.")
http://www.nlm.nih.gov/medlineplus/encyclopedia.html (Click on "Bl-Bz," then scroll down to "blood culture.")

◈   ◈   ◈

BLOOD OXYGEN LEVEL (BLOOD GAS)

A blood gas measures the amount of oxygen and carbon dioxide in the blood, as well as the acidity of the blood.

A blood gas is drawn from an artery. This type of blood vessel is sometimes difficult to access — it is deeper and therefore less visible than a typical vein. In fact, it is easier to feel an artery than to see it. This is because the artery pulsates, reflecting the beating of the heart. Veins do not do this.

The normal blood oxygen level is typically above 85 mmHg and may be much higher, especially when supplemental oxygen is given. When there are problems in the heart or lungs, the level may fall quite low. This is not necessarily obvious: you cannot always tell by looking at someone that his blood oxygen level is low.

If the oxygen level falls below 55 to 60 mmHg, however, the skin often looks pale, and supplemental oxygen may be necessary. When the oxygen level is critically low, the heart and lungs begin to work increasingly hard to try to get more oxygen into and around the body.

A blood gas will often need to be rechecked, especially if the first test showed abnormal results. The test also needs to be repeated if an intervention was made, such as giving oxygen. Each time a blood gas is repeated, a new needle stick is required. The exception to this is with a **central line,** a semipermanent catheter that is placed in an artery. Some seriously ill children have these catheters placed to provide easy access for blood draws. This spares the child repeated poking with a needle.

Sometimes a **pulse oximeter** can be used instead of drawing a blood gas. Because a pulse oximeter measures only the percentage of red blood cells that are carrying oxygen, it provides less information than a blood gas. Pulse oximeters are discussed later in this chapter.

Additional Resources:
http://www.labtestsonline.org/ (Go to "search" in upper right-hand corner and type in "blood gas.")

COMPLETE BLOOD COUNT (CBC)

A complete blood count is a test that looks at the basic components of blood: **red blood cells,** which carry oxygen (reported as the hematocrit, or HCT); **white blood cells (WBCs),** which fight infection; and **platelets,** which help blood to clot. The CBC is an excellent screening test to look for a variety of medical problems, including anemia, infection, bleeding problems, and blood cancers.

The blood for a CBC must be drawn from an artery or vein; it cannot be done using a finger (or heel) stick. The puncture site is cleaned with alcohol or another antiseptic, and a tourniquet is placed just above the area where the blood is to be drawn. This pressure restricts blood flow through the vein, causing the vein to fill with blood. After the needle is inserted into the vein, blood is collected in a syringe or vial. Once the blood has been collected, the tourniquet and needle are removed, and the puncture site is covered with a piece of gauze or a bandage.

The blood must be sent to the laboratory shortly after it is drawn, or it may clot, making the test unreliable. A clotted CBC must be redrawn. Redrawing blood is unfortunate with any patient, but it is especially difficult with toddlers.

The HCT measures the proportion of whole blood that is made of red blood cells. In other words, it estimates how many red blood cells are circulating in the blood. Another measure of red blood cells is the hemoglobin (HGB). The HCT is simply a multiple of the HGB — both numbers measure circulating blood levels. For simplicity, this section refers only to the HCT, but the HGB could be substituted.

Anemia is the medical term for a low HCT. The normal range for the HCT is generally considered to be between 30 and 40. However, this varies a bit depending on age, gender, and ethnicity. When a child is anemic, the cells that carry oxygen have a lower than normal carrying capacity. This means that the amount of oxygen distributed to various parts of the body is less than it should be, and in some cases the metabolic needs of the body cannot be met.

WBCs are part of the body's immune system. When there is infection or inflammation in the body, the WBC number will usually be elevated. This can also happen in times of stress. There are also cases during which the WBC number is actually lower than normal. Viral infections may lower the number, as may certain medicines, problems with the bone marrow, cancers, and diseases of the immune system. The normal WBC range is 5,000 to 11,000 cells/microliter.

Different types of WBCs serve different purposes. Therefore, most laboratories differentiate these cells to help determine why their count is higher (or lower) than normal. Following are the various types of WBCs:

Neutrophils (also known as polymorphonuclear leukocytes, or "polys") tend to be elevated when there is a bacterial infection, although they can be elevated for a number of different reasons.

Bands are the most immature form of WBCs. When they are significantly elevated, there is almost always a bacterial infection.

Lymphocytes are the type of WBCs that fight viral infections. Therefore, they tend to be elevated during viral infections.

Monocytes are elevated in the presence of a variety of infections, the most famous of which is mononucleosis, or Epstein-Barr virus.

Eosinophils are often elevated when there is inflammation or allergy.

Platelets help the blood to clot. The normal range of platelets is 150,000 to 450,000 per microliter. When the number is low, the blood does not clot well; the skin bruises easily; and there may be bleeding from the nose, in the stool, or internally. The converse is also true: when the platelet number is high, blood clots can form easily. A stroke is an example of a complication from too much clotting.

In addition to the HCT, WBCs, and platelets, many other characteristics of the blood are measured in the CBC. These are covered in the resources listed below.

Additional Resources:
http://www.labtestsonline.org/ (Go to "search" in upper right-hand corner and type in "CBC.")
http://www.nlm.nih.gov/medlineplus/encyclopedia.html (Click on "C-Cg," then scroll down to "CBC.")

◆　　◆　　◆

COMPUTED TOMOGRAPHY (CT) SCAN

A computed tomography scan — also called a CAT scan or CT scan — is performed by a 3-D X-ray machine. A computer integrates multiple images to make a cross-sectional picture, showing "slices" of the body. It uses the same basic technology as an X-ray machine.

CT can be used anytime a detailed picture of the body is required. The most common use of CT in the toddler population is head CT to look at the brain, especially after a child has fallen and hit her head. Abdominal CT is also quite common to visualize organs such as the appendix, liver, and spleen when certain illnesses are suspected.

The scanner is shaped like a giant, narrow doughnut (it is not elongated like an MRI scanner) with multiple small X-ray cameras. The patient lies on a narrow table that slides into and out of the "doughnut." This machine is not claustrophobic because it is not an enclosed space. Rather, only the part of the patient's body being imaged is "inside" the machine.

Older CT scanners took a while to shoot the various X rays, but newer models take only seconds. This is important because a toddler used to require sedation to have a CT scan. Now, with the faster machines, most children can lie still for 30 to 120 seconds while the machine takes pictures, obviating the need for sedating medicines and pediatric anesthesia.

Occasionally, a child will need to be given a ***contrast material***, a liquid that will show up on the CT scan. This liquid is called a contrast material because it helps show contrast between certain internal structures. Typically, an IV is placed in the child's arm, and the liquid is injected into the vein before the pictures are taken. Some images require an oral contrast, and some even require a rectal contrast. Depending on the suspected problem, sometimes the CT scan is done immediately after the contrast material is given, while other times two to four hours must pass before the picture is taken. A radiologist — a doctor who specializes in medical imaging — will decide whether and what type of contrast to use, as well as how long to wait between giving the contrast and completing the CT scan.

It is possible to have an allergic reaction to the contrast material. Reactions can range from hives to allergic respiratory failure (*anaphylaxis*). Children with an iodine or shellfish allergy are at increased risk for a reaction to the contrast.

CT can image just about any part of the body. It is a painless procedure, but there are small risks of radiation exposure. One way to think about this is in terms of normal daily radiation exposure. A single chest X ray is equivalent to the amount of radiation a person is exposed to over two and a half days of just walking around on earth. A CT scan, which uses multiple X-ray images, ranges from 240 to 1,200 days of radiation exposure.

Additional Resources:
http://brighamrad.harvard.edu/patients/education/ct/ctguide.html
http://www.fda.gov/cdrh/ct/risks.html
http://www.nlm.nih.gov/medlineplus/encyclopedia.html (Click on "Cp-Cz," then scroll down to "CT.")

ELECTROLYTES

The term "electrolytes" refers to the salts in the bloodstream and the minerals found in tissues. These charged particles are responsible for the general balance of the body in the most basic way, helping to eliminate waste products from individual cells, while neutralizing the body's acid and water levels. The electrolytes measured in an electrolyte panel include sodium (Na), potassium (K), chloride (Cl), and bicarbonate (CO_2). Water balance is most influenced by sodium. Acidity is affected by bicarbonate.

An electrolyte panel must be drawn from an artery or vein; the test cannot be done using a finger (or heel) stick. The puncture site is cleaned with alcohol or another antiseptic, and a tourniquet is placed just above the area where the blood is to be drawn. This pressure restricts blood flow through the vein, causing the vein to fill with blood. After the needle is inserted into the vein, blood is collected in a syringe or vial. Once the blood has been collected, the tourniquet and needle are removed, and the puncture site is covered with a piece of gauze or a bandage.

The blood must be sent to the laboratory shortly after it is drawn, or the results may be unreliable. Occasionally, the blood is drawn through such a small needle that cells break apart, leading to inaccurate values. This is especially true for potassium. In this case, the blood must be redrawn.

Electrolyte levels are often checked when an illness involves a major organ (such as the heart or kidney) or when the fluid balance in the body is in question (for instance, when a child is dehydrated). Electrolyte levels are affected by diet, and they can also be regulated by various hormones in the body. If the levels are too low, electrolytes can be replaced using oral or IV solutions in the hospital.

If your child has an IV, sometimes blood tests can be drawn using this IV, sparing the child a needle stick. However, this cannot be done when an electrolyte panel is checked because the saline solution that runs through an IV contains sodium and often potassium. Therefore, using these lines typically results in inaccurate lab results.

Additional Resources:
http://www.labtestsonline.org/ (Go to "search" in upper right-hand corner and type in "electrolytes.")

◈   ◈   ◈

GLUCOSE (BLOOD SUGAR)

Glucose is sugar that serves as the body's primary fuel source. It circulates in the blood, and its level rises after eating a meal and drops between meals. **Hypoglycemia** means low blood glucose, and **hyperglycemia** means high blood glucose.

To measure blood glucose, blood can be drawn from the artery or vein or from a finger (or heel) stick. When a vein is used, the puncture site is cleaned with alcohol or another antiseptic, and a tourniquet is placed just above the area where the blood is to be drawn. This pressure restricts blood flow through the vein, causing the vein to fill with blood. After the needle is inserted into the vein, blood is collected in a syringe or vial. Once the blood has been collected, the tourniquet and needle are removed, and the puncture site is covered with a piece of gauze or a bandage to stop any subsequent bleeding.

When the finger (or heel) is used, the surface is cleaned with alcohol or another antiseptic and a small hole is made in the skin. The blood will drip out. Either way — vein or finger — the blood must be sent to the laboratory soon after it is drawn.

Normal blood glucose is 60 to 120 mg/dl. Hypoglycemia is generally considered to be less than 60 mg/dl. Severe hypoglycemia is less than 40 mg/dl. Hyperglycemia is generally considered to be greater than 120 mg/dl if the blood is not checked immediately following a meal.

Severe or rapidly developing hypo- or hyperglycemia can be life threatening. Infections that have spread throughout the body can cause either hypo- or hyperglycemia. Diabetes causes hyperglycemia, while inadequate calorie intake causes hypoglycemia. Either very low or very high blood glucose can cause organ failure, brain damage, seizures, coma, or even death.

Additional Resources:

http://www.labtestsonline.org/ (Go to "search" in upper right-hand corner and type in "glucose.")

http://www.nlm.nih.gov/medlineplus/encyclopedia.html (Click on "G," then scroll down to "glucose test.")

MAGNETIC RESONANCE IMAGING (MRI)

Magnetic resonance imaging (MRI) uses magnets and radio waves instead of X rays to take pictures of the human body. The images generated are similar to CT scan images in that they are cross sections (or slices) of parts of the body. However, these images usually have much better resolution than CT scans and therefore often show greater detail, especially in certain parts of the body.

Although the physics of this machine are complex, this is a safe and effective way of imaging. Perhaps more important, unlike CT and X ray, there is no radiation involved.

Unfortunately, the MRI scanner can be claustrophobic for many people. It is a long, narrow tube surrounded by strong magnets. The patient must lie very still while a series of images is collected. The process is slow — an MRI can take an hour or more. Because of the way the machine is constructed and because of the time it takes for an MRI to collect images, patients often need to be given sedating medicines during the scan. Toddlers usually need to be sedated; otherwise they will be unable to cooperate with the test. Newer "open" MRI scanners may cause less claustrophobia.

As with the CT scan, the MRI scan may be enhanced with a dye injected into the veins. This ***contrast material*** helps to light up certain structures inside the body. A radiologist — a doctor specializing in imaging — will determine whether the contrast is needed. The contrast material used for MRI scans is different from that used for CT scans and carries a lower risk of allergic reactions.

Additional Resources:
http://www.cincinnatichildrens.org/ (Go to "search" in upper right-hand corner and type in "MRI scan.")
http://www.nlm.nih.gov/medlineplus/encyclopedia.html (Click on "Mg-Mz," then scroll down to "MRI.")
http://www.fda.gov/cdrh/safety/mrisafety.html

PULSE OXIMETER

A pulse oximeter is a noninvasive device used to monitor the percentage of ***hemoglobin*** — a component of red blood cells — saturated with oxygen. In short, it tells your doctor quickly and painlessly whether there is enough oxygen in your child's body.

The device consists of a probe attached to the patient using either sticky tape or a painless clip. The probe is connected by a long, narrow wire to a small computer. The percentage of hemoglobin saturated with oxygen is displayed, along with the heart rate and an audible signal for each pulse beat. Alarms ring when the oxygen level or pulse changes significantly.

The pulse oximeter illuminates the skin with a red light and measures how much of the light is absorbed. It is effective only if it is put on a part of the body where there is sufficient blood flow. Otherwise, the pulse oximeter cannot accurately measure the oxygen level in the blood. Other factors — including certain medical conditions and the presence of specific toxins in the blood — may reduce the accuracy of the pulse oximeter.

A measurement of 100 percent means that the red blood cells are carrying 100 percent of the oxygen that they can possibly carry. The blood is fully saturated with oxygen. A level below 100 percent means that the blood is not carrying all of the oxygen it can possibly carry. The normal oxygen saturation is 95 to 100 percent while awake and may be lower during sleep. In most cases, an oxygen saturation of less than 95 percent while awake is considered too low.

Additional Resources:
http://www.nda.ox.ac.uk/wfsa/html/u05/u05_003.htm

◈　　◈　　◈

SPINAL TAP (LUMBAR PUNCTURE)

A spinal tap, also called a ***lumbar puncture,*** is a test of the fluid surrounding the brain and spinal cord. This fluid is called ***cerebrospinal fluid (CSF).*** A spinal tap will be done anytime a doctor suspects that there is an infection in the brain (***encephalitis***) or around the brain (***meningitis***).

A spinal tap is most often performed with a toddler lying on one side, knees curled up to the abdomen, and chin tucked into the chest — the "fetal" position. One person holds the child in this position while another actually does the procedure. Holding the child in the proper position is essential to completing the spinal tap quickly and successfully. The skin covering the lower spine is washed with antibacterial soap, and sometimes a local anesthetic is injected. A needle is inserted between two of the vertebrae. A sample of fluid is collected, the needle is removed, and pressure is applied to the site using gauze or a bandage.

Normal spinal fluid is clear yellow. Cloudy fluid is likely infected. The fluid may look bloody if the needle punctured a vein during the procedure. It can also look bloody if there is actual blood in the CSF.

Once the fluid is collected, it will be sent for several different tests. It is checked for red blood cells (RBCs) and white blood cells (WBCs), which can be indicators of an infection. Normal CSF has no RBCs and very few WBCs. The CSF is also checked for protein and glucose. These are normal components of the CSF, but the amount of each will be higher or lower than usual with certain illnesses. The fluid is often cultured, using plates and techniques similar to blood and urine cultures. In some medical centers, the fluid is sent for ***polymerase chain reaction (PCR),*** a test that can identify specific infections.

A normal CSF contains the following:

RBCs	0
WBCs	0–5
Glucose	40–70 mg/dl
Protein	<40 mg/dl

Additional Resources:
http://www.nlm.nih.gov/medlineplus/encyclopedia.html (Click on "Cp-Cz," then scroll down to "CSF collection.")

ULTRASOUND

An ultrasound, also called a **sonogram,** is a machine that uses high-frequency sound waves to construct images of the body's interior. No radiation is involved. You are probably familiar with ultrasound, which is used throughout pregnancy to look at the developing fetus.

The test is done with the child lying down. A gel is applied to the part of the body to be imaged. The gel conducts the sound waves of the machine. A probe, ranging in size from a golf ball to a paintbrush, is placed on top of the gel. As the probe is moved over the area, a picture is generated on the machine's screen. This procedure does not hurt, but the gel may feel cold on the skin.

Some ultrasound machines have **Doppler,** a mode that can simultaneously measure blood flow. Doppler machines can determine whether there is blood flowing to a specific area and the direction in which it is moving.

Ultrasounds can also be done inside the body. In these cases, the probe is inserted into the mouth, vagina, or rectum to look at specific parts of the body. These specific ultrasound tests are rarely necessary in children. A radiologist — a doctor specializing in imaging — will determine the type of ultrasound that will be done before the procedure.

Additional Resources:
http://www.nlm.nih.gov/medlineplus/encyclopedia.html (Click on "U,"
    then scroll down to "ultrasound.")

URINALYSIS

A urinalysis is a test of the urine. Waste products are normally eliminated from the body through the urine or stool. Although some waste products are normal, urine can contain abnormal elements as well. Urinalysis helps identify these abnormal elements. Chapter 11 covers the urinary tract and causes of abnormal urine in detail.

Urine can be collected in one of three ways. The least invasive method, called a **clean catch,** involves having a child urinate directly into a cup. If your toddler is not potty trained, or if your child is not in the mood to comply with the collection, another method will be used. A **bag urine** is done by taping a sterile plastic bag around the vagina or penis so that when a child urinates, the urine is collected. The area is cleaned before the bag is taped on. Alternatively, a **catheterized urine** can be done by inserting a catheter — a narrow plastic tube — into the urethra and up into the bladder. Again, the area is cleaned before the urine is collected. Although the bag is a less intrusive means of collecting urine, it can take a long time for a child to urinate, and the specimen can easily become contaminated. The catheter is more invasive, but it is also faster, more sterile, and often more accurate.

A urinalysis checks for several characteristics. The acid level in the urine is measured using the pH scale. A normal urine has a pH of 4.5 to 8.0. The specific gravity is also measured, reflecting how concentrated or dilute the urine is. A normal specific gravity is 1.005 to 1.025. Urine with a specific gravity less than 1.005 is too dilute, whereas urine with a specific gravity greater than 1.030 is too concentrated.

Urinalysis also looks for white blood cells (WBCs) and red blood cells (RBCs), glucose, and other byproducts of normal bodily functions (such as protein, nitrites, bile, and ketones). The presence of any of these helps determine whether there is a metabolic irregularity, kidney disorder, infection, or other problem. A normal urinalysis does not contain any of these byproducts.

Additional Resources:
http://www.labtestsonline.org/ (Go to "search" in upper right-hand corner and type in "urinalysis.")

URINE CULTURE

A urine culture looks specifically for the bacteria that can cause an infection in the urinary tract. Normally, urine is sterile — it has no bacteria growing in it. The causes of ***urinary tract infections (UTIs)*** are covered at length in chapter 11.

Urine can be collected in one of three ways. The least invasive method is to have a child urinate into a sterile cup, called a ***clean catch*** collection. The external genital area is cleaned with a sterilizing solution prior to urination.

If your toddler is not potty trained, or if your child is not in the mood to comply with the urine collection, a bag can be taped around the vagina or penis. When your child urinates, the urine is collected in the bag. This is called a ***bag urine*** collection. Again, the external genital area is cleaned with a sterilizing solution prior to bag placement. Unfortunately, despite thorough cleaning, normal bacteria that grow on the skin can easily contaminate the bag specimen. Therefore, although a bag collection is often sufficient for a ***urinalysis,*** it is not the best method for a urine culture.

The most invasive approach to collecting urine for a culture is with a catheter, called a ***catheterized urine*** collection. In this case, the external genital area is cleaned with a sterilizing solution. Then a narrow plastic tube is inserted into the urethra and up into the bladder. This is a sterile approach, because the urine is extremely unlikely to become contaminated with the bacteria that normally live on the skin.

A urine culture requires only a few drops of urine. When both a urinalysis and a culture must be done, the specimen can be collected all at once, with part placed in a sterile cup (for the culture) and the rest in a nonsterile cup (for the urinalysis). Remember, however, if the urine must be sterile for a culture, the whole collection process must be sterile. Therefore, if a nonsterile approach is used for the collection — for instance, if the area is not cleaned with a sterilizing solution or if the primary collection container is not sterile — a urine culture cannot be performed with that specimen.

The urine collected for culture is carefully put on a culture plate, and the plate is placed in a warm incubator for 24 to 48 hours. If there are bacteria in the urine, they should grow on the plate. Antibiotics can be added to the plate to determine which drug will be most effective in eliminating the infection.

A urinalysis can be a good early indicator of an infection. If the urinalysis shows signs of an infection, a urine culture is likely to grow bacteria.

Additional Resources:

http://www.labtestsonline.org/ (Go to "search" in upper right-hand corner and type in "urine culture.")

http://www.nlm.nih.gov/medlineplus/encyclopedia.html (Click on "U," then scroll down to "urine culture.")

X RAY

An X ray is a type of radiation. The X-ray machine focuses on one specific part of your child's body, and when a picture is taken, X rays travel through him onto special film behind his body. Depending on the tissues and organs in the body, all, some, or none of the X rays will pass through. This generates a picture on the film. Dense structures, such as bones, look white on an X ray, while air looks black.

Only technicians and doctors (radiologists) perform X rays. The actual image takes just a second or two to film, but the patient must be perfectly still for the technician to capture the best image. Parents may stay with their children during an X ray, but they are usually asked to wear lead coats to protect them from unnecessary radiation exposure.

Sometimes patients will be asked to drink a liquid called a **_contrast material_**, which shows up as white on the X ray. This liquid can help to outline certain structures in the body.

Just about any part of the body can be x-rayed. It is a painless procedure, but there are small risks of radiation exposure. One way to think of this is in terms of normal daily radiation exposure. A single chest X ray is equivalent to the amount of radiation a person is exposed to over two and a half days of just going about daily life. One chest X ray also is equivalent to about five round-trip plane trips from Los Angeles to New York.

Additional Resources:
http://www.nlm.nih.gov/medlineplus/encyclopedia.html (Click on "X," then scroll down to "X-ray.")

20

Vaccines

Vaccines, also called **immunizations,** are designed to boost your child's immune system against specific infectious agents, protecting him from serious and sometimes life-threatening diseases.

Vaccines come in many varieties. Some are lab-manufactured replicas of a piece of a bacterium or virus. These are called **recombinant vaccines.** Others are made by attaching proteins to parts of a bacterium. These are called **conjugated vaccines.** These two methods of manufacturing vaccines use only small pieces — or even replicas of small pieces — of organisms that cause infections. The recipient is not exposed to the entire bacterium or virus, just to one little part of it. This gives the immune system the illusion that the body is infected when it really isn't.

A few vaccines are produced by altering an entire bacterium or virus — using heat to denature its proteins, thereby rendering it inactive. These are called **inactivated** or **killed vaccines.** Finally, some vaccines are made from a living virus. The virus is weakened, so that when it is given in the form of a vaccine, it cannot cause a full-blown illness. These are called **live-attenuated vaccines.**

All four kinds of vaccines work by tricking your child's immune system into thinking the body has been exposed to a true bacterial or viral infection. The immune system then makes the appropriate antibodies to fight off that particular infection. Therefore, when the child is exposed to the true virus or bacterium, the body has been primed, giving the immune system memory that will provide rapid antibody production.

Over the past few decades, the number of vaccines recommended by the Centers for Disease Control (CDC) and the American Academy of Pediatrics (AAP) has increased significantly. The vaccines are listed on an immunization schedule that is revised regularly. Most schools require completion of the schedule prior to entry. Although these vaccines are strongly recommended, they are not required by law.

Many parents have raised concerns about the long-term effects of vaccines on children's health and development. Their concerns range from the use of preservatives in vaccines to the administration of multiple vaccines during one doctor's visit. For some parents, weighing the risks and benefits has complicated what was, in the past, a simple rite of passage. This chapter is meant to summarize basic information about the vaccines given over the first five or six years of life. If you care to do additional research, see the resources at the end of this chapter. Although some of the vaccines described here are routinely administered before a child's first birthday, booster doses often are given in the toddler years. Therefore, all of the vaccines listed on the AAP vaccine schedule are included here.

Given the recent attention focused on preservatives used in vaccines — specifically, the mercury-containing compound *thimerosal* — this topic deserves an extra note. In 1999, the AAP voted to remove thimerosal from the routine childhood vaccines. Since 2001, each vaccine listed on the recommended schedule has been available thimerosal-free. Although there are still some vaccines produced using thimerosal as a preservative, almost all of the vaccines stocked in pediatric offices are thimerosal-free. The vaccines that may still contain thimerosal are noted in the following sections.

DIPHTHERIA, TETANUS,
AND ACELLULAR PERTUSSIS (DTAP)

DTaP combines vaccines against diphtheria, tetanus and pertussis. It is currently given as a series of five doses, recommended at 2 months, 4 months, 6 months and 12 to 18 months, with a booster dose between 4 and 6 years.

Diphtheria generally causes a throat infection, although it also can lead to problems in other parts of the body. The mucous membranes of the throat swell and then become thin and fragile. The infection can cause blockage of the airway, or it can spread into the bloodstream and then to the heart, nerves or brain. Diphtheria is not common in the United States, but pockets of outbreak do occur. It is far more common in developing countries. It is considered important to have a diphtheria vaccine prior to any international travel.

Tetanus is well known. If you step on a rusty nail or get a dirty cut, the bacteria that carry the tetanus toxin can enter the skin and multiply. The wound must be deep for these bacteria to grow, because they can survive only in an environment without any oxygen (called **anaerobic**). The bacteria release a nerve toxin that causes muscle spasms sometimes so severe that the muscles become completely rigid. **Lockjaw** (also called **trismus**) is a classic symptom of tetanus. The breathing muscles can become spastic as well, a potentially life-threatening complication.

Pertussis is more commonly known as **whooping cough.** In older children, teens, and adults, pertussis causes a persistent (or staccato) cough that goes on for so long that the infected person must gasp and inhale deeply to catch his breath. This is the "whoop" of whooping cough. In infants, especially those under six months, pertussis can cause regular breathing to stop suddenly (called **apnea**) even before a cough is heard. In some studies, it is estimated that 25 to 30 percent of adults who have been coughing for more than three weeks carry pertussis. One reason pertussis is so prevalent is that the immunity against the infection disappears several years after the last dose of the vaccine. Until 2005, teens and adults had not routinely been vaccinated against pertussis. Instead, they received a booster diphtheria-tetanus vaccine without pertussis. Therefore, many adolescents and almost all adults serve as reservoirs for this bacteria. Since 2005, however, a new tetanus booster vaccine that includes protection against pertussis has been available for adults up to age 65. Although older children and adults can get morbidly sick with pertussis, this is quite rare. Infants are at greatest risk when they are infected.

The DTaP formulation of the vaccine has been widely available since 1996. Before that, DPT was used instead. DPT had whole-cell pertussis, not acellular pertussis. The old DPT form was fraught with side effects. It often caused fevers up to 104° to 105°F, which in turn led to febrile seizures in some children. DPT was also responsible for several infant deaths due to shock. When the formulation of pertussis was changed, the side effects of the vaccine became significantly less severe. DPT is no longer used in the United States.

The most common adverse reactions reported with DTaP include pain or soreness at the injection site (5 in 100 children), low-grade fever (5 in 100), fussiness (30 in 100), and swelling at or around the injection site (8 in 100). Only 1 in 3,000 children experiences a high fever. These symptoms resolve in one to three days. Other adverse reactions include continuous screaming or crying for more than three hours (1 in 2,000), seizures (6 in 10,000), and allergy to one of the components.

Many people ask whether the components of DTaP are available separately. Although some countries do carry pertussis vaccine on its own, it is neither manufactured nor available in the United States this way. For now, the only way to be vaccinated against pertussis is to have the combined DTaP vaccine. Tetanus vaccine is available either alone (T) or with diphtheria (TD), but neither T nor TD is recommended for children under seven. In addition, both of these forms tend to contain significant amounts of thimerosal.

HAEMOPHILUS INFLUENZAE TYPE B (HIB)

Haemophilus influenzae type B vaccine (HiB) is currently given as a series of three or four doses, recommended at 2 months and 4 months, with booster doses at 6 months and/or 12 to 18 months depending on the manufacturer of the vaccine.

Haemophilus influenzae type B (also called **H flu**) accounted for 10,000 to 20,000 cases of **meningitis** each year until the vaccine became available about two decades ago. It caused at least 500 deaths annually. Although *H flu* is just one cause of meningitis, until the vaccine was available, *H flu* was the most common cause of bacterial meningitis in infants and young children.

H flu also can cause **epiglottitis,** an infection at the entrance to the airway. When *H flu* causes epiglottitis, the flap that normally protects the lungs swells, and air cannot get down to the lungs easily. *H flu* can cause infections in the joints (called **septic arthritis**), skin (**cellulitis**), lungs (**pneumonia**), bones (**osteomyelitis**), and bloodstream (**bacteremia**).

The vaccine became available in 1985, and today *H flu* is responsible for only about 100 cases of meningitis each year. Every case of *H flu* meningitis occurs in a child who was not fully vaccinated with HiB.

HiB vaccine can cause redness, soreness, and swelling at the site of injection in 1 in 4 children. Many fewer children — about 1 in 20 — have fever and irritability within 24 hours of receiving the vaccine. All of these symptoms resolve in one to three days.

HiB is available on its own or in combination with other vaccines. Comvax combines HiB and Hep B vaccine. TriHiBit combines HiB and DTaP.

HEPATITIS A (HEP A)

The hepatitis A vaccine is not given until a child is at least one year old. It is given in a series of two injections 6 to 12 months apart. It can be given anytime after a child's first birthday.

Hepatitis is an inflammation of the liver that is often caused by a viral infection. The viruses have been named alphabetically: hepatitis A, B, C, and so on all the way up through G, and more will certainly be identified. Hepatitis B and C are the most well known, largely because they can cause long-term liver damage. By contrast, hepatitis A is far more common, much easier to catch, and usually less serious (although deaths do occur).

In teens and adults, infection with hepatitis A can cause vomiting and diarrhea for several weeks, in some cases up to several months. However, many children who get the illness have no symptoms at all. Though uncommon, liver failure can occur. Hepatitis A is shed in the stool and passed hand to mouth, allowing rapid spread, especially among day care workers who frequently change diapers and restaurant workers who don't wash their hands after using the bathroom. Hepatitis A can also be spread through water; shellfish are a known reservoir for this virus.

The vaccine is now recommended for all children in the United States, with an emphasis in certain geographic areas known to have greater disease prevalence (namely the southwestern states). Because this virus is found throughout the world, the vaccine is considered important for travelers.

The side effects of Hep A vaccine are common but mild. They include soreness at the site of injection (1 in 5 children), headache (1 in 20), and decreased appetite (1 in 12). These all resolve shortly after the vaccine is given. Rare cases of allergic reactions to the vaccine have been reported.

HEPATITIS B (HEP B)

Hepatitis B vaccine is given in a series of three injections. It is the only vaccine known to be effective when given immediately after birth. The recommended schedule for Hep B is at birth, 1 month, and 6 months. However, if the mother is known to be hepatitis B negative (that is, she does not have evidence of current or past hepatitis B infection), this schedule is often treated flexibly, with

Hep B given on the same schedule as the other infant vaccines (at 2 months, 4 months, and 12 to 18 months).

Hepatitis B infection can cause lifelong disease. "Hepatitis" means inflammation of the liver. It is usually caused by a virus, and because there are so many viruses that can cause it, they have been named alphabetically: hepatitis A, B, C, and so on all the way up through G, and more will certainly be identified. Hepatitis B is transmitted through sex, needle sharing, and blood transfusions. It can also be passed from a pregnant woman to her child during labor and delivery. There seems to be an unknown vector of transmission for hepatitis B, as several cases of infection occur in people with none of these risk factors.

Chronic hepatitis B infection is a worldwide problem. It is estimated that between 200 million and 300 million people have the disease, with the majority of cases in Africa and Asia. About 95 percent of people infected with hepatitis B eventually recover, but the 5 percent remaining may go on to develop liver cancer or **cirrhosis** (liver failure).

Hep B vaccine has a few mild side effects, including soreness at the site of injection (1 in 11 children), fever (1 in 14 to 100, statistics vary), and allergic reaction to one of the components. There have been reports that Hep B vaccine is associated with rheumatoid arthritis, diabetes, and multiple sclerosis, but none of these reports has been verified with studies.

Some manufacturers of Hep B vaccine use thimerosal as a preservative, but there are also mercury-free forms on the market. Ask your pediatrician which form your child will receive. Hep B is available on its own or in combination with other vaccines. Comvax is Hep B plus HiB vaccine. Pediarix is Hep B, DTaP, and IPV.

INFLUENZA (FLU SHOT)

Influenza vaccine is an optional vaccine offered each year at the beginning of the flu season (usually between October and December). It is not part of the routine childhood immunization schedule and is not required by schools for admission. Since 2004, however, it has been strongly recommended by both the CDC and the AAP for all children ages 6 to 23 months.

The vaccine cannot be given before a child is 6 months old. Children under 9 years who are getting the flu shot for the first time need two doses at least four weeks apart. In subsequent years when the shot is given (or the first time in children over age 10 and in adults), only one dose is necessary.

Influenza is the virus that causes the flu. This virus changes slightly each year, so that every winter different strains are spread throughout the world.

Influenza causes high fever, upper respiratory symptoms (such as cough and runny nose), and muscle aches that can be so profound they make it difficult to stand or walk. Flu causes more symptoms in older children and adults than in infants, but it is far more dangerous for the very young and the very old. In infants, influenza is one of the most common causes (if not the most common cause some winters) of respiratory distress and hospitalization. Historically, flu epidemics have killed millions of people. Flu is spread easily from person to person, especially from children to older adults.

Children who are at higher risk for respiratory failure, hospitalization, or even death from influenza include children born prematurely and children with a history of asthma, cystic fibrosis, chronic pulmonary or cardiac disease, sickle-cell anemia, chronic renal disease, or immune system diseases such as HIV. Women in their second and third trimesters of pregnancy are often encouraged to get a flu shot at the beginning of the flu season. This vaccine will protect the mothers from febrile illness during pregnancy and protect their fetuses by providing antibodies that get passed through the placenta.

Each year, as the strains of influenza evolve, the shot changes. Therefore, the vaccine is useful for only one year at a time. Because its effectiveness depends on how well the scientists who design the vaccine can predict the upcoming winter flu strains, some years it is more effective than others.

The flu shot is a killed vaccine. A nasal spray called FluMist is a live-attenuated vaccine similar to MMR and varicella vaccine. Flu-

Mist is currently only available to healthy people ages 5 to 49. Side effects occur within 12 hours of receiving the shot. With the flu shot, redness and swelling can occur at the site of the injection. One batch of flu vaccine used in 1976 was associated with the development of temporary paralysis of the nerves called **Guillain-Barré syndrome;** this has not been reported since. FluMist has been reported to cause fever and muscle aches in many recipients.

Because flu vaccine is prepared in embryonated eggs, it should not be given to anyone with a severe egg allergy. If it is, a serious allergic reaction, including **anaphylaxis,** can occur. Most children with a mild or moderate egg sensitivity can be safely immunized with flu vaccine.

Many formulations of flu vaccine contain thimerosal as a preservative, but mercury-free forms also are available. FluMist is thimerosal-free, but it has not yet been approved for use in children under five years of age.

MEASLES, MUMPS, AND RUBELLA (MMR)

MMR vaccine is given in two doses, the first at 12 to 18 months and the second at 4 to 6 years.

MMR vaccine has become one of the most controversial vaccines. It protects against three diseases: measles, mumps, and rubella (German measles). Viruses cause all three of these diseases. Each of these diseases was once a common childhood illness, with periodic major outbreaks in the United States — tens of thousands (up to millions) were infected at the same time. Epidemics of these serious diseases still occur in developing countries where the vaccine is not available. In the United States, the vaccine has decreased the incidence of these diseases by more than 90 percent, and epidemic outbreaks are very rare.

The **measles virus** causes a bright red, splotchy rash that starts at the hairline and moves down the face and body. The hallmark of measles is a triad of cough, runny nose, and eye infection (**conjunctivitis**), along with a rash and fever. The accompanying fever makes most children fussy and sleepy.

Although the vast majority of children get through measles with few problems, 1 in 1,000 children who have measles is hospitalized with severe complications, the most dangerous of which is a brain infection (**encephalitis**) that can be fatal.

The **mumps virus** causes inflammation and swelling of the internal organs. The swelling of the salivary glands gives children with mumps the signature jowly look. The pancreas, ovaries or testicles, and area around the brain (meninges) are also subject to swelling. Among boys, one or both testicles will swell (called **orchitis**) in up to 25 percent of mumps cases. Rarely, orchitis leads to sterility. As with measles, the high fever seen with mumps can make children irritable.

Rubella (also called **German measles**) is a milder illness than measles or mumps. Often there are no symptoms at all. Some children will have common cold symptoms, accompanied by swollen glands and a rash. However, rubella is not considered benign during pregnancy. If a pregnant woman gets rubella and passes it to her fetus, the fetus can suffer from **congenital rubella syndrome.** If carried to term, a baby with this disease may be born mentally retarded, deaf, or blind. Many of these pregnancies end in miscarriage. Prior to the era of vaccination, approximately 20,000 babies per year were born with congenital rubella syndrome.

MMR vaccine was originally three separate vaccinations. In 1979, it was combined into one. Today both forms of the vaccine are produced. Most children receive the combined vaccine, but some pediatric offices still carry separate measles, mumps, and rubella immunizations.

MMR is one of the two live-attenuated vaccines still on the immunization schedule for toddlers. The other live-attenuated vaccine is varicella. The nasal spray FluMist is also live, but it is not given to children under five years of age.

The most common side effects of MMR are mild: fever (1 in 6 children), rash (1 in 20), and swollen glands in the neck (rare). The vaccine is also associated with seizure (1 in 3,000) and temporary low platelet count, causing bruising or bleeding (1 in 30,000). A small number of patients report allergic reactions to one of the components. Because MMR is prepared in the fluid of chicken embryos, it should not be given to anyone with a severe egg allergy. If it is, a serious allergic reaction, including **anaphylaxis,** can occur. Most children with a mild or moderate egg sensitivity can be safely immunized with MMR.

There is a great deal of controversy over the question of a causal relationship between MMR vaccine and the rising incidence of autism. Numerous studies have shown that there is no correlation between MMR vaccine and autism, but the debate remains highly contentious.

PNEUMOCOCCAL CONJUGATE (PREVNAR)

Pneumococcal conjugate vaccine (also known by its trade name, Prevnar) is given in four doses: at 2 months, 4 months, 6 months, and 12 to 18 months. For children who did not get the vaccine as infants, there is a catch-up schedule, with two doses if given for the first time after 12 months of age and one dose if given after 24 months of age.

Pneumococcal conjugate vaccine protects against the bacterial infection *Streptococcus pneumoniae* (or pneumococcus). It is a member of the same streptococcus family that causes other infections, like strep throat. This is the most recent vaccine to be added to the childhood immunization schedule, approved by the FDA in 2000.

Pneumococcus causes lung infection (***pneumonia***), blood infection (***bacteremia***), infection of the fluid around the brain (***meningitis***), and millions of ear infections annually. There are many strains of pneumococcus, but a small number account for the majority of illnesses. Therefore, the vaccine protects against only the seven most common strains.

Although pneumococcus infects people of all ages, it is most dangerous in children 6 to 18 months old. It is the leading cause of bacteremia and ear infections in this age group, and it is a common cause of bacterial meningitis.

In many communities throughout the United States, pneumococcus has a tremendously high rate of antibiotic resistance. Up to 25 percent of pneumococcal strains have some degree of

resistance. This means that even when the infection can be identified, it cannot necessarily be treated with standard antibiotics.
Antibiotic resistance is a result of the overuse of antibiotics during
the past several decades. Pneumococcal vaccine becomes increasingly important when viewed in this light, because it offers a
means to reduce the incidence of infection in the community,
thereby reducing the reliance on antibiotics to treat the infection
and eventually limiting the development of further antibiotic
resistance.

The short-term side effects of pneumococcal vaccine are well
studied. These include tenderness, redness or swelling at the injection site (1 in 5 to 8 children), and fever (1 in 3). Long-term side
effects are less well established, given that the vaccine is so new.

Pneumococcal conjugate vaccine has no mercury preservative.
However, the form of pneumococcal vaccine given to older children, Pnu-Imune 23, does contain thimerosal. Pnu-Imune 23 is
only indicated for certain children over the age of two. Ask your
doctor if your child will receive this vaccine.

POLIO (IPV)

Until recently, the polio vaccine came in two forms: a live-
attenuated form (OPV) given as a drink and a killed form (IPV)
given as an injection. Since 2000, only the injectable form has
been available in the United States. It is given in a series of four
doses: at 2 months, 4 months, 12 to 18 months, and a booster at 4
to 6 years.

Polio is a virus that can destroy nerve cells in the spinal cord
and brain. Before the vaccine was available in 1955, polio caused
thousands of cases of paralysis. In some cases, it paralyzed the
breathing muscles and led to suffocation and death. The last case
of natural (wild) polio in the United States was documented in
1979. Between 1980 and 1994, there were 125 reported cases of
polio caused by the oral form of the vaccine. Most of these cases
were in adults whose immune systems were in some way compromised, such as patients receiving chemotherapy or people
with HIV infection. A few cases were in children with undiag-

nosed immune deficiencies. Because the oral polio vaccine caused these few cases of polio, and because wild-type polio has been eradicated in the United States, the oral vaccine is no longer used.

Worldwide, wild-type polio is still a problem. It is primarily found in Southeast Asia, Africa, and the Mediterranean, although there have also been outbreaks elsewhere. Because of the persistence of the virus in parts of the world, the vaccine is always recommended for travelers. The World Health Organization has a goal for worldwide eradication of the virus. To attain this goal, most of the world's population must be vaccinated.

IPV has very few side effects. The only reported reactions include redness or soreness at the injection site (1 in 7 children) and fever (1 in 3). No severe reactions have been reported.

VARICELLA (VARIVAX)

The varicella (chicken pox) vaccine is given in a single dose anytime after a child is one year old. However, if the vaccine is given after a child is 12 years old, two doses are required.

Chicken pox is among the most common childhood illnesses. Most children who contract chicken pox naturally (also known as ***wild-type chicken pox*** or ***varicella zoster virus***) experience fever and an itchy, blistery rash lasting several days. It is estimated that 1 in 2,000 children will experience more serious complications. Vigorous scratching of the pox can break the skin and lead to a secondary skin infection and scarring. The most serious type of skin infection is caused by a type of streptococcus bacteria called ***flesh-eating strep.*** The varicella virus can also circulate through the bloodstream, spreading to the lungs (***pneumonia***), liver (***hepatitis***), and brain (***meningitis*** or ***encephalitis***). The risk of these serious complications increases with age. It is estimated that 1 in 5 adults with wild-type chicken pox develops pneumonia, and an adult is 25 times more likely to die from chicken pox than a child is.

Varicella vaccine is one of only two live-attenuated vaccines on the childhood immunization schedule (the other is MMR). The nasal spray FluMist is also live, but it cannot be given to children under five.

The side effects include tenderness or swelling at the injection site (1 in 5 children), fever (1 in 10), and rash (1 in 20). The rash looks similar to actual chicken pox, with small red bumps turning to blisters and then scabbing over. Unlike wild-type chicken pox — in which several hundred pox can appear all over the skin, as well as in the mouth, esophagus, and vagina — the varicella vaccine only causes a handful of nonitching pox. The rash typically appears 7 to 10 days after the child receives the shot, but it has been reported to appear up to one month later.

It is estimated that 1 in 10 children who have received the varicella vaccine will get chicken pox when exposed to it months or years later. However, like the vaccine rash, chicken pox in vaccinated children is extremely mild. There are only a handful of pox, they do not itch, there is rarely an accompanying fever, and the pox are usually completely gone within a couple of days. Unvaccinated children, by contrast, can have hundreds of itchy pox and a high fever lasting 7 to 10 days or longer.

If your child has not received the varicella vaccine and is exposed to another child with the disease, he can get the vaccine within 72 hours of exposure. This will help minimize the extent of his illness. However, receiving the vaccine after exposure is not as effective as receiving it weeks or months (or years) earlier. In addition, parents are rarely notified of a child's exposure. More likely, your child will be exposed in a public place where you do not know the other families, who consequently cannot alert you when a child develops the illness.

Children under one year of age cannot receive the vaccine because it is not proven effective in this age group. Therefore, if a child under one year old gets chicken pox, all you can do is give him a fever-reducing medicine as needed, an oatmeal bath for comfort, and often an oral antihistamine to help with the itching. Your child's nails should be cut short to minimize skin breakage with scratching. For severe cases of chicken pox, an antiviral medication called acyclovir (Zovirax) can be used. This is covered in the section on chicken pox in chapter 1.

Varicella vaccine has been used in Japan since the 1970s. It was approved by the FDA for use in the United States in 1995.

Additional Resources:
http://www.vaccine.chop.edu
http://www.cdc.gov/nip
http://www.immunofacts.com
http://www.who.int/immunization/en
http://www.nlm.nih.gov/medlineplus/childhoodimmunization.html
http://www.vaccine.org
http://www.immunizationinfo.org

Part Three

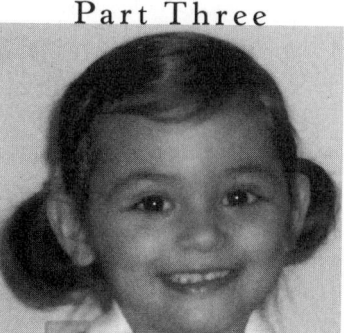

Development

21

The Developmental Milestones

Watching your child develop and mature is one of the great gifts of parenthood. But at some point, most parents wonder whether their child's developmental progress is normal. How can you tell if your child is precocious or delayed? And when do you need to be concerned?

Pediatricians use a number of tools to assess child development. General pediatricians are responsible for getting an overall sense of a child's progress during routine checkups. Developmental pediatricians specialize in child development, observing children carefully and measuring their progress objectively using codified tests. They help parents and other health care providers determine whether there is a delay and, if so, what interventions are necessary to help a child overcome it.

There are many different scales that measure "normal" developmental milestones. Probably the most widely used is the ***Denver Developmental Screening Test (DDST).*** This tool was developed to help general pediatricians assess developmental milestones thoroughly and quickly. It divides the developmental tasks into four categories: gross motor, language, fine motor (or adaptive), and personal (or social). The Denver Developmental Screening Test II (DDST-2) is the most recent version of the scale. The DDST-2 is easy to use. The pediatrician draws a vertical line down the page at the appropriate age point. Tasks that a child should be engaging in at that age bisect the line. A child of a given age should already have mastered the tasks to the left of the line and should not yet have mastered the tasks to the right. This snapshot view provides a quick and reliable assessment of overall development.

This chapter is divided into sections by developmental category. The developmental tasks are listed by average age of accomplishment. It must be emphasized that a delay in one task is not a cause for concern. However, delays in multiple tasks or delays across categories should prompt parents to consider the possibility of a developmental issue.

In each section, I have listed the signs of developmental delay. Again, it cannot be overemphasized that an isolated delay is not uncommon in a developmentally normal child. Multiple signs of delay, however, should raise concern.

In the United States, it is estimated that 10 percent of children have a delay in at least one area of development: gross motor, fine motor, language, cognitive, or psychosocial. This figure includes all children who qualify as delayed, whether mildly or severely.

Recently there has been increased attention paid to **autism.** Autism accounts for a very small proportion of all developmental delays. Only 0.2 to 0.4 percent of all children (or 2 to 4 percent of children diagnosed with a developmental delay) are autistic. "Autism" means many things to many people, and there is a wide range of issues and intensity among children with autism. For this reason, children are rarely called "autistic" and instead are said to have **autistic spectrum disorder (ASD)** or **pervasive developmental disorder (PDD).** Children with ASD/PDD generally have abnormal or impaired development in social interaction and language, including a decidedly restricted repertoire of interests and activities, but the severity of ASD/PDD ranges widely.

GROSS MOTOR DEVELOPMENT

Early in the toddler years, your child goes from being largely dependent on you to being almost completely independent, particularly in terms of getting around. Each child hits her motor milestones at her own pace. The earliest mover may walk at 9 months and climb stairs seamlessly by the time she is 18 months old. Another child may not walk until she is 17 or 18 months old and may not climb stairs independently until she turns 3. Both of these patterns are normal.

Gross motor tasks include everything from walking and running to climbing and hopping. They are movements that incorporate many large muscle groups at once. In general, children who tend to reach gross motor milestones fastest become children who can get what they want and don't have to ask for it. Therefore, many of these early movers — though by no means all — tend to develop verbal skills a bit more slowly. They get their own milk rather than having to say "milk" or "bottle." For this reason, I often warn parents that early walkers may be late talkers and vice versa.

Gross Motor Milestones	Age Range	Average Age
Walks	9–17 months	12 months
Walks backward	12–18 months	14 months
Runs	13–20 months	15 months
Jumps on 2 feet	17–34 months	24 months
Throws ball overhand	17–36 months	20 months
Kicks ball	18–30 months	24 months
Climbs stairs (alternates feet)	28–36 months	30 months
Performs broad jump	27–39 months	30 months
Balances on 1 foot for 1 second	27–39 months	32 months
Peddles tricycle	30–48 months	36 months
Hops	39–51 months	42 months
Heel-toe walks	4–5.75 years	4.5 years

Signs of Gross Motor Delay

Not pulling to sit by 4.5 months
Not rolling by 6 months
Not sitting without support by 8 months
Not standing while holding on by 10 months
Not walking by 18 months
After several months of walking, has not mastered mature heel-toe
    pattern or walks exclusively on toes
Cannot push wheeled toy by 2 years
Not climbing up or down stairs by 2 years
Not jumping with both feet by 2.5 years
Frequent falling or difficulty with stairs by 3 years
Unable to stand on 1 foot momentarily by 3 years
Cannot throw a ball overhand by 4 years
Cannot jump in place or hop by 4 years
Cannot ride a tricycle by 4 years
Unable to walk in a straight line back and forth or balance on 1 foot for
    5–10 seconds by 5 years

FINE MOTOR DEVELOPMENT

Fine motor maturation is sometimes harder to appreciate than gross motor development. The evolution of hand-eye coordination is critical to mastering tasks of daily living, such as dressing (and undressing) and feeding.

Fine motor tasks also include visual motor skills, such as drawing and eventually writing. The progression from scribbling to drawing a stick figure to writing letters and eventually words is part of fine motor development.

It is extremely common for a child who is precocious in gross motor development to be slower in fine motor development or vice versa. It may have more to do with personality and temperament than with skill set. Think about the best athlete you know. Is he the best artist you know as well? Likely not.

Fine Motor Milestones	Age Range	Average Age
Helps with dressing	10–16 months	12 months
Spoon-feeds	12–18 months	15 months
Uses open or sippy cup	10–18 months	15 months
Imitates housework	14–24 months	18 months
Uses 1 hand predominantly	18–30 months	24 months
Helps with undressing	22–30 months	24 months
Potty trains	24–36 months	30 months
Undresses self	30–40 months	36 months

Signs of Fine Motor Delay
Persistence of grasp reflex (in the hands) at 3.5 months
Unable to hold rattle at 5 months
Unable to hold an object in each hand by 7 months
Absence of pincer grasp by 11 months
Unable to remove socks or gloves by self at 20 months
Unable to stack 5 blocks or not scribbling by 2 years
Not turning a single page of a book by 2.5 years
Unable to stack 8 blocks or draw a straight line by 3 years
Unable to stack 10 blocks or copy a circle by 4 years
Unable to copy a square by 4.5 years
Unable to build a staircase of blocks or copy a cross by 5 years

LANGUAGE DEVELOPMENT

Although all realms of development are remarkable to watch, verbal development may be the most awesome, because a baby who does not speak and cannot understand becomes a child who can do both. Your child goes from being someone who gives you cues to someone who tells you precisely what she wants or what is the matter.

The language milestones are probably the most variable, though, because they are influenced by so many factors, such as how well a child hears, how many languages she is hearing, how she learns to use her mouth and tongue, whether there are influences (like older siblings) around to motivate her to speak sooner, and whether she can communicate so well nonverbally that she doesn't need to speak very much at all.

For parents, measuring verbal development is usually more subjective than measuring any of the other developmental milestones. Many one-year-olds have no understandable words at all. Some say a few words clearly, but the majority use jargon that a parent can understand but a stranger cannot. So the answer to the question "When did your child say her first word?" is usually arbitrary.

Pediatricians measure verbal development much more objectively. A child can easily demonstrate how talkative — and how understandable — she is during an office visit. Teachers are an even better source of language assessment. They watch children over time, in groups and alone. Sometimes a very chatty toddler is quiet in the doctor's office because she is nervous or tired, but at school she is more verbal.

There is a noticeable difference between unilingual and bilingual children. The more languages a child is learning, the later

Language Milestones	Age Range	Average Age
Says 1 word	9–15 months	11 months
Says 2 words	10–16 months	12 months
Says 3 words	11–17 months	14 months
Points to body parts	12–24 months	18 months
Says 6 words	16–23 months	18 months
Names 1 picture	18–25 months	19 months
Knows 6 body parts	18–27 months	20 months
Speech is half-understandable	18–33 months	24 months
Puts 2 words together	20–30 months	24 months
Speech is entirely understandable	21–48 months	30 months
Uses pronouns inappropriately	22–30 months	24 months
Follows 2-step command	22–30 months	24 months
Knows 2 adjectives	27–42 months	32 months
Names 1 color	27–44 months	32 months
States full name	30–40 months	34 months
Uses pronouns appropriately	30–42 months	36 months

Signs of Language Delay
Not babbling by 5–6 months
Not saying "da" or "ba" by 9 months
Not saying "dada" or "baba" by 11 months
Has fewer than 3 words with meaning by 18 months
Not speaking at least 15 words (regardless of meaning) by 18 months
No 2-word phrases or repetition of phrases by 2 years
Not using at least 1 personal pronoun by 2.5 years
Speech only half-understandable by 3.5 years
Not understanding prepositions by 4 years
Not using proper syntax in short sentences by 5 years

she is likely to pick up a large vocabulary and put words together. This happens because the brain is integrating more than one word for a given concept. The brain is also learning to juggle different grammatical rules. While initial language acquisition is slower among children learning more than one language, future reading and writing skills are the same as, if not better than, those of peers who learn a single language. By school age, bilingual children will catch up and often surpass unilingual children.

◈ ◈ ◈

SOCIAL AND EMOTIONAL (PSYCHOSOCIAL) DEVELOPMENT

Environment can shape a child's social and emotional development tremendously. For instance, children in day care tend to be more social and adaptive in new settings than children who are cared for alone at home. Firstborn children are raised and behave differently than second and subsequent children, partly because parenting styles change and partly because younger children are influenced by older siblings. Even short-term environmental factors, such as moving to a new home or watching parents argue, can affect psychosocial development. Remember, the longer and more intense the environmental factor, the more likely it is to have a lasting impact on social and emotional development.

Social and emotional development are sometimes hard to assess because they are so influenced by temperament. However, there are some clear markers of psychosocial maturation that have nothing to do with your child's personality.

Social and Emotional Milestones	Age Range	Average Age
Independence	12–36 months	18 months
Parallel play	12–30 months	24 months
Associative play	24–48 months	30 months
Cooperative play	24–48 months	36 months

Signs of Psychosocial Delay
Not smiling socially at 3 months
Not laughing in playful situations by 6–8 months
Hard to console or stiffens when approached at 12 months
Kicks, bites, and screams easily and without provocation; rocks back and forth in crib; no eye contact or engagement with other children or adults at 2 years
In constant motion; resists discipline; does not play with other children by 3–5 years

COGNITIVE DEVELOPMENT

Cognitive development refers to the process of learning. As toddlers mature, their brains become more organized, and they develop thinking skills. Eventually, they can reason, imagine, and solve problems.

Cognitive Milestones	Age Range	Average Age
Follows 1-step command with gesture	10–16 months	12 months
Follows 1-step command without gesture	12–20 months	15 months
Begins to sort shapes and colors	by 24 months	
Begins to have imaginary play	by 24 months	
Completes puzzles with 3 or 4 pieces	by 36 months	
Understands concept of "two"	by 36 months	
Correctly names some colors	by 4 years	
Understands concept of counting	by 4 years	
Understands concept of same/different	by 4 years	

Signs of Cognitive Delay
Does not search for hidden object by 12 months
Not interested in cause-and-effect games by 15–18 months
Does not categorize similarities (e.g., animals vs. vehicles) by 2 years
Does not know own full name by 3 years
Cannot pick shorter or longer of 2 lines by 4 years
Cannot count sequentially by 4.5 years
Does not know colors or any letters by 5 years
Does not know own birthday or address by 5.5 years.

Additional Resources:
http://www.dbpeds.org/ (Go to "search" in upper right-hand corner and type in "milestones.")
http://www.nlm.nih.gov/medlineplus/infantandtoddlerdevelopment.html
http://www.cdc.gov/ncbddd/child/devtool.htm

For Information About Developmental Delay and Testing:
www.genetests.org
www.nichcy.org
www.ncbi.nih.gov/omim/

Bibliography

http://www.aaai.org
http://www.aafp.org
http://www.aap.org
http://www.aapd.org
http://www.biosci.ohio-state.edu
http://www.caps.ca
http://www.cdc.gov
http://www.choc.com
http://www.chop.edu
http://www.cincinnatichildrens.org
http://www.clevelandclinic.org
http://www.cpmc.columbia.edu
http://www.dbpeds.org
http://dermatlas.med.jhmi.edu
http://dermatology.cdlib.org
http://www.duj.com
http://www.emedicine.com
http://www.fda.gov
http://www.fpnotebook.com
http://www.headlice.org
http://www.healthcentral.com
http://www.hopkinsmedicine.org
http://www.immunofacts.com
http://www.info.med.yale.edu
http://www.keepkidshealthy.com

http://www.labtestsonline.org
http://www.mayoclinic.com
http://www.medem.com
http://www.nda.ox.ac.uk
http://www.niddk.nih.gov
http://www.ninds.nih.gov
http://www.nlm.nih.gov
http://www.orthoseek.com
http://www.packardchildrenshospital.org
http://www.pediatricneurology.com
http://www.pedisurg.com
http://www.pueblo.gsa.gov
http://www.tch.harvard.edu
http://www.uaaf.org
http://www.umich.edu
http://www.umm.edu
http://www.urologychannel.com
http://www.who.int

Index

(Page references in *italic* refer to illustrations.)

Cara Familian Natterson, MD, author of *Your Newborn: Head to Toe,* practices medicine at Tenth Street Pediatrics in Los Angeles and is on staff at Cedars-Sinai Medical Center, St. John's Hospital, and Santa Monica UCLA Hospital. She graduated from Harvard College and the Johns Hopkins School of Medicine, and she completed her residency at the University of California at San Francisco. She and her husband, Paul, have two children: a newborn named Ry and a toddler, Talia.

A one-of-a-kind primer for new parents

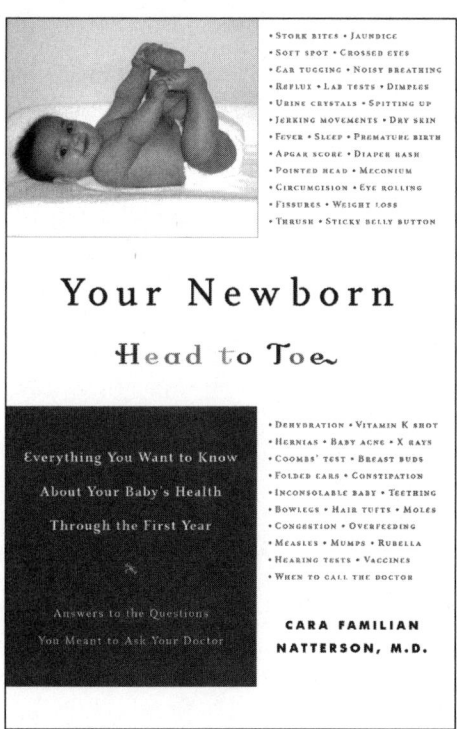

Read it before delivery

Unlike virtually any other book that covers childbirth, *Your Newborn: Head to Toe* focuses not on the mother's experience but on the child's.

Take it along to the hospital

Why is a newborn's head pointy? What's an Apgar score? This fact-packed reference helps to allay parents' concerns as it explains the purpose and scope of common medical procedures and tests administered at birth.

Consult it throughout baby's first year

From vaccines to a slow-healing belly button, from constipation to baby's sleep habits, this book addresses the questions about infant health that preoccupy parents most.